The Curriculum
Experiment

The Curriculum Experiment

MEETING THE CHALLENGE
OF SOCIAL CHANGE

John Elliott

Open University Press
Buckingham · Philadelphia

Open University Press
Celtic Court
22 Ballmoor
Buckingham
MK18 1XW

and
1900 Frost Road, Suite 101
Bristol, PA 19007, USA

First Published 1998

A catalogue record of this book is available from the British Library

ISBN   0 335 19429 X (pb)   0 335 19430 3 (hb)

Library of Congress Cataloging-in-Publication Data
Elliott, John, Dip. Phil. Ed.
    The curriculum experiment : meeting the challenge of social change
/ John Elliott.
        p.   cm.
    Includes bibliographical references and index.
    ISBN 0–335–19430–3 (hc). — ISBN 0–335–19429–X (pbk.)
    1. Curriculum planning—Social aspects—England.   2. Curriculum
change—England.   3. Teacher participation in curriculum planning—
England.   4. Educational change—England.   5. Elliott, John, Dip.
Phil. Ed.   6. Teachers—England—Biography.   I. Title.
LB2806.16.E45   1997
375′.001—dc21   97–12960
                                                                      CIP

Typeset by Graphicraft Typesetters Ltd, Hong Kong
Printed in Great Britain

For
Christine and
Dominique, Jessica, Katy

Contents

Acknowledgements

The ideas and experiences reported in this book have been shaped in conversations and projects I have been privileged to enjoy over the last thirty years. Their foundations reside in my teaching experience at Senacre Secondary School during the 1960s. At Senacre I gained my first experience as a curriculum developer under the visionary leadership of its head teacher, Norman Evans. I am grateful to the staff at Senacre during that period, particularly John Hipkin, and other Kent teachers such as Michael Head. Together we embarked enthusiastically and perhaps over-optimistically in transforming the curricular experiences of large numbers of young people who were disaffected by their experience of schooling.

I owe an enormous intellectual debt, as this book testifies, to the Director of the Humanities Project, Lawrence Stenhouse. Lawrence taught me to view curriculum development as a form of research, a social experiment in education. Also, to Barry MacDonald, the project's evaluator and my colleague at CARE for nearly thirty years, for his insights into the way power operates in educational change contexts. I also owe a tremendous debt to philosophers of education I have associated with, such as my old supervisor Richard Peters, and David Bridges, Hugh Sockett, and Wilf Carr.

During the bleak 'curriculum years' that followed the 1989 Education Reform Act in the UK, my vision of curriculum change was sustained by Professor Peter Posch, at the University of Klagenfurt, and our work together over a long period on the OECD's 'Environment and School Initiatives' project.

I would like to thank my partner Christine O'Hanlon and daughters, Dominique, Jessica and Katy. Christine's critiques of early drafts of some of the material in this book did not spare my 'ego' and I am grateful to her. My conversations with my daughters about their recent experiences of schooling, and my attendance at parents evenings, has made me realize that very little has changed for young people below the numerous surface changes that have occurred over the last thirty years and the political rhetoric that has accompanied them.

Thanks are also due to Laura Tickner and Lesley Newman for help in preparing the manuscript for this book and to my friends in County Donegal for letting me in on 'their craic' in the autumn of '95 as I attempted to write my initial draft.

Finally, I am grateful to the following for permission to reproduce published material covered by copyright:

The Editor of *Curriculum Studies* for 'The Teacher's Role in Curriculum Development: an unresolved issue in English attempts at curriculum reform', *Curriculum Studies*, vol. 2, no. 1, 1994, Triangle Publications.

The Collaborative Research Network (CARN) for 'What Have We Learned from Action Research in School-based Evaluation', *Educational Action Research: an international journal*, vol. 1, no. 1, 1993, Triangle Publications.

Carfax Publishing Company for 'School Effectiveness Research and its Critics: alternative visions of schooling', *Cambridge Journal of Education*, vol. 26, no. 2, 1996.

Routledge Journals for 'The politics of environmental education: a case study', *The Curriculum Journal*, vol. 6, no. 3, 1995.

John Elliott

Introduction

Most of the themes and ideas explored in this book are raised in the professional life story presented in Chapter 1. I am grateful to Eileen Francis, who invited me to write a story about my experience of educational change for a symposium at the 1995 Annual Meeting of the British Educational Research Association. Eileen gave contributors the interesting task of structuring their story around the idea of 'institutions in the mind'.

Reflecting on this task, I decided that five 'institutions' had been salient in shaping my thinking about educational change: Senacre Secondary School, the Schools Council's Humanities Curriculum Project (HCP), the 'Cambridge Group' of philosophers of education, the Centre for Applied Research in Education at the University of East Anglia, and the OECD (CERI) Project on 'Environment and School Initiatives'.

Moreover, each of these 'institutions' I have belonged to significantly interacted with one or more of the others, and this was not simply due to my agency. I found myself appointed to the Humanities Project because others perceived a connection between the curriculum innovations at Senacre School and the curriculum problem the Humanities Project was established to address. The project's director, Lawrence Stenhouse, had from the beginning attempted to involve philosophers of education in the Peters and Hirst 'stable' in a debate about the theories of education and knowledge which underpinned it, and, in spite of initial hostility, discovered that there were a number who wanted to engage with the curriculum and pedagogical issues the project was raising in the practical domain. Some of them settled in Cambridge and formed what became known in philosophy of education circles as the 'Cambridge Group'. Their philosophical agenda represented a significant challenge to the dominant 'logic of education' being developed by many philosophers of education, but resonated with the ideas of Stenhouse and his team. The Centre for Applied Research in Education (CARE) emerged out of the HCP with the intention of developing the thinking about curriculum change which had been tested in HCP and applying it to new contexts of change. The Cambridge Group found an alternative reference group, 60 miles up the A11 in the opposite direction from London. I found myself working in Norwich and living in Cambridge, which enabled me to belong to both groups. Two years after CARE was established at the University of East Anglia, I was involved in a three-week seminar, led by Stenhouse, on the study of curriculum for German-speaking academics. One of them was Peter Posch from the University of Klagenfurt. Fourteen years later, in 1986, the Austrian Government persuaded the OECD to launch an international curriculum and school development project in the field of 'the environment'. Its architect was Peter Posch and its significance as a change project of a certain kind was easily recognized by those familiar with the thinking and ideas which underpinned the research and development work at CARE. At various points in the now ten-year history of ENSI, the staff in CARE have played an active role in supporting its development.

The significance of my participation in a certain tradition of thinking about the problems of educational change, as it was represented and developed in the 'institutions' which have influenced my own ideas, should be only too clear to the reader of this book. It is not a scholarly review of the field. Nor does it comprehensively acknowledge the contribution of all those who have played a major role in the development of this tradition in the UK and more internationally. What it attempts is to depict a tradition of thinking about educational change, to display the interconnectedness of its key themes and ideas, and to locate them in the context of contemporary social change as preferable to technical-rational solutions which assume that the problems of educational change can be reduced to problems about means rather than ends. In doing so, I shall draw on sources that have been personally significant, which is not to deny that others might equally appropriately draw on rather different sources to depict, display and socially locate the same way of thinking about social change.

The key themes and ideas which belong to the tradition of thinking represented in this book can briefly be summarized as follows:

1 Social change is no longer an episodic set of events interspersed by periods of social stability. Advanced societies are now open to continuous change which is difficult to predict scientifically and control socially. They are dynamic rather than static, and complex rather than simple entities.

2 Advanced societies are 'risk societies'. Social change has ambiguous consequences for the individual, it opens up new possibilities for human fulfilment, and multiplies the risks and hazards which confront the individual in finding it. In these circumstances, responsibility for shaping the conditions of existence in society should be devolved down to the grassroots, to the people themselves. Decisions about what is good for people can no longer be left to governments, even 'democratically' elected ones, or any other social authorities, including those who invoke scientific knowledge as the basis of their authority.

3 Education can only meet the challenge of social change if it enables all pupils to appropriate our cultural resources in a form which enables them to take responsibility for actively shaping the economic and social conditions

of their existence. The organization of the curriculum in terms of academic subjects, for the purpose of systematic instruction, is ill-suited to the aim of a general education, because it structures our cultural resources in a form that renders them accessible to the few rather than the many. More consistent with such an aim is a curriculum which organizes cultural resources in usable forms for the purpose of enabling pupils to deepen and extend their understanding of the problems and dilemmas of everyday life in society, and to make informed and intelligent judgements about how they might be resolved. Such a curriculum will be responsive to pupils' own thinking and their emerging understandings and insights into human situations. It will therefore be continuously tested, reconstructed and developed by teachers as part of the overall development of the pedagogical process itself, rather than in advance of it. Hence, the idea of 'pedagogically driven' curriculum change as an 'innovative experiment' which is central to this book.

4 *Educational* change implies a focus on both curriculum and pedagogy, and on the development of teachers as experimental innovators or action researchers. In my experience, the idea of 'teachers as action researchers' emerged from a conception of the curriculum as an innovative pedagogical experiment in making the cultural resources of society equally accessible to all pupils. In recent years, the idea has become detached from this curriculum change context and treated simply as a useful professional development strategy regardless of the curriculum context. In this book, I have attempted to relocate the teacher as action researcher in the idea of the curriculum as an innovative pedagogical experiment.

5 Educational change originates in the reflexive and discursive consciousness of teachers as they deliberate together about the problematics of their curriculum and pedagogical practices. It is teachers who change the structures which shape their practices and not organizational systems. Systems changes are not necessarily accompanied by structural change in the patterns of belief and value which shape the selection, organization and representation of content for the purpose of learning. Systems may, however, support or frustrate structural change. Teachers are the primary agents of structural improvements in education. I shall argue that such improvements imply radical changes in schools as social systems. They will need to become less tightly bounded and insulated from a dynamic social environment, and form the coordinating nodes of *learning networks* which penetrate that environment and thereby *connect* learning with the lived experiences of students in a rapidly changing society. In the course of this book, I shall examine school effectiveness research and its outmoded assumptions about school improvement in the light of this view of educational change. In the final chapter, I will provide a detailed justification for the generative role of teachers as agents of structural change in educational systems.

6 Different conceptions of education and of the curriculum presuppose different conceptions of society and the principles governing access to its 'goods'.

The ideas of the curriculum as an innovative pedagogical experiment, and of the teacher as an experimental innovator, presuppose a certain vision of the social ends of education; namely, the development of society as a community of educated people who feel equally at home in deploying its cultural resources to promote both their own and other people's well-being. I shall link this vision with John Rawls' liberal-egalitarian theory of justice and contrast it with the alternative views of justice as an end of education which underpin the technocratic and market-based conceptions of education.

7 Planning the curriculum by objectives distorts the nature of knowledge and leaves little room for individuals to use our culture as a medium for the development of their own thinking in relation to the things that matter in life. By standardizing and predetermining learning outcomes 'objectives' inhibit the expression of individuality and creativity in learning, and thereby prevent young people from personally appropriating culture as a resource for making sense of their experience. This approach to curriculum planning may be appropriate in a context where people need to acquire specific skills and techniques, but more is required in the context of a general education aimed at developing young people's capacities for discernment, discrimination and judgement in the complex and unstructured situations they will encounter in life.

In the following pages, I shall attempt to weave these strands of thinking together by exploring their appropriateness as a basis for educational and curriculum policy-making in advanced modern societies.

Norwich, August 1997

1

Institutions in the Mind: Autobiographical Fragments

Looking for my school

The head's secretary came into the staffroom and said, 'John, the headmaster wants to see you'. It was a short walk up the corridor, past the deputies' offices, to Norman's office. As I entered he sat facing me, a short but stocky, red-haired and ruddy faced man. Even sitting down he physically exuded a kind of restless energy.

'John, have you seen the advertisement in the *Guardian* for a job with the Schools Council's Humanities Project. I want you to apply for it'.

Norman never wasted words. He always came briskly and quickly to the point. No small talk with Norman. He found it rather distasteful, I think.

'Yes, I saw it but I'm off to Keele'.

I had decided after five years at Senacre to go off and do an Advanced Diploma in Counselling: I was interviewed at three universities. Two rejected me but I had been offered a place at Keele. The local education authority (LEA) had agreed to release me for a year on secondment. Norman barked at me:

'You are introverted enough without doing a counselling course. What you need is a good healthy bit of curriculum development. Don't worry, I'll fix things with Keele'.

I felt the burden of responsibility lifted from my shoulders and conceded. Norman had a lot of connections. In the staffroom we were all aware of that. He had appointed a number of the teachers at Senacre through his grapevine. Not me though, at least to my knowledge.

'Apply, have a bath, buy a suit and go to the interview', he commanded brusquely.

The meeting at this point came to an end and I returned to the staffroom. It was rumoured that Norman had once commanded a minesweeper and he appeared to run the school sometimes as if he were still in charge of one. A public schoolboy himself, he had left his job as housemaster in one of these institutions to make his way in the secondary modern school system. I once heard a fellow teacher describe him as 'on a mission to the working class'.

I was called for an interview one fine winter's day in 1967 at Nuffield Lodge, the London headquarters of the Nuffield Foundation. The Foundation was helping to sponsor the Humanities Curriculum Project as a joint initiative with the newly formed Schools Council for Curriculum Reform and Examinations, that now defunct institution that attempted to bring central government, LEAs and the teachers unions into a partnership for the purpose of promoting change in the school curriculum. The Nuffield Foundation had been a key player in promoting innovation in the teaching of maths and science prior to the establishment of the Council in the early 1960s. It was now directing its attention to the humanities, but recognized the fact that the Council would increasingly take over its role as the agent of curriculum change in schools.

I remember Nuffield Lodge as a rather grand Regency building full of elegant period furniture. Brian Young, the head of the Foundation and ex-headmaster of Winchester, welcomed the interviewees and introduced us to Lawrence Stenhouse, who was leaving his post as head of education at Jordanhill College of Education to become the director of the project. He was on the short side and dapper. I remember he was wearing a light grey suit, white shirt and red tie, and thinking that it was the typical 'uniform' of the training college lecturer. I thought I knew the type of male, especially in education departments, having been one of the last two-year trained teachers to go through training college. I had experienced them as pleasant, bland, earnest, mildly liberal and certainly as dull as ditch water. I turned out to be wrong about Lawrence. Like Norman, he exuded a kind of restless energy, but whereas Norman released it in getting things done, Lawrence released it in a flow of ideas.

I was eventually invited into the interview room and introduced to the panel. There sat Stenhouse himself, Eric Briault, the deputy chief and eventually chief of the now defunct ILEA, Jocelyn Owen, one of the Council's joint secretaries and eventually the chief of Devon LEA, and two or three others whose names escape me. They were not unfamiliar with some of my work at Senacre. As head of humanities in the school, I had played a leading role in developing a curriculum for 14 to 15-year-old pupils organized around life themes and taught by an interdisciplinary team of teachers. Traditional class grouping practices had been abandoned, the team working with a whole-year group in blocks of time where we were able to bring the whole together for lectures, or break the year down into small groups for discussion and project work or send them out of the school to do 'field research' in the community. Our work on 'The Family' had been picked up by a visiting field officer at the Council who was co-authoring the Council's Working Paper 11 on 'The Humanities and the Young School Leaver'. It was eventually reported in this publication, which had also recommended a national initiative to support widespread curriculum development along similar lines. Hence the Humanities Project was born.

Jocelyn Owen asked me who I would select if I were putting together curriculum materials around the theme of the Hero. 'James Bond', I replied. He looked shocked and asked why.

'Because he exemplifies the predicament of human beings in our society today', I said somewhat pretentiously.

'And what is that?'

'How to play a diversity of roles and keep a sense of yourself at the same time. Not lose your integrity'.

'What about the Greek Heroes? Would they have a place in your curriculum?'

I 'flannelled' a response and he didn't persist. I learned afterwards that he was fond of the classics. I didn't know too much about them. They didn't teach Greek literature in my grammar school and I was not put in the Latin set. This is the only exchange at the interview I remember. Afterwards I went into a cinema and watched a western, *The Professionals* with Burt Lancaster, before catching a train home. I had always loved westerns and spent the major part of my GCE English literature lessons at grammar school reading them under the desk. On the top lay the set texts – *The History of Mr Polly*, *As You Like It* and *The Golden Treasury of Longer Poems* – unread.

Norman greeted me in the corridor the next day. 'Well done John, you got the job', he said breezily and simply.

I was delighted but surprised to hear the news from him, rather than Owen. 'How did you find out', I asked knowing he would be embarrassed by the question.

'Oh', he responded somewhat bashfully, 'I was in town last night with Briault. He said you performed very well, and although it was finally up to Stenhouse, felt confident you would get it'.

A few days later a letter came from Owen formally offering me the job of project officer and I accepted. Some four years later, I was interviewed by Barry MacDonald, HCP's evaluation director. He had been doing an investigation of how the HCP team came to be appointed. The National Union of Teachers (NUT), a powerful force on Schools Council Committees, had raised questions about why only one practising schoolteacher had been appointed to the team, namely myself. At the time, MacDonald had developed a model of evaluation as an information service to all those interest groups who had a major stake in the success or failure of the innovation. The teacher unions were considered to be major stakeholders and the evaluation team had been talking to them about their information needs. In this context, the NUT's concern about the appointments was considered a very appropriate thing for the evaluators to investigate. MacDonald and his colleagues developed some interesting micro-political stories around some of the appointments, including mine, which went something like this.

Aware of the decision to launch HCP, the National Council of the Christian Education Movement (CEM) – a professional association of religious education teachers – discussed at one of their meetings the possible implications of HCP for the teaching of religious education as a subject in schools. Concern was expressed about the possibility of the project's interdisciplinary approach threatening the subject's already marginal status in the school curriculum and further eroding pupils' opportunities to develop their understanding of religious beliefs and practices. The CEM Council felt that it was important that the project team appoint a religious education specialist to safeguard the interests of the subject. My headteacher Norman, Jocelyn Owen and Eric Briault were all members of the Council. I was a religious education specialist.

The story shocked me out of my naivety about how I came to be involved in HCP. It threatened my belief in my ability to construct and control my own professional career. When Stenhouse heard the story, he angrily denied the implication that he also had exercised little control in the appointment process and argued that I was his choice. But it taught me a great deal about the innovation process. How innovations shape up is as much a product of what happens 'backstage' as what happens within the formal and public process of decision-making 'on-stage'. It gave me some initial insights into the power of interpersonal networks, which create strategic alliances between individuals across formal organizational structures, to effect or subvert a process of change. Social power to effect change cannot be contained in formal organizational structures alone. As Foucault argued, power is not so much a property possessed by certain individuals or organizations. It is a social strategy constructed in the alliances individuals create across social structures and institutions.

Norman and I left Senacre together, he to become head of education at a church training college in the Midlands and I to London where HCP was housed, in a training college. We have retained a personal friendship for nearly thirty years, and our paths have continued to cross professionally. He eventually left teacher training by taking crombie as the principal of a training college, and established the Experiential Learning Trust, moving his sphere of action into innovations in higher education institutions (HEIs), which breaks down the boundaries between the types of learning valued and promoted through the academy and those valued and promoted in the context of everyday experience in work and life. His mission has remained constant throughout his professional life. Whether it be schools or HEIs, his aim as an innovator has been to transform educational provision in our society and the values which underpin it, so that it benefits all young people rather than simply catering for an elite.

In our subsequent encounters over the years, Norman never referred to our Senacre years. He had moved his mission on from the schools to the guardians of the educational values they promote. I had also moved on from

Senacre to support a curriculum innovation in schools across the country. But perhaps unlike Norman, I was unable to leave the Senacre in my mind. I went out and worked with teachers in schools across the land expecting to find other Senacres. I was disappointed and disillusioned. From the stories I have heard, the Senacre in my mind no longer mirrors the school of that name as it exists today. So what is the Senacre I have carried with me for nearly thirty years?

Senacre

It is an image of continuing, unremitting engagement in curriculum experiments that were the subject of constant discussion within the staffroom and with 'the kids' on the receiving end. At Senacre, we were always involving pupils in the search for curricular solutions by eliciting and reflecting upon their accounts of their curricular experiences. It was a school in which the pupils' voices were frequently heard and attended to.

I remember one particular session when I was attempting to get one of my fourth-year groups to critique their curricular experiences with me and the humanities team. After giving me some lively and hard-hitting feedback which I managed to take without reacting too defensively, although I was feeling pretty bruised by it, they got to the crunch question. It was all very well them being allowed to say what they honestly felt, but what was the point of it. Nothing would change. We teachers retained control over curriculum decisions. I argued that although this was so, and would remain so, they were able to influence our decisions by the kind of critical feedback they had voiced, and were able to monitor the extent of that influence. It was in this session that I first began to articulate a view of the relationship between the exercise of authority and accountability in teaching. I was saying to the pupils that we had authority over curriculum decisions but that they could influence them by calling us to account. It was a different view of teachers' accountability for the curriculum to one that emerged in later years in the context of the National Curriculum; namely, that teachers are responsible for implementing curriculum decisions made by others (e.g. the State) and are held accountable not for the decisions but for implementing them.

Senacre was also an image of teachers experimenting with curricular solutions together as teams rather than as individuals working in isolation from each other and locked into interpersonal networks which influenced their thinking. It was a well networked school. Many of us belonged to strategic alliances which constituted movements for change across institutional boundaries. John, our head of English, had come out of the London Institute stable of Jimmy Britton and Nancy Martin, and with others from the same stable had formed a local association of English teachers, which drew on their ideas to promote new approaches to teaching language and literature in schools.

Similarly, I was linked to the CEM, which at the time was busy promoting Harold Loukes' inductive approach to religious education in schools. One joke that circulated in the staffroom was that at Senacre, the Bible was first introduced to pupils in their fifth year as a special treat. Both these networks shared a common vision of education as a process which enabled pupils to use the subject as a resource for constructing personal meaning in their lives. And there were teachers of other humanities subjects, such as history and geography, who were locked into networks, sharing a not dissimilar curriculum philosophy. Within the school we formed a kind of innovation beachhead.

As usual in winter, most of us assembled around the electric fire at one end of the staffroom in a semi-circle. (There was space enough for all twenty-five of us to sit together like this.) Dan, our head of maths, sat opposite me explaining the golf swing to Stephen, the head of science, whom he periodically coached on the playing field. He looked across me to John, our trendy head of English, who was walking past on the way to the school office.

'You look tired out John', Dan called with a twinkle in his eye and a side glance at those of us identified as sidekicks to this spearhead of innovation.

'I most certainly am Dan, had the fourth years all morning, and they are full of good ideas'.

'Yes, it must be very exhausting teaching silent reading', Dan went on. Some of the staff, including me, laughed and a few others smiled with satisfaction as Dan's little dart winged its way across the room.

John smiled. 'Us English types don't have much time for g-u-l-f', he retorted crisply, mimicking an upper crust accent. He giggled and so did Dan, who may have been a golfer but displayed no trace of a plummy accent. While a bastion of traditional education, subject-centred, didactic and streamed by 'ability', he gently and with humour mediated the reactions of the traditionalists to innovatory practice. On behalf of the innovation camp, John responded to good-humoured scepticism with wit. It was only when a traditionalist became indignant about innovations producing a decline in standards of learning or behaviour that John's wit became devastatingly biting and arrogant. But when Dan was around, the debate was always transformed into the medium of a good-natured banter expressing mutual tolerance and respect for one another.

The banter about silent reading arose from the perception of pupils sitting around in English spending a lot of time reading books they had selected from a departmental library and not being taught anything. Pupils exchanged books, discussed them together, wrote reviews and used them as a stimulus for their own creative writing endeavours. Reviews and writing were frequently published in a specially edited magazine for pupils and staff. For some these magazines were a convincing demonstration of the intellectual and creative potential being released and developed in English, while for others it demonstrated a serious lack of concern for standards, evidenced by sloppy spelling and punctuation in many cases. The English department refused to 'correct' pupils' work prior to publication. In doing so, it hoped to change some teachers' understanding of standards in education and knowingly risked criticism in the process.

The magazine enabled the staff as a whole to call innovatory practice to account and the English department to foster a debate in the staffroom about the meaning of standards. The setting for these debates was not so much the formal meeting, but the informality of the staffroom and the semi-circular gatherings around the electric fire.

Senacre taught me that innovations didn't have to be implemented on the basis of policies that represented a bureaucratically manufactured professional or public consensus in order to succeed. This way of institutionalizing educational innovations kills innovation and tells a pathological story, because it defines them in terms of the level of consensus achieved and fails to confront the fact that genuine innovations generate conflict and expose the fundamental value-issues which divide people. Bureaucratically managed 'innovation and change' is so often a conflict-avoiding rather than a conflict-handling strategy.

I must confess to a degree of scepticism over the currently fashionable 'school development planning', 'target setting', etc., if it simply involves improving, in the words of Lyotard (1979) 'the performativity of the system' – that is, achieving the best equation between the maximum level of outputs and the minimum level of inputs. 'Performativity' implies a consensus about organizational goals, and reduces them to tangible and measurable outcomes. It implies reforming the organization into a smoothly running, or efficient, system. Such a system will have little tolerance for fundamental questioning and disagreements over the aims and purposes of the organization, and for the value complexity and conflict they reveal. *Reform* and *innovation* are qualitatively different kinds of change. One way of distinguishing them is the extent to which the future is accommodated to the past or vice versa.

At Senacre I learned that educational innovations are best treated as controversial experiments that are open to continuous readjustment through open discussion and debate grounded in evidence about their effects. Senacre's innovative style was to allow groups of teachers to propose curricular solutions and then subject them to a process of experimentation in which the solutions were continually revised through open discussion of the evidence gathered about their effects on pupils. Professional accountability to peers and research were integral elements of this process rather than additional options. Curricular solutions were not implemented and then subsequently evaluated for the purposes of *post-hoc* accountability. Rather, they were developed through *research* in a context where the evidence it generated was discussed openly and made available for critical scrutiny among all the staff. Innovations were not imposed on unwilling teachers but increasing numbers became involved as their values and attitudes were influenced by the discussions of evidence. I subsequently learned that this kind of discursive experimentation was called 'action research'. For me, action research is not one of the 'supporting cast' or even an 'extra' in a curriculum change scenario, but plays the leading role. If one believes as I do that one's efforts to effect curriculum change, as opposed to reform, are best theorized/conceptualized as innovative experiments, then action research is integral to the process of change and action research theory constitutes a theory of change.

HCP and 'going into care'

Stenhouse had been educated at an elite institution: Manchester Grammar School. He frequently argued that he wanted to make his experience of education as a student in that institution accessible to all young people in schools. It was the experience of treating knowledge as problematic, provisional and open to questioning. His view of his teachers was that they refused to transmit knowledge, as if it were a certain and unchanging body of facts. Instead, it was treated as material for discussion with the aim of developing their students' powers of judgement, discernment and discrimination. For Stenhouse, it was discussion rather than instruction which made his experiences at Manchester Grammar educationally worthwhile.

The image of this institution which he carried around in his head, however over-idealized it may have been, shaped his thinking about HCP. I remember him visiting Senacre before I departed to see our humanities curriculum in action. He was clearly disappointed and I was upset that he was. Perhaps he was looking for Manchester Grammar at Senacre. But we instructed pupils in the facts we believed they ought to know before they discussed a topic or issue. What he observed were not discussions where teachers invited pupils to question the information we had given them. They were discussions where pupils were invited to treat the facts as given and to focus their discussion on the conclusions they might draw from them, on the value-judgements they could be used to defend.

Stenhouse had come to understand factual information not so much as a report of objective truth but as evidence of an evaluative point of view on human events and situations, and he believed that this is how it should be handled by teachers of the humanities. For him the humanities curriculum in schools should be viewed as a framework which supported the study of human values rather than 'objective facts'.

The image of Manchester Grammar that Lawrence carried around in his head also shaped his conduct in academic circles. His style in any seminar was to play the clever boy in the class, turning arguments on their heads whatever their disciplinary basis and whatever the prestige and authority-status of those who pronounced them. Such exchanges were often initiated by a question which targeted some basic and unexamined value-assumptions underpinning the argument and catching their author off-guard. Often these exchanges were not welcomed by those 'knowledgeable authorities' he engaged with. He experienced a great deal of rejection from the educational academics whose approval he sought, perhaps naively believing they would value a critical discussion of ideas. He was simply doing what he had learned to do at school, rendering 'knowledge' problematic by exercising his powers of judgement, discernment and discrimination. While some saw him as a renaissance man in his ability to express intelligence in any sphere of academic discourse, without being qualified as a subject specialist in most of them, others saw him as too clever for words. But he was unable to stop being something he had been encouraged to become at school, described by a reviewer of his major work as a 'chess player in a world of draughts'. Indeed, one way of expressing his aspirations for teachers and schools is that he wanted them to help young people to play chess rather than draughts with our cultural resources.

Stenhouse was convinced that the problem the Schools Council in its early years was seeking curricula solutions to could be solved if the schools shifted away from an instruction-based towards a discussion-based pedagogy. The school leaving age was being raised from 15 to 16, and alarm was spreading among the schools about how young school leavers were going to take an extra year of compulsory schooling when many had already 'switched off' by the time they were 14, particularly in the humanities subjects, as a Council survey had convincingly demonstrated. Many schools had established elaborate systems of containment and control to cope with the widespread hostility and disaffection adolescents of below-average and even average academic ability were displaying. For Stenhouse, the curriculum problem was not so much a problem of content but how content was represented and mediated by teachers in their transactions with students.

Stenhouse used the work of the philosopher Richard Peters to articulate the logic which underpinned the design of HCP and claimed that it was the first curriculum project to be grounded in a philosophically defensible rationale. He used Peters' well-known distinction between the teacher as *an authority* on a subject and the teacher as *in authority* over the educational process, and linked it with Peters' account of educational aims as implying the values and principles which define the process of education rather than its extrinsic outcomes. Stenhouse argued that since values constituted the subject-matter of the humanities, in a pluralistic democracy like ours it would be undemocratic for a teacher to see him or herself as *an authority* on human issues where questions of value were at stake. Instead, he or she should view his or her role in terms of being *in authority* within an educationally worthwhile process for handling morally, socially and politically controversial human acts and social situations aimed at the development of understanding. He was not concerned to clarify this aim in terms of any specific learning outcomes referring to the content of understanding. For Stenhouse, the pre-specification of what pupils needed to understand about controversial human acts like war or controversial social situations like poverty would imply a value-position on the part of the curriculum planner and imply an intention to indoctrinate. If in a demo-cratic society pupils had a responsibility to make up their own minds by con-structing a value-position for themselves, then pre-defining understanding as a curricular aim in terms of content objectives was inconsistent with it. Such a responsibility suggested a different account of the development of under-standing in terms of the power to exercise independent and autonomous judgement.

Following Peters' account of educational aims, Stenhouse argued that the aim of developing understanding referred to an educational process to be realized in classrooms rather than a set of specific content objectives, and proceeded to clarify it in this light, in terms of what Peters called 'procedural principles'. Developing understanding involved discussion rather than instruc-tion at the core of the pedagogy, in which the teacher protected divergence of opinion, ensured that minority views were represented, safe-guarded crit-ical standards of reasoning about evidence, and adopted a procedurally neut-ral position on the issues under discussion. Such a process would focus on content conceived as evidence for or against a particular value-position, and took the form of written and other texts fed into the process at appropriate points by the teacher. He or she would be helped by access to a resource archive indexed to ensure rapid retrieval.

Stenhouse emphasized that the principles specified did not prescribe con-crete procedures for handling information; these were for teachers to develop in their particular circumstances. Their function was to provide criteria for monitoring the consistency of such procedures with the aim. The idea of the teacher as a researcher of his or her own practice was integral to HCP's design. Teachers were asked to tape-record discussions and to analyse their interventions in the light of the procedural principles by asking such ques-tions as, 'Am I protecting divergence' or 'Am I using my authority position here to promote my own views?' They were asked to identify interventions that were inconsistent with these principles and to experiment with altern-ative courses of action by monitoring their effects on the quality of discussion (see Stenhouse 1970a). The experience in HCP of supporting teachers to change the curriculum through self-reflexive experimentation in their class-rooms was continuous with my experience at Senacre. From these formative experiences, I later formulated a distinction between *educational research* and *research on education*. In the former, teaching and research were unified as the attempt to realize an educational ideal through an innovative curriculum experiment; in the latter, teaching as an 'educational' activity is viewed as the object of research and extrinsically rather than intrinsically related to it. Hence, I came to see educational research as a form of action research, which is not simply research *on action* but research *in action*.

From HCP, Stenhouse generalized his 'process model of curriculum de-velopment' to the whole curriculum, and used it as a basis for producing a powerful critique of *planning by objectives* (Stenhouse 1975), which he argued was anti-educational, since it distorted the nature of all knowledge by rendering it unproblematic and value-free. It was also undemocratic because it prevented young people from developing those powers of judgement and discrimination which enabled them to influence actively as citizens the social conditions which shaped their lives.

The process model of curriculum planning did not get a warm reception from philosophers of education in the Peters and Hirst stable at the London Institute of Education, which at the time was exercising an enormous influence on initial teacher training in the teacher training colleges. Peters himself displayed interest and served on HCP's Steering Committee, but his close associate, Paul Hirst, had, according to reports, refused to serve as a consultant to the project on the grounds that he would have nothing to do with a curriculum that lacked clear objectives. However, Stenhouse suggested that I should enrol on the advanced diploma course in the philosophy of education at the London Institute of Education as a part-time student. I needed to compensate for the lack of a first degree. Through the course, I joined the Philosophy of Education Society and attended its annual conference.

After I completed the diploma course, the HCP team moved from London to Norwich in 1970 where it established the Centre for Applied Research in Education (CARE). For domestic reasons, I moved to live in Cambridge, but drove 60 miles to Norwich to my work in CARE. In Cambridge, I discovered the Cambridge Group.

The Cambridge Group

Although most of the philosophers of education I came across were conservative and scholastic, expounding a logic of education which legitimated the organization of the curriculum in traditional academic categories and traditional teaching methods, the group in Cambridge were attracted to HCP and the curriculum theory which drove it. They wanted to bring philosophical inquiry into a more interactive relationship with the practical problems curriculum developers were grappling with in the educational system and saw themselves as part of a newly emerging discipline in higher education; namely, curriculum studies, an offshoot of the involvement of academics in curriculum development projects funded by Nuffield and the Schools Council.

Most of the philosophical group I and HCP generally started to network with were by the early 1970s living and working in Cambridge and became known as the 'Cambridge Group'. There was Hugh Sockett, who introduced curriculum studies into inservice courses for teachers at the Cambridge Institute of Education, where he worked on a philosophical critique of 'Rational Curriculum Planning'. He was joined by Richard Pring from Goldsmiths College, where he had begun a philosophical critique of various kinds of integrated curricula taking shape in schools. David Bridges at Homerton College developed an interest in HCP's model of discussion and embarked on a philosophical inquiry into the logic underpinning different forms of discussion. His colleague at Homerton, Peter Scrimshaw, developed an interest in HCP's notion of 'understanding' as an educational aim. Another colleague, Charles Bailey, took issue with the idea of the neutral teacher and embarked on an extensive philosophical debate with me about it. HCP provided the Cambridge Group with a philosophical agenda which formed the basis for regular seminars and a number of publications and books, and the group provided the HCP team with additional support in developing a strong philosophical defence for its ideas.

I participated in the activities of the Cambridge Group and helped to establish close links between it and the team at CARE. The interaction between the members of CARE and the original members of the Cambridge Group has had a significant influence on my professional career and development over the past 25 years. It has also made a significant impact on theirs I believe.

In 1976, Hugh Sockett left Cambridge for a Chair at the New University of Ulster. I left CARE to occupy his curriculum studies post at the institute. In the early 1980s, he went to a Chair in the newly created School of Education at UEA, of which CARE became a part. Lawrence died in 1982, and was eventually succeeded as CARE's director by Barry MacDonald, HCP's evaluation director. The latter had been asked to undertake a major review of the police training curriculum in England and Wales in the wake of the Brixton riots. The curriculum was a fine example of rational planning by specific content objectives, but it appeared to be failing to develop officers capable of making intelligent decisions on the streets in a rapidly changing and complex pluralistic society. Police interventions were becoming increasingly controversial and a knowledge of law and procedure was no longer a sufficient basis for training. MacDonald was asked to recommend changes in the curriculum and asked me to return to CARE to join the team he was getting together. I returned in 1984.

By this time, Sockett had become dean of the School of Education at UEA. He left two years later to create a centre for promoting educational change at an American university. In 1990, David Bridges left his post as vice-principal at Homerton for a Chair at UEA, and after working in close collaboration with CARE on a number of research and development projects, including the Police Project, while still at Homerton, he succeeded me as dean of the School of Education and Professional Development, as it is now called, for a short while before becoming pro vice-chancellor. Peter Scrimshaw left Homerton in the late 1970s for a post in the Open University, and recently collaborated with me and others in CARE on a joint research project into the impact of computers in classrooms on the quality of children's talk. All the members of the old Cambridge Group are still doing philosophy but in the context of applied research and educational development projects. Only

David Bridges strives to build bridges back into mainstream philosophy of education, and not without some latter-day success.

I have dwelt on the major ideas which constitute Stenhouse's theory of curriculum change and which he embodied in HCP because they articulate · much of the theory which underpinned our search for curriculum solutions at Senacre. These ideas then became embedded in the culture of CARE and continue to shape its work to the present day, twenty-three years after HCP as a funded project finished. As a member of CARE over that period, with the exception of a break of eight years working at the Cambridge Institute of Education, my image of Senacre is now contained within my image of CARE as a centre for the study of educational innovation and change. I am not saying that my ideas have remained the same. The move from Senacre to HCP developed my understanding of the political context of curriculum innovation and of the epistemological assumptions that underpin traditional curricula and pedagogy and which are so difficult to shift. It also developed my understanding of curriculum innovation as a form of research. In the context of HCP, I was able to develop the kind of action research methods we had used at Senacre; for example, by integrating the elicitation of pupil and peer perspectives on teachers' curricular and pedagogical practices into a more systematic and structured process of grounding teacher experimentation in the analysis of triangulation data. My involvement with a certain group of educational philosophers has enabled me to sustain a vision of curriculum change through the past decade when it has increasingly been regarded by politicians, officials and some educational researchers as unfashionable. It has done so by helping me to be aware that fashionable views often rest on untenable assumptions which gradually become obvious, like the assumption that educational excellence resides in the passive acquisition of subject knowledge rather than in the use of that knowledge as structures within which to think about the problems of living in a complex and rapidly changing society.

ENSI

I have discovered that there are always contexts in which it is possible for me and my colleagues in CARE to work with the vision of education embedded in HCP. In the 1980s, the failure of a rationally planned and centralized police training curriculum to develop the powers of discrimination and judgement officers need to exercise on the streets in relation to complex situations, provided a context for developing a process model of training which gave trainers a greater role in reflectively developing teaching strategies that developed the capacities of police recruits to make intelligent judgements in operational situations.

The Education Reform Act seriously limited our opportunities to support innovative curriculum experiments in schools from the late 1980s onwards. But as our government began to centralize curriculum decision-making, other countries began to decentralize responsibility for curriculum development and encourage initiatives in schools.

Nearly ten years ago, I was asked by the OECD to serve as a pedagogical consultant to an international curriculum project in the field of environmental education entitled 'Environment and School Initiatives' (ENSI). The overall curriculum framework took the form of a process model specifying educational aims and procedural principles, and within this framework schools were encouraged to develop their own curriculum strategies through action research. The design of ENSI by Peter Posch at the University of Klagenfurt in Austria was influenced by the ideas of Stenhouse. The project has been a great success in the eyes of policy-makers within the participating countries. It has created an international network which enables teachers and schools to share information about their innovative experiments across national boundaries. The government in the UK has supported the project in Scotland and Northern Ireland since 1989, but not until recently in England and Wales, since at one time, according to one official I met, its interdisciplinary nature and focus on local environmental issues was considered to be incompatible with National Curriculum requirements.

I can still draw on my experience of Senacre, HCP, CARE and the Cambridge Group as institutions embedded in my mind. I have found enough opportunities to use it through the networks I am linked to in a variety of curriculum change contexts, in spite of the fact that opportunities to do so in the context of curriculum change in English schools is limited. However, my experience tells me that a national curriculum planned by content objectives, and in which knowledge is divorced from any consideration of value issues and teachers are viewed as technical operatives, cannot work. Dearing (1993) has done his best to make it work in its own terms. Soon teachers and schools will be able to engage in innovative experiments once again, and there will be work for me and my colleagues in CARE to do with them. In the meantime, I carry around with me the voices of the students I listened to at Senacre and of my own daughters, who have only recently completed their schooling.

One day HCP received a cry for help from a large comprehensive school in the North. I was sent up there. The pupils were resolutely refusing to discuss the evidence contained in the HCP resource packs. I observed a group and the teacher was confronted with a blanket of silence after he asked them to respond to some material he had placed before them. At the end of the session, I interviewed them without the teacher being present and tape-recorded it:

'What do you feel about these materials you are being asked to discuss?'

'We don't like them'.

'Is that because you find them difficult to read, or even boring? The teachers think this may be the case'.

Some looked surprised.

'No, you see we disagree with them'.

'Great, then why don't you discuss them'.

They looked at me, as one who had just stepped off Mars, and patiently explained that teachers didn't give you information to disagree with but to accept as true.

With the group's permission, I played the recording back to the teachers. They were amazed. They had failed to understand that pupils' experience of schooling generally is one where teachers give them information to agree with and accept uncritically and that a sudden invitation to discuss late in their school careers is going to be met with a high degree of scepticism. They began to realize that the new ground rules had to be made explicit to the pupils, and continually discussed in relation to specific teaching strategies, if they were to believe that their teachers sincerely intended them to render knowledge problematic in the classroom.

HCP trial schools generally complained about the 'evidence' being too difficult for 'average' and 'below average ability' pupils. A typical response to this in the classroom was to do a comprehension session on the bits the teacher thought were difficult before proceeding with the discussion. I observed this pattern operating in a classroom in the Midlands. The teacher even carried out a comprehension test before allowing discussion. When he did say 'Right, let's now discuss it', he received a nil response. Afterwards I spoke with some of the pupils:

'Why did the teacher do that comprehension exercise?'

'He thinks we find the stuff difficult'.

'Is it?'

'Well bits, but most of us get the gist of it. If only he would let us discuss it straight away we could help each other understand the bits we find difficult. But after twenty comprehension questions to answer we get too fed up to discuss it'.

Through helping teachers get access to this kind of perspective from pupils, which they articulated on a nationwide basis, many began to change the theory of information handling which shapes traditional pedagogy; namely, present information, ensure comprehension and then, if there is time, invite discussion. The new theory went: *read–discuss–understand.*

About six years ago, a group of teachers on the CARE MA course in applied educational research were discussing a transcript one of them had made of his attempts to elicit his pupils' experience of life in his classroom. My eldest daughter was on work experience in CARE from the college of further education she was attending and sat in the seminar reading a magazine, waiting for me to take her home. The group generally felt that the teacher was not getting at the authentic voice of his pupils, and pointed out how he was manipulating their responses by asking leading questions. No-one asked my daughter, who had only recently left secondary education, what she thought about the problem. At one point she rose to her feet and left the room. I could tell she was angry and followed her.

'What's the matter Dominique?'

'If they think they can find out what we really think of their lessons, they are wrong?'

'Why?'

'We don't even see them as human'.

'Go in and tell them that'.

She declined.

The problem of helping teachers to gain access to the authentic voice of their pupils persists. It is the central methodological problem in educational action research, and my enduring commitment to helping teachers become action researchers is based on the knowledge that worthwhile curriculum change will only occur when those on the receiving end are given a voice and thereby enabled to influence the conditions which shape their experience of schooling.

2

The Teacher's Role in Curriculum Development: An Unresolved Issue in English Attempts at Curriculum Reform

Introduction

In this chapter, I place the autobiographical reflections in the last chapter in the context of a broader analysis of curriculum change in the UK during the second half of the twentieth century. I shall compare the British curriculum reforms of the 1960s with contemporary government-initiated reforms, and argue that the central problem of pedagogical change persists because the latter adopted one of the two solutions to the problem which emerged from the former – namely, the objectives model of socially engineered change. The other solution, proposed by Lawrence Stenhouse, which views curriculum change as a social experiment in which teachers play a central role, has been neglected. I will argue for the validity of Stenhouse's contention that there can be no curriculum development without the professional development of teachers as researchers of their own practices in schools and classrooms.

Since 1945, schools in the UK have experienced two giant waves of curriculum reform. The first wave burst through the schools in the 1960s and early 1970s and the second followed it over a decade later in the form of the 1988 Education Reform Act, which established the National Curriculum. It is now fashionable to see these two events as radically discontinuous with each other, and underpinned by quite contrary assumptions about the teacher's role.

The first wave is often characterized as teacher-initiated in contrast to a second wave operationally directed by the state. The intervention of the state in curriculum development is frequently justified in terms of the failure of teachers and their associations to improve educational standards in schools. Indeed, government ministers and the popular press have tended to point to the 1960s reforms as a cause of declining standards. Evidently, the first wave of reform left a sediment of 'progressive' practices in schools – topic-based curricula, mixed-ability classes, small-group teaching, discovery and project learning – which the second wave needed to break up and wash away if standards were to be raised. Moreover, the ideas that inform these 'progressive' practices are believed to stem from educational theorists in universities, who disseminate them through teacher training programmes. Such beliefs may explain why government ministers tended to avoid much discussion and negotiation with teachers and academic educationalists generally over arrangements for implementing the requirements of the National Curriculum in schools. They may also explain government attempts to subordinate teacher training to the requirements of the National Curriculum by weakening its higher education base and locating it more in the schools. School-based training is not simply a way of making training more practical, but of ensuring that it becomes the servant of national curriculum implementation rather than an instrument of subversion and resistance.

Any tendency for officials, charged with implementing the National Curriculum, to accommodate the voices of teachers and academic educationalists was, until many teachers and schools revolted against the tests for 14-year-olds in 1993, viewed by government ministers as a sign of weakness. Although they were involved and consulted in the construction of the original draft orders for each national curriculum subject area, they have seen the results of their efforts continually modified by ministers. The trend has been to dissociate the acquisition of knowledge and skills from a consideration of value issues, an understanding of other cultures and culturally diverse points of view, and from the uses of inquiry and discussion as modes of learning. Knowledge has been increasingly reduced to information, and skills to techniques for processing it. The direction of the curricular reforms initiated by teachers during the first wave has been rapidly reversed by the state during the second wave.

Stuart MacLure, formerly editor of the *Times Educational Supplement*, has pointed out (TES, 22 February 1993) the Conservative government's tendency to interpret the role of the professionals as a conspiracy against society. Given the political diagnosis of our educational ills, it was inevitable that national curriculum reform came to adopt a confrontational stance towards teachers and other professional educationalists. As MacLure (1993) argued, the secretary of state for education expected them to 'do anything they are told without question, even if it goes against their professional judgment'. As a parent, he concluded, 'I certainly would not have wanted my children to be taught by compliant teachers with no conscience, nor any ultimate criteria of their own about what is professionally right'.

Much of the contention surrounding the implementation of the National Curriculum revolved around the arrangements for testing children's progress in learning at the various key stages outlined in the Reform Act of 1988. The first big row focused on the testing of 7-year-olds. Teachers protested that children of this age were too young to cope with the stress of testing and that it would not produce an accurate and fair picture of their achievements in the circumstances. Those involved in the 'pilot assessments' protested about the extent to which testing intruded on teaching time in classrooms and the generally unmanageable nature of the procedures they were required to follow. In 1993, English teachers protested about government plans to test 14-year-olds at Key Stage 3. They objected to the secrecy and lack of consultation which had surrounded the piloting of the tests (the Key Stage 1 pilot schools had made their views public and in doing so had won concessions for the rest). Teachers knew that increasingly they were being required to teach for the tests. Rather than tests being used to support and validate teachers' judgements about independently defined learning outcomes, they were used to define such outcomes and replace the teacher as the agent of assessment. The report of the Task Group on Assessment and Testing (TGAT), under the chairmanship of Professor Paul Black, had recommended a blend of internal teacher assessment and external testing as a basis for providing both diagnostic feedback to teachers and more summative information for parents and the public about children's progress (see DES 1989). However, later at the implementation phase, testing became uncoupled from teacher assessment, with the result that diagnostic assessment for purposes of teaching became dissociated from summative assessment for the purpose of providing public information.

Michael Marland, a London headteacher and renowned educationalist, entered the 'testing debate' about Key Stage 3 English, by arguing that the problem was not the tests but the uses to which they were put. He cogently represented the professional perspective when he argued that, 'Tests should not be seen as full pictures; they are limited devices to assist further consideration of the young person's needs' (*The Observer*, Schools Report, 17 January 1993). He made a strong plea for a proper analysis of the use of tests for teaching purposes as a basis for an agreed position between the government and teachers. Any such agreement would reinstate the teacher's voice as an integral part of educational assessment, and compromise the government's project of using assessment as a device for bringing teachers under the control of the educational consumer. In which case, the government would have to revise its views of the teaching profession as a conspiracy against society. To what extent did Sir Ron Dearing's 1993 review contribute to such a revision?

The report of the review recommended no fundamental changes in the basic structure of the National Curriculum, but reduced it to allow schools 20 per cent discretionary time for self-initiated curricula. It opted for a more slimline version of what existed, particularly with respect to reductions in the content of, and time spent on, subjects outside the 'core' (maths, English, science), and for a greater flexibility at post-16 to incorporate more vocationally oriented subjects for some students. Dearing also opted for reducing the amount of testing, and therefore the time teachers spend administering tests rather than teaching. The emphasis was to be placed on more streamlined tests within the core subjects alone, and much was made of giving teacher assessment equal status to test results. Both would be reported to parents and published in school annual reports and prospectuses. Test results would only be reported in aggregated form and not as school performance tables.

The government accepted these broad recommendations in a published response (DfE 1993) to the Interim Report of the Review (July 1993). It claimed the effect would be to improve substantially the 'manageability for teachers' of National Curriculum implementation. It argued that the revisions would also do something to reduce the hostility of teachers to tests in terms of their use to make 'unfair comparison' between schools. In spite of all this, I would argue that the Dearing Report did not significantly change the role of teachers in relation to the curriculum. In my view, the reforms still – albeit by a more 'softly, softly' approach – aim to deprofessionalize teachers and to reduce their role to the status of technicians.

To revise its view of the teaching profession, and its role in national curriculum reform, the government would need to reassess what happened during the first wave of reform. In the remainder of this chapter, I will try to indicate how a more positive account of the teachers' role might be constructed from a study of the earlier reforms.

Curriculum change: What we should have learned by now

The current fashionable view that curriculum change in the 1960s was largely teacher-initiated and unplanned is over-simplistic but it contains an element of truth. However, there was more centralized intervention than the Conservative government of the 1980s and 1990s was prepared to admit. In this section, I will attempt to analyse the central problems which emerged and argue that some interventions from the 'centre' to address these problems were based on a false set of diagnostic assumptions and therefore only served to perpetuate the problems. What we should have learned from the 1960s is that centralized social engineering does not work when it comes to effecting fundamental change to the quality of pupils' learning experiences in schools. What does work was actually discovered during the 1960s and 1970s but remains unacknowledged by politicians and government officials. The second wave of reform has simply strengthened and toughened up the social engineering model which emerged as central agencies increased their influence during the earlier 'first-wave' reforms. Having summarized the argument, I shall now expound it in some detail.

In 1976, MacDonald and Walker gave the following account of the origins of the reform movement in England and Wales:

> In the summer of 1961 a private British charity called the Nuffield
> Foundation was persuaded to donate some money to a group of teachers

who wanted to 'do something' about the grammar school science curriculum. The teachers belonged to the Science Masters' Association, one
of whose leading members had just come back from a visit to Russia
and America where he had been astonished to find school courses in
nuclear physics. The Nuffield Foundation's involvement in the development of new school curricula was soon to become a land mark in the
education system. Suddenly, in England and Wales, much of the planning and energy that since the Second World War had been devoted to
implementing the Education Act of 1944 was switched to the problem
of curriculum obsolescence. Whitehead's dictum 'The rule is absolute:
the nation that does not value trained intelligence is doomed' assumed
the status of an imperative, and a decade of planned educational change
began.

The Nuffield initiative set the wheels of the State turning, and in 1964
a new institution appeared, one that has since become a familiar if still
contentious feature in the formal structure of the school system. This
was the Schools Council for Curriculum Reform and Examinations. In
the space of twelve years the Schools Council has initiated and supported more than 160 projects whose major concern has been to lend
speed and quality to the ongoing process of curriculum change in the
classroom by centralising the functions of intervention and production.
The implicit model of planned change was thus centre peripheral: innovation is accelerated at the centre, then disseminated to the outposts.
(MacDonald and Walker 1976: 1)

The representatives of the Science Masters' Association who approached
the Nuffield Foundation were seeking to emancipate themselves and their
fellow science teachers from the prison of the traditional grammar school
syllabus. In this respect, the curriculum reform movement of the 1960s was
teacher-initiated. Note the introduction of the term 'curriculum' rather than
'syllabus', suggesting a need to get away from some of the connotations of
the latter. The reform movement involved more than an aspiration to change
the topics covered on a syllabus. It embodied a different conception of the
nature of school knowledge and how it should be represented to students by
teachers.

MacDonald and Walker (1976: 909) argued that Nuffield Science:

> can be seen as one stage of a continuing debate in which the tension
> lies between a view of science as a source of technical knowledge, and
> a view of science as a contribution to culture . . . between science as
> information and techniques to be learnt, and science as knowledge to
> be gained by the extension of imagination and understanding.

They also argued that the debate was not a new one and referred back to the
Devonshire report of 1870, which proposed that true science teaching should

consist of 'habituating the pupil to observe for himself, to reason for himself on what he observes, and to check the conclusions at which he arrives by further observation and experiment' (MacDonald and Walker 1976: 93). It was this view of science education as the reconstruction of the process of discovery in the classroom, rather than the acquisition of inert information, which characterized Nuffield Science and spread to other subject areas as the reform movement evolved. As I indicated earlier, it was not a movement to change the curriculum conceived as a syllabus. The traditional syllabus of the British school was not simply a list of pedagogically neutral content. It represented content in a form that served the purpose of systematically transmitting information and technical skills to children. Mere changes in syllabus content do not require fundamental pedagogical change, but *curriculum change* based on a fundamental reappraisal of the nature of school knowledge does, since it implies a new way of representing knowledge to the student.

Curricula are representations of knowledge for the purpose of teaching. They are the languages teachers employ to talk about things and events in the world and as such they imply what Bruner (1986: 125) calls 'a stance' – a point of view about the use of the mind in relation to these things and events. The curriculum, as the language of education, not only refers to things in the world, its content, but also marks the stance the teacher is to adopt towards the use of the student's mind in relation to them. Bruner recalls a statement one of his own teachers made in the classroom. She said, 'It is a very puzzling thing not that water turns to ice at 32 degrees Fahrenheit, but that it should change from a liquid into a solid'. He then recounts how she went on to provide an intuitive account of Brownian movement and of molecules which invited 'me to extend my world of wonder to encompass hers. She was not just informing me . . . She was a human event, not a transmission device' (p. 126).

The stances to knowledge marked down in curricula either invite teachers to express and extend their powers of understanding in the ways they represent knowledge to children, or they imprison teachers as transmission devices which represent knowledge as inert information. The curriculum reform movement of the 1960s, at least initially, was as much about teacher development as it was about changing the content of education. It was about changing the ways knowledge was represented in schools to children; not as information to be transmitted but as structures of ideas, principles and procedures which support creative and imaginative thinking about human experience. This, of course, does not necessarily imply changes in content. Knowledge of the same content can be represented in different ways to children, as Bruner's example illustrates; what his teacher did was to adopt a different stance towards it than he had been led to expect from teachers.

Nevertheless, changes in the way knowledge is represented by teachers in classrooms has implications for the selection and organization of content. The 'syllabus' organizes information around content categories. It enables teachers to transmit large amounts of information in an efficient and orderly way. But when knowledge is represented as structures which support inquiry, the traditional syllabus is a quite inappropriate form of content organization. This mode of representing knowledge is incompatible with a requirement for teachers to cover large amounts of information. It requires a more parsimonious organization of content around the central questions and problems which define the various disciplines by which human beings have attempted to make sense of their experience.

We can therefore interpret the initial impetus behind the curriculum reforms of the 1960s as an attempt to develop the professional role of teachers by reconstructing the curriculum which traditionally shaped their practice in the classroom. As the most creative curriculum developer of that period, Lawrence Stenhouse proclaimed: 'No curriculum development without teacher development'. Stenhouse (1975: 68) pointed out that this did not mean 'we must train teachers in order to produce a world fit for curricula to live in'. The message of the 1960s was that we needed to develop curricula fit for teachers to grow in, because the quality of children's education depended on the quality of the people teaching them. Stenhouse argued that it was the task of the curriculum developer to represent knowledge in a form that 'by virtue of their meaningfulness curricula are not simply instructional means to improve teaching but are expressions of ideas to improve teachers' (ibid.).

Such a view stands in marked contrast to the government's present stance on teacher training; namely, that it should equip teachers to implement the requirements of the National Curriculum. For Stenhouse, curricula were resources to help teachers reconstruct their view of knowledge and in its light their pedagogical relations with students in classrooms. They provided support for reflective practice rather than a 'straitjacket' into which the practice was required to fit. The phrases 'curriculum planning' and 'curriculum implementation' suggest that teachers' role is one of conforming their practice to a set of external curricular requirements or plans. 'Curriculum development', on the other hand, suggests the continuing reconstruction of the forms in which teachers represent knowledge in classrooms as they, in collaboration with their students, reflect about their teaching. Here the classroom is not so much an implementation site as a laboratory for pedagogical experimentation.

From the teacher-initiated curriculum reforms of the 1960s, an idea about the teacher's role in curriculum development emerged in Britain, which has subsequently spread throughout the world, namely that of 'the teacher as researcher'. The idea is usually attributed to Stenhouse (1975, 1980), and he certainly expounded it with enormous eloquence and insight. However, I have argued (Elliott 1991a: ch. 1) that what Stenhouse did was to articulate the logic of teacher-initiated curriculum reform. Stenhouse realized, perhaps more clearly than other curriculum developers working with teachers, that the professional transformation they were trying to accomplish implied a research stance towards their practice. This research stance was not separate from the pedagogical stance that characterized the reform movement of the 1960s. The latter aimed to enable pupils to appropriate knowledge in a form which supported independent (autonomous) thinking and the growth of understanding. But this required teachers to reconstruct the view of knowledge implicit in their traditional practice and the assumptions it embodied about how knowledge was to be represented to pupils in classrooms.

Stenhouse, reflecting on the problems of curriculum reform when he entered the field in the late 1960s, realized that a condition of teachers realizing their pedagogical aspirations was that they adopt a research stance towards their practice. This involved reflecting jointly about pedagogical ends and means (the assumptions which underpinned their practice concerning both the nature of knowledge and the ways of relating that knowledge to the minds of their students). Stenhouse (1983: 183) wrote about the relationship between information and the mind in the following terms:

> Of course we need instruction. And textbooks too. The key is that the aim of discovery and discussion is to promote understanding of the nature of the concessions to error that are being made in that part of our teaching where we rely upon instruction or textbooks. The crucial difference is between an educated and an uneducated use of instruction. The educated use of instruction is sceptical, provisional, speculative in temper. The uneducated use mistakes information for knowledge. Information is not knowledge until the factor of error, limitation or crudity in it is appropriately estimated, and it is assimilated to structures of thinking . . . which gives us the means of understanding.

What Stenhouse observed in schools was the inability of 'innovatory' teachers, in spite of their aspiration, to adopt a certain stance towards the information they provided students with. It was transmitted as not open to question, to the reconstruction of its meaning and significance for the issue at stake, and yet teachers expected their students to use it as a basis for judgement. Teachers were unaware that their practice, in spite of all the changes many had made to the organization of curriculum content and social arrangements in classrooms, was very continuous rather than discontinuous with the traditional curriculum. They persisted in the assumption that information was knowledge while expecting students to use it as a resource for their thinking. The only way they could have changed, to realize a greater consistency between aspirations and practice, would have been to analyse their practice together in the light of systematically gathered evidence.

The so-called progressive methods of the 1960s are now seen by those who embrace the New Right agenda in Britain, including New Labour politicians, to be responsible for a 'decline' in educational standards. The kind of stance towards knowledge and its representation, which I have referred to as the aspiration of the first wave of curriculum reform, was never fundamentally realized on any significant scale. What passes for progressive methods in schools – topic work, small group work, active learning projects – represent surface curricular changes that have been accommodated to traditional ways of representing content to students. For example, topic work is often reduced to children looking up information in books and copying it down in their workbooks quite mindlessly, and active learning methods are often reduced to providing contexts for children to apply information they have received rather than to evaluate it. As Alexander *et al.* (1992) pointed out in their government-commissioned report on primary school practice, such 'progressive methods' have become part of the taken-for-granted practice of teachers. It is my contention after 25 years of observing classrooms, that they are tacitly employed as methods of representing information as knowledge and differ only from more didactic methods by making concessions to children's interests. The so-called child-centred nature of these methods treats children's interests as extrinsic motivational hooks on which to hang informational content rather than intrinsic conditions of meaningful learning about content. All meaningful learning in relation to content involves students coming to see the content as intrinsically interesting. Many teachers are unaware of the gulf between their progressive rhetoric and their practice.

It may well be the case that the surface changes in curriculum practice I have cited are less effective and economical ways of transmitting information than didactic whole-class teaching. If *transmission* is how information ought to be handled in schools, then some recent secretaries of state for education have been right to want a return to more didactic teaching in classrooms. However, such a view is indicative of how the National Curriculum is being politically reconstructed at the implementation phase. To meet the requirements of simple, cheap and unambiguous forms of standardized testing, to provide performance indicators to educational consumers, the National Curriculum will increasingly redefine content as knowledge to be mastered rather than ideas which support creative and imaginative thinking. In spite of political claims that the implementation of the National Curriculum is raising educational standards, I would claim that it cannot if it is reinforcing an uneducational use of instruction, by denying students access to our culture in a form that develops their powers of understanding.

At the early stages of national curriculum implementation, ministers and officials assured teachers, that although the government prescribed content in the form of targets and programmes of study linked to them, it left teachers free to select teaching methods. The rhetoric appeared to respect a measure of professional autonomy for classroom teachers. But it is now changing fast. The government is increasingly using 'evidence' gathered by the Office for Standards in Education (Ofsted) as a basis for pronouncing on questions about appropriate teaching methods for implementing national curriculum requirements. It has begun to acknowledge the fact that a curriculum plan, which primarily organizes knowledge as informational content, can only be implemented effectively if it also controls pedagogy. In doing so, the government is having to abandon any pretence of safeguarding teachers' professional autonomy.

I have to agree with the government that the curriculum reforms of the 1960s failed to raise educational standards, not because progressive methods (e.g. discovery learning) were responsible, but because they were largely unrealized. The solution to the problem of standards is not the one provided by the current National Curriculum but the one discovered by Stenhouse towards the end of the 1960s; namely, helping teachers to adopt a research stance towards their teaching. Stenhouse designed his humanities curriculum as a research programme for teachers. In doing so, he was not only aware of the problems the science education developments encountered in realizing their aspirations in practice, but also of the solution being proposed by some to these problems, namely planning by objectives. Stenhouse believed that the 'objectives model of curriculum planning' being imported from the USA would seriously distort the nature of the knowledge teachers represented to students. This same planning model was later adopted by the government to design the National Curriculum.

Putting on the blindfold: Planning by objectives

According to the objectives model, rational curriculum planning begins with a specification of educational aims and then proceeds to break them down into behavioural objectives – statements of intended learning outcomes which are sufficiently precise and unambiguous to enable measurement. A programme of curriculum content, and learning tasks related to it, could then be rationally organized in the light of these statements, and criterion-referenced tests developed for assessing the extent to which the intended learning was achieved.

The first systematic use of the objectives model in the context of the 'first-wave' British reforms was the Schools Council's (1972) Science 5–13 Project. The majority of primary school teachers had undertaken little advanced study of science, and a large-scale curriculum development programme to promote science teaching with pre-secondary school children needed a device for focusing their attention on what scientific learning meant in this context. The objectives model appeared to meet this need. It was also seen as a device for shifting teachers' representations of knowledge towards a discovery mode. Hence, we find Hilda Taba (1962), one of the great advocates of discovery learning in the USA, pointing out that since 'education does not consist solely of the mastery of content, objectives also serve to clarify the types of powers, mental or otherwise, which need to be developed'. The 5–13 Project certainly saw its objectives in these terms. They largely referred to the development of children's conceptual powers and inquiry skills through discovery learning. To emphasize the use of the model to transcend a 'knowledge as information' perspective, the proponents of the objectives model often referred to 'process' as well as 'content' objectives. Moreover, the emphasis on the development of conceptual powers led 'rational' curriculum planners to incorporate stage theories of concept learning into their designs. For example, the objectives of Science 5–13 were grouped around Piaget's stages of conceptual development, giving teachers a vision of 'progression' in learning from one stage to another, and helping them to 'match' learning tasks to children's learning needs at each stage.

The following example from 5–13's plan (Schools Council 1972) illustrates the main features of the planning model it adopted. The general curriculum aim was to develop 'an inquiring mind and a specific approach to problems'. This was then analysed into eight 'broad aims', including 'developing basic concepts and logical thinking'. The latter was further analysed into more specific objectives organized around four stages of development. The objectives listed for the early stage of concrete operations were:

1.33 Ability to predict the effect of certain changes through observation of similar changes.
1.34 Formation of the notions of the horizontal and the vertical.
1.35 Development of concepts of conservation of length and substance.
1.36 Awareness of the meaning of speed and of its relation to distance covered.

Science 5–13 represents the use of the objectives model as a basis for centralized intervention in the curriculum development process. It emerged at the turn of the decade as the problems of securing curriculum change at the level of classrooms became only too clear to the Schools Council. The project marked a borderline between central support and central control. It was aimed at structuring the ways teachers thought about children's learning in their classrooms. But, at least at the initial stages of implementation, it left teachers to decide on the learning activities for achieving the objectives. Materials were produced for teachers in the form of ideas and suggestions for appropriate learning activities and ways of organizing them in classrooms, but ultimately responsibility for decision-making was theirs. Later it became clear that specifications of objectives and teacher materials were not enough to 'engineer' fundamental change in the ways teachers represented knowledge to pupils, and a supplementary project emerged to prescribe learning tasks and activities. The movement within the framework of the objectives model was towards the construction of a 'teacher-proof' curriculum involving greater centralized intervention in the specification of teaching/learning methods.

There is a remarkable continuity between the use of the objectives model in Science 5–13 and the design of the National Curriculum. The statements of broad aims are similar in form to the 'targets' stated for each subject area. The National Curriculum takes over the idea of 'progression' in learning through developmental levels. Rather than four there were ten levels specified for the National Curriculum, but unlike Science 5–13 their theoretical basis and rationale is far from clear. Statements of attainment against which progress towards each target can be measured were specified at each of the ten levels. These are very similar in form to the statements of objectives employed in Science 5–13. Finally, for each national curriculum target there is a prescribed programme of study in the form of learning tasks linked to attainment levels.

As a device for socially engineering improvements in the quality of teaching and learning in classrooms, there are a number of reasons why the planning model adopted by the National Curriculum is unsatisfactory. These were well-argued and documented in the educational change literature of the 1960s and 1970s.

Let us revisit the critique of the objectives model as a central planning device which emerged from the first wave of reform. I will provide three main arguments for rejecting it.

1 First, we have the powerful argument employed by Stenhouse (1975) that it distorts the nature of knowledge. Although it is true that the model is often used to emphasize the importance of developing children's powers of understanding in terms of concepts and inquiry skills, the way it does this carries forward many of the assumptions embedded in traditional ways of representing knowledge. Concepts, for example, are treated as having unambiguous and precise meanings. Their meaning is not something that is open to question. Children either understand or misunderstand a concept and this can easily be assessed by observing how it is used. According to Stenhouse, however, concepts are not so much objects of mastery as a focus for speculation. Within any discipline of inquiry, the key ideas which structure thinking are intrinsically problematic and open to a variety of interpretations. Disagreements about facts cannot simply be explained in terms of insufficient evidence, because people may disagree on what is to count as evidence (i.e. in their understanding of concepts). Thus historians may disagree over the causes of a past event, not because they lack sufficient evidence to resolve the issue, but because they have different understandings of the concept of historical causality, and these differences can be linked to personal values which inevitably bias and condition all human thought.

From Stenhouse's point of view, teaching children to learn through discovery involves inducting them into various forms of social discourse, which have evolved in our culture to address significant questions about our experience of the natural and social environment. Education becomes an induction into ways of discussing these questions. For Stenhouse, discovery learning is not a matter of getting children to reconstruct for themselves the precise and unambiguous ideas which are falsely assumed to underpin a 'knowledge of the facts'. Such a view of discovery learning, reinforced by the objectives model, ultimately subordinates the aim of developing the powers of understanding to the aim of acquiring certain and indubitable knowledge. It becomes a subtle means of representing knowledge as information. This became very clear when teachers experienced what became known as 'the discovery teacher's' dilemma on a large scale. What were they to do when the children adopted a different line of thought to the one which generated the correct answer? Should they simply tell the child? My response is 'why not?' If what you want from the child is right answers, then informing them may be a more effective and efficient means of getting them than discovery learning.

In reinforcing the view of concept learning I have described, the objectives model constitutes a misrepresentation of knowledge, because within our *postmodern* culture we now tend to experience all knowledge as uncertain and unstable, as provisional and open to revision. This experience of knowledge as a *dynamic* rather than *static* quality may be positively embraced or it may evoke a desire to return to the old certainties and their promise of a rational foundation for living. The objectives model was first employed in both the USA and UK in planning science curricula, and became more problematic as curriculum reform spread into the arts and humanities. However, it is now increasingly clear from historical and philosophical inquiry into the nature of scientific discovery, that the positivist account of science which has underpinned the development of science education in schools is now culturally, if not politically, obsolete.

2 A second reason for rejecting the objectives model of curriculum planning lies in its view of learning as a highly individualistic activity. Children are assumed to make progress in learning as isolated individuals who relate only to a sequence of prestructured tasks mediated by a teacher. The model reinforces an individualistic theory of discovery learning which is quite contrary to Stenhouse's view of learning as a process of induction into the various ways of discussing human experience which have evolved in our culture. But it is highly consistent with the ideology of possessive individualism, which underpins a production–consumption model of schooling.

Increasingly, we find contemporary learning theorists following on from Stenhouse the curriculum theorist, in emphasizing the social aspects of learning and the educational significance of reflective discussion in schools. Hence, we find Bruner (1986: 127) giving the following account of the development of his own theory of learning:

> Some years ago I wrote some very insistent articles about the importance of discovery learning on one's own, or as Piaget put it later (and I think better), learning by inventing. What I am proposing here is an extension of that idea, or better, a completion. My model of the child in those days was very much in the tradition of the solo child mastering the world by representing it to himself in his own terms. In the intervening years I have come increasingly to recognise that most learning in most settings is a communal activity, a sharing of the culture. It is not

just that the child must make his knowledge his own, but that he must make it his own in a community of those who share his sense of belonging to a culture. It is this which leads me to emphasise not only discovery and invention but the importance of negotiating and sharing, in a word, of joint culture creating as an object of schooling and as an appropriate step en route to becoming a member of the adult society in which one lives out one's life.

For Bruner, culture is being constantly created in the forums which enable participants in a culture to distance themselves reflectively from their presumed knowledge, to look at things from different points of view, and construct new visions of the world. The educational implications of this view of culture closely follow those argued by Stenhouse. For Bruner, education as an induction into culture must 'also partake of the spirit of a forum, of negotiation, of the recreating of meaning'. He is aware, as Stenhouse was, that such a conclusion 'runs counter to traditions of pedagogy that derive from another time, another interpretation of culture, another conception of authority; one that looked at the process of education as a transmission of knowledge and values by those who knew more to those who knew less and knew it less expertly'. He is critical of the presumption that learning follows a hierarchical sequence towards the achievement of more and more abstract knowledge: a presumption that underpins most curricula planned by objectives including the National Curriculum in the UK. Instead, Bruner offers an alternative account of the development of mind by reflecting about shifts in his own understanding of Shakespeare's play *Othello*. It is not that he now understands the play more abstractly than when he first encountered it as an adolescent, or that he knows more about the human emotions pride, envy, and jealousy that motivate the characters in the play. The play is not a statement about the human condition through the telling of a story, but rather the way the story is told, its language and craft, 'makes the drama reverberate in our reflection'. It is, Bruner argues, an invitation for us 'to reflect about manners, morals, and the human condition'. Such reflection is not abstract thought in the usual sense, but rather gives one 'a sense of the complexities that can occur in narratives of human action' (Bruner 1986: 128).

For Bruner, progress in learning is not primarily a matter of reaching higher and higher levels of abstract thought, although this may be involved, he argues, in physics and algebra. Even in these areas, the growth of understanding is indicated not by an increasing capacity to master the 'uncontaminated language of fact and "objectivity"', but by shifts in the stance the learner adopts towards the content he or she is presented with. In fostering such development in the form of understanding, Bruner argues that the educational process 'must express stance and must invite counter stance and in the process leave space for reflection, for metacognition'. It is this process 'of objectifying in language or image what one has thought and then turning around on it and reconsidering it', that permits the learner to reach higher ground (Bruner 1986: 129).

Only if the school curriculum permits students to reach this higher ground where they become, in Bruner's words, 'an agent of knowledge making as well as a recipient of knowledge transmission', will they be able to take responsibility as adults for developing the culture which shapes their lives. The implementation of a national curriculum constructed through an object-ives model and representing knowledge as non-problematic, as an individual rather than social achievement, and as something acquired by progressively moving through higher and higher levels of abstraction, will suppress rather than enhance the intellectual development of the majority of children in our schools. As a vision of what is involved in providing the mass of the citizenry with equality of educational opportunity, it is seriously flawed.

Moreover, politicians in Britain have not yet begun to see a problem of implementation that is already beginning to emerge. Crime and violence among schoolchildren has become a major social issue, and people are attributing responsibility to the breakdown of family and community life. For some this breakdown is attributed to political policies which cast citizens entirely in the role of possessive and acquisitive consumers of social goods and services. It is being suggested that such policies are destructive to the development of a sense of community in the young. What has yet to be appreciated is that our national curriculum framework constitutes a denial of the social being of children in favour of turning them into possessive individuals. This is the 'hidden curriculum' in our National Curriculum. As such, implementation will only reinforce the social alienation of children because it denies them the chance to develop a sense of what it means to participate with others in the construction of shared values and beliefs. Indeed, the National Curriculum threatens to undermine the culture itself, by transforming its elements into commodities which can be individually possessed rather than viewing them as common goods which bind individuals together.

3 The third reason for rejecting the objectives model is that it is an engin-eering model of change. The engineer designs a system which will fulfil cer-tain precise functions or goals, and then supervises its implementation. The plan enables the engineer to control the process of development by commun-icating his or her requirements to the workforce, and providing criteria for monitoring and supervising progress. The objectives model implies what Donald Schon (1971), in *Beyond the Stable State*, calls a centre–periphery system of social change. It is particularly attractive to those governments who cast their role in society in the form of the engineering metaphor. The problem with the objectives model is that it fails to take into account the complexities of human action and interaction in society. It 'blinds' the state to the complexity of the society it governs.

In the context of curriculum change, Stenhouse (1975: 77–8) argued that 'the objectives formula sidetracks and blurs the ethical and political problems associated with the control of education', and ignores the concrete experience of teachers in schools. It pre-empts discussion, for example, of such questions as: Can quality in education be defined in terms of common standards when the practical experience of many teachers suggests that the highest achievements of students are expressions of their individuality? Or, can educational events and effects be predicted when the experience of teachers suggests that 'our classes and teaching vary from year to year and in nominally similar classes in any one year'? Another way of putting this is to say that the assumptions about control which underpin and define the objectives model, and indeed the very notion of 'centrally engineered' curriculum change, appear to contradict the experience of teachers. They are also inconsistent with enabling pupils to participate in adult life in a democratic society. Such a society certainly presupposes equality of educational opportunities, but this does not imply the standardization of learning outcomes. A democratic form of social life requires citizens who are self-determining and therefore capable of actively shaping the conditions of their existence, and this presupposes that they have had equal educational opportunities to develop those dynamic personal qualities which constitute powers of self-determination. Equality of educational opportunity therefore implies respect for the individuality of every student. The problem with the standardization of learning outcomes in the form of objectives is that it reinforces the development of passive qualities in students, thereby inhibiting the development of their powers of self-determination and the cultivation of their individualities.

Schon (1971) argued that centre–periphery systems are prone to failure because the demands made on the centre by the periphery invariably outstrip its capacity to manage an appropriate supply of human and material resources to meet them. The centre also outstrips its capacity to stimulate and manage feedback from the periphery. In these circumstances, the centre tends to compensate by flooding the periphery with large quantities of information. Lacking adequate feedback mechanisms, it tends to misinterpret problems at the periphery as either problems of communication or 'resistance to change' on the part of vested interests. According to Schon, centre–periphery systems for delivering social change are characterized by *exhaustion*, *overload* and *mismanagement* at the centre. It is a vicious circle. Such systems promote this state of affairs by a lack of adequate feedback mechanisms, and this state of affairs provides the systems-managers with little 'space' in which to reflect about the feedback problem.

The objectives model of planning reinforces the view that implementation problems can be resolved through increasing the flow of information from the centre. It encourages the presumption that if things are not going according to plan, it is because the people at the periphery do not understand the plan. Once they understand it, they will simply do what is required. And when flooding the system with more and more information does not work, the centre responds by increasing its direct interventions in the socio-cultural context of action at the periphery. Such interventions will involve attempting to secure behavioural conformity to the plan. The assumptions built into the plan continue to blindfold the centre by preventing it from understanding the points of view, the values and beliefs, of those at the periphery and why they adopt them. When judged non-reflectively in the light of these assumptions, the culture at the periphery is simply wrong.

A very good example of the blindfolding effects of the objectives model is provided by a report on the implementation of the National Curriculum in primary schools, drawn up by the National Curriculum Council for the Secretary of State for Education (NCC 1993). It drew on a range of evaluation findings that suggest teachers have the following concerns:

1 The curriculum is proving to be unmanageable, too complex and over prescriptive (with 450 statements of attainment alone for stages 1 and 2, and 39 end of stage statements).
2 Depth is being sacrificed for breadth of learning.
3 Teachers feel they do not know enough to handle all the prescribed content, especially in science and technology.
4 Adequate resources (e.g. texts) are not available to support teaching in some subjects.
5 Adequate conditions in schools, such as lack of non contact time and a class based teaching system which requires each teacher to teach all nine National Curriculum subjects to their class, pose significant problems.
6 The arrangements for testing and assessment are impacting negatively on curriculum decisions and seriously reducing the amount of teaching time in schools.
7 The government is attempting to implement the curriculum too hastily.

The report interpreted some of these concerns – speed of implementation, the lack of resources and feelings of inadequacy about subject knowledge – as mere teething problems which will diminish with time. Whether teachers saw them in these terms is not at all clear. One could argue that such problems are inevitable consequences of a centre–periphery system of change; namely, that it necessarily underestimates time-scales, levels of resourcing and the degree of competence required to achieve meaningful change. In my view, they are unlikely to diminish significantly. What the report focused on as more fundamental is the concern about the manageability of the curriculum content and the issue of depth in the quality of teaching. But it provided no decent analysis of the nature of these concerns from the standpoint of teachers. For example, is the problem of content overload understood by teachers as one of having too many targets and statements of attainment, or is it due to the fact that in classrooms such statements are inadequate as criteria for selecting content? We are not told. Blindfolded by the assumptions which underpin the planning model, the National Curriculum Council proposed a solution in terms of a reduction in the number of objectives to be covered to 'the essentials', whatever that might mean.

Again, is the issue of breadth rather than depth in learning one that can be resolved by slimming down the number of objectives and getting teachers to reorganize their classrooms so that the only function provided for is the achievement of these objectives? For example, by more subject-based whole-class teaching, more setting of children according to ability, and less topic-based teaching in small groups. Learning as meta-cognition, as the social activity of constructing and reconstructing understanding, is not a concept such proposals acknowledge because the planning model excludes it. However, teachers' expressions of concern over quality rather than depth may well be grounded in something like this view of learning. The report displays some awareness of this concept at work in teachers' resistance to giving up topic-based curricula, mixed-ability teaching and learning in groups. But such approaches were summarily rejected as non-rigorous and intellectually unchallenging. Arguments teachers might put to show why this is not necessarily the case were presumed not to exist.

In possibly misrepresenting many teachers' expressed concerns about the implementation process, the National Curriculum Council report recommended forms of intervention in the organization and process of teaching and learning that are unlikely to effect improvements in the quality of education. This is because such interventions will not shift attitudes, although they may effect surface structural and behavioural changes. The report identified teacher culture as a problem for curriculum change at the level of practice, but failed to recognize that cultural change can only occur in the context of a reflective dialogue about practice: a dialogue shaped by the willingness of both parties to render the assumptions which underpin their respective practices problematic. This kind of dialogue between government and teachers, however, is impossible when the former interprets its role as a change agent in terms of social engineering and blueprint planning by objectives.

One particular manifestation of the objectives model operating in the context of centre to periphery curriculum reforms initiated by the UK Government, with respect to both the National Curriculum for basic education and, more recently, teacher training are the interpretative devices used to legitimate the power-coercive role of the state. The first device is to negatively stereotype the professional practitioners and thereby undermine public confidence in their activities. The second device at the 'consultation' stage, following the publication of proposed legislation to make certain curriculum objectives mandatory, is to interpret objections as resistance to change on the part of certain vested interests. The third device, at the implementation stage, involves interpreting 'silence' at the periphery as the achievement of consensus in favour of the reforms rather than simply acquiescence based on shared feelings of powerlessness. Through such devices, a 'legitimating discourse for the use of power' is constructed which marginalizes the 'voice' of teachers and produces an appearance of successful curriculum change.

Beyond social engineering: A vision of curriculum reform as a social experiment

How do we get out of the impasse which the experience of two waves of curriculum reform in the UK should have taught us we are in. Neither teacher-driven nor state-driven change appears to work. My own answer is that we must adopt a third option, described by David Marquand (1988: ch. 8), an ex-politician turned political theorist, as the negotiated adjustment of society. A 'negotiated' national curriculum would be continuously constructed and reconstructed in an interlocking network of local (school level), regional (local government level) and national forums. At each level, representatives of functional groups in our society – teachers, parents, employers, employees – and of appropriate levels of government, would share and negotiate in dialogue their respective visions of educational aims and processes, and attempt to translate the common understandings which emerge into forms of practice that leave room for further debate.

On this view, teachers and schools are accountable to regional and national forums in which the citizenry endorse, examine and evaluate curriculum change proposals and in the process educate each other about education. It is the kind of political process which Marquand calls 'mutual education'. As such, it reflects the educational theories of Stenhouse and Bruner. Curriculum development becomes the process by which the citizenry in partnership with teachers create and recreate an educational culture to support their deliberations about what it means to induct children into the culture of the society. Viewed in this light, national curricula are designs for an experiment in education to be carried out by teachers.

In our attempts to understand what a curriculum conceived as a social experiment might look like, we would do well to reach back over two decades to examine afresh Stenhouse's practical response to the impasse, apparent even then, between teacher-driven and socially engineered curriculum change, namely the Humanities Curriculum Project.

Stenhouse (1975: ch. 7) appealed to different sectors and groups in society in creating a humanities curriculum for young adolescents about to enter into adult roles and responsibilities as citizens. He posed the problem of how controversial moral, social and political issues within society could be handled in an educationally worthwhile way in schools. In doing so, he placed himself in the positions of parents, teachers and children belonging to various social groups that held different points of view on such issues. For example, he felt that a military parent might reasonably object to a teacher promoting pacifism in the classroom, while a pacifist parent might equally reasonably object to a teacher promoting the idea of a just war. The solution he proposed was one he felt they could agree to accept; namely, to induct students into the discussions of such issues within our pluralistic culture. He rejected the idea that the solution was to avoid handling value issues in the school curriculum which, I have argued, is the position of the National Curriculum (see Elliott 1994).

Having consulted society – in imagination if not in reality – Stenhouse proceeded, not to formulate aims and objectives, but to use the criterion that controversial value issues should be taught in schools as a basis for mapping out curriculum content. He proposed that controversial social situations and human acts could be grouped into such categories as 'War and Society', 'Law and Order', 'People and Work', 'Poverty', 'Relationships between the Sexes', 'Education' and 'Living in Cities'. The idea was to select products from the culture – poetry, literature, film, photographs, historical writing, works of art, research accounts from the behavioural sciences – which represented a diversity of points of view on these situations and activities. Stenhouse wanted teachers to play an active role in selecting such cultural artefacts, but given limitations of time and resources, he asked his team to produce a foundation archive which teachers and students could begin to use, and subsequently extend.

After the content had been basically mapped, Stenhouse proceeded to formulate an aim for using it in classrooms. It provided a vision of the purpose of humanities teaching as a whole rather than a map of objectives for specific subjects, as the National Curriculum Council proceeded to do twenty years later. Many teachers argued that the National Curriculum failed to provide them with a coherent view of the whole curriculum. Stenhouse (1975: 93) proposed that the overarching aim for humanities teaching should be 'to develop an understanding of social situations and human acts and of the controversial value issues which they raise'. He pointed out two important implications of this aim:

> First, it is implied that both students and teachers develop understanding; that is, the teacher is cast in the role of a learner. Second, understanding is chosen as an aim because it cannot be achieved. Understanding can always be deepened. Moreover, there must always be dispute as to what constitutes a valid understanding. The teacher and the group have to expect as part of their task an exploration of the nature of understanding.
> (Stenhouse 1975: 94)

From the evidence cited earlier, that the National Curriculum is making teachers feel intellectually inadequate, it is clear that what is meant by 'understanding' in the statements of attainment is very different from what Stenhouse meant. Indeed, it is different from what Bruner (1970) meant when he designed, at about the same time, a behavioural science curriculum for 10- to 12-year-olds in American elementary schools, entitled 'Man: A Course of Study'.

Although it was about teaching the concepts of the behavioural sciences – life cycle, social organization, structure and function, innate and learned behaviour, etc. – Bruner like Stenhouse saw concepts and ideas as resources to support reflective thinking about one's own experience. There was therefore no reason why teachers should presume mastery of the concepts before introducing them to children. They should cast themselves in the role of senior learners alongside their students. It is only when ideas are misrepresented as objectives, as objects of mastery, that teachers are made to feel guilty and inadequate about their lack of understanding.

For Stenhouse, to analyse 'understanding' as a set of knowledge objectives would misrepresent the nature of evidence in the humanities, for it invited reflection and discussion about one's own views of the human condition, rather than the drawing of fixed and certain conclusions. In other words, it suggested not so much a learning outcome as a learning process and a stance for teachers to adopt in relation to it. This is why Stenhouse proceeded to analyse the aim in terms of pedagogical principles governing the teacher's stance in handling evidence in the humanities, as opposed to objectives. Following the philosopher R.S. Peters (1966), he argued that aims like developing understanding were ideas which embodied values about what constituted an educationally worthwhile learning process. From them, one could derive a logically consistent set of principles of procedure which defined the teachers' stance to content. Stenhouse (1975: 93–7) specified the following principles for the study of controversial value issues within the humanities:

1 That controversial value issues should be taught in schools;
2 That discussion rather than instruction should be at the core of the learning process;
3 That divergent views should be respected and minority opinions protected;
4 That teachers should refrain from using their authority position in classrooms to promote their own views;
5 That teachers should accept responsibility for critical standards in discussion.

Given their similar vision of education, it should not be surprising to learn that across the Atlantic during the same period, Bruner (1970) had also specified the teacher's stance in relation to content for 'Man: A Course of Study'. The content was selected to enable 10- to 12-year-old children to explore three questions:

♦ What is human about human beings?
♦ How did they get that way?
♦ How can they be made more so?

It consisted of high-quality observational evidence on film of the behaviour of the Pacific salmon, the herring gull, the baboon and the Netsilik Eskimo. In relation to this evidence, children were continually invited to explore their response to it in the light of the conceptual framework of the course. To safeguard against the possibility of teachers treating this framework as a set of objectives rather than a resource for reflection, principles of procedure, called 'pedagogical aims', were devised to define their basic stance in the classroom, namely:

1 To initiate and develop in youngsters (10–12 years) a process of question posing (the inquiry method);
2 To teach a research methodology where children can look for information to answer questions they have raised and use the framework developed in the course (e.g. the concept of life cycle) and apply it to new areas;
3 To help youngsters develop the ability to use a variety of firsthand sources as evidence from which to develop hypotheses and draw conclusions;
4 To conduct classroom discussions in which youngsters learn to listen to others as well as to express their own views;
5 To legitimate the search; that is, to give sanction and support to open ended discussion where definitive answers to many questions are not found;
6 To create a new role for the teacher, in which he becomes a resource rather than an authority.

(Hanley *et al.* 1970: 5)

The similarities between the procedural principles of Stenhouse and Bruner are marked. Both curricula represent what Stenhouse called the 'process model of design' in contrast to design by objectives. It is a model our national curriculum planners ignored, and yet as a model of curriculum design it promises to offer a coherent vision of the whole curriculum through a specification of the educational aims and principles which ought to govern the handling of information in classrooms. Moreover, it leaves a great deal of space for the professional judgement and decisions of teachers. The aims and principles of procedure provide teachers with an orientation in the classroom without prescribing their concrete behaviour. They invite reflection about their meaning and significance for practice, and can only be realized on this basis. Stenhouse grasped this implication better than Bruner. He viewed his curriculum design not as a plan to be implemented by teachers, but as a framework to support an educational experiment. The Humanities Project, argued Stenhouse, encapsulated a theory about the relationship between knowledge, teaching and learning for teachers to test in the laboratory of their classrooms, and for society to examine in the light of the experiment. He expected teachers not simply to realize the theory in practice but also to reconstruct it through the study of practice.

During the pilot phase of the Humanities Project, Stenhouse asked teachers to regularly tape-record and analyse episodes from discussions. They were encouraged to look at their actions and interactions with students in terms of their consistency/inconsistency with the procedural principles. Recordings were sent to members of the central team (of which I was a member) and we also analysed them, feeding such analyses back to teachers to compare with their own and making follow-up visits for observation and discussion. During our visits, we frequently held tape-recorded interviews with students to elicit their self-understandings of their classroom experiences and their interpretations of teacher behaviour. With their permission, the interviews were released to teachers.

The research strategy that evolved came to be known as triangulation, or 'looking at evidence from different angles'. Observational evidence was recorded and the teacher analysed it by looking for patterns of action and interaction. He or she would then compare the analysis with accounts provided by central team members and/or peers, and by students. Teachers were generally encouraged to discuss divergent interpretations with peers and students.

As this collaborative research process progressed (see Elliott 1991a: 152–9), the central team members and participating teachers were able to identify problematic patterns of teacher action and interaction that generalized to a very significant degree across classrooms and schools. The teachers were asked for an experimental period to replace such practices with alternative action strategies that appeared to be more consistent with the procedural principles, and to monitor their effects in the classroom using the same triangulation strategies as before. For example, it was suggested that they replace the widespread habit of asking students if they agreed with a point of view (and commonly interpreted by the latter as pressurizing them to agree), by asking if anyone disagreed with it. Teachers were asked to make these changes on the basis of an analysis of teaching which they had collaborated in, not as authoritative prescriptions from on high, but as experimental action hypotheses to test over a particular period of time and to be further modified in the light of evidence. The experiment had dramatic effects on the quality of discussion and students' contributions to it in many classrooms.

Following the pilot experiment, the project moved into a period of national dissemination. It not only disseminated its teaching materials and an account of the pedagogical rationale which underpinned their selection and use, but through practical workshops all over the country it introduced teachers and schools to the action research methodology it had developed to support pedagogical change in classrooms, and to the significant questions that needed to be addressed in realizing such change. The project produced a self-training manual to assist teachers to study their own teaching (Stenhouse 1970a). It not only outlined a research strategy for gathering and analysing data, but in the light of the pilot experiment posed a list of questions to ask in relation to the data.

The curriculum, as Stenhouse conceived it, specified not only content, aims and pedagogical principles, but also an action research programme to support teacher reflection and discussion about the aims and principles and the problems of realizing them in forms of appropriate action. Through action research in the context of the process model, pedagogical aims and methods constitute joint objects of reflection. Teachers are involved in a reflective process of reconstructing not only their methods but also the vision of education that underpins them. Such involvement provides the key to resolving the problem which has beset both teacher-driven and state-driven change; namely, of transforming the professional culture that shapes practice.

However, Stenhouse was only too aware that the traditional ways of representing knowledge in classrooms are reinforced by schools as organizational systems. Realizing that it was difficult for teachers to critique the constraints of 'the system' on their capacity to change classrooms, he appointed a schools study officer, Barry MacDonald, to set the problems of classroom change in a broader institutional context. MacDonald embarked on a series of case studies of schools in a search to understand the institutional conditions that supported and constrained pedagogical change in classrooms. He became aware of the ways in which the expectations of external groups in the wider society – parents, employers and policy-makers – influenced these conditions and decided that they needed better information against which to judge the problems and potential of curriculum innovations like the HCP. He gathered data about their perceptions and judgements of the HCP, and from them identified issues which were then explored in the school case studies. The idea was to provide the various interest groups with a database to inform intelligent public discussion with schools and teachers about the problems and potential of curriculum change proposals. It was an idea that MacDonald (1974) further developed in his model of 'democratic evaluation'.

It is not difficult to see the connection between MacDonald's evaluation model and Marquand's idea of politics as a form of 'mutual education'. This form of evaluation constitutes a political process which enables different agencies and groups in society to share, discuss, test and renegotiate their visions of education in dialogue with the teaching profession. Educational action research is the complementary activity of enabling teachers to participate fully, confidently and openly in this dialogue.

The HCP played a major role in constructing the cultural resources we need to develop an alternative vision of a national curriculum. It is a curriculum where both discipline-based and interdisciplinary content will be selected by society in terms of its relevance to the great debates that have occurred and recur in different forms within our culture. It is a curriculum that will induct children into those debates in a way that enables them to make sense of their experience of the world together, and in doing so to play their part in recreating our culture. It is a curriculum that will be open to the professional judgement of teachers and support the development of their capacities for judgement. Over the last 20 years, action research, as an approach to teacher professional development, has been an integral component of many higher education and local government-based part-time courses for teachers, and has influenced the professional culture in many schools through the development over time of a 'critical mass' of reflective practitioners. Finally, it is a curriculum designed to yield public information about the quality of processes and procedures in schools: conceived in terms of their consistency with educational aims and values rather than their productivity in generating predetermined learning outcomes.

This in no way implies that the quality of learning outcomes cannot be assessed in such a curriculum context. But the assessment of learning is an intrinsic part of teaching, and cannot be divorced from it without distorting the process of education. That teachers should take responsibility for critical standards in the classroom was a key pedagogical principle of the HCP. For Stenhouse, such standards did not predict outcomes by standardizing them, but consisted of criteria for responding critically to students' thinking as it unfolded and manifested itself in often unanticipated ways within their work:

> The worthwhile activity in which teacher and students are engaged has standards and criteria immanent in it and the task of appraisal is that of improving students' capacity to work to such criteria by critical reaction to work done. In this sense assessment is about the teaching of self assessment.
>
> (Stenhouse 1975: 95)

Our current National Curriculum distinguishes teachers' formative assessments from summative assessment for public consumption in the form of standardized test results. This has evidently happened because teacher assessments were deemed to be too variable and therefore untrustworthy. Here lies the heart of the problem. Testing implies not trusting teachers. Stenhouse recognized the same problem when he argued that critical assessment implies complex and difficult judgements, and therefore exposes the strengths and weaknesses of teachers. Students want criticism against criteria when they trust their teachers, he argued, and marking against objectives when they do not (Stenhouse 1975: 95). Our National Curriculum and assessment system can be sympathetically portrayed as our government's attempt to protect children from weak teachers. Stenhouse simply proposed an alternative solution to the problem by designing a curriculum to develop teachers as reflective professionals. Both alternatives, the objectives and process models of curriculum design, emerged as solutions to the problems of poor teaching during the first wave of curriculum reform. Twenty years later, the UK Government opted for one of them. As a basis for national curriculum design, the other solution awaits the time when our society is prepared to risk seeing the curriculum as an innovative experiment which develops teachers.

3

The Curriculum Dimensions of Student Disaffection

Introduction

In the previous two chapters, I have portrayed two contrasting models of curriculum change. The first model views curriculum change as a social experiment in education, in which teachers as researchers of their own practices play a major generative role and render their experiments open to public scrutiny and critique. The second model views curriculum change as a piece of social engineering in which control is located outside the teaching profession and made possible by prespecifying measurable outcomes of schooling and holding teachers accountable for their production. It has not been an unbiased portrayal and Chapter 1 makes clear why it could not be otherwise. Given my formative experience as a teacher in a highly innovative secondary modern school, how could I subsequently deny the validity of that experience by accepting a model of curriculum change that places little trust in the generative capacities of teachers, and in spite of a rhetoric about the minimum entitlement of students gives them little space to articulate their experience of the curriculum provision they are supposed to benefit from?

In Chapter 2, I attempted to depict how the objectives model of socially engineered curriculum change, which emerged alongside the idea of change as a social experiment in education, became taken up as the basis for state-controlled curriculum reform in the UK. I argued that the use of the model 'blindfolds' the state and renders it incapable of comprehending the complexity of the society it governs. It is therefore unable to see how the National Curriculum reinforces rather than reduces a sense of alienation from society on the part of students. At the same time as the UK Government is claiming that the National Curriculum is 'driving up standards' in schools, it is having to deal with the manifestations of disaffection on the part of students in schools – violence, disruptive behaviour and non-attendance – on an unprecedented scale. The problem is increasingly being represented in the media as a matter of widespread public concern. At the time of writing (October/ November 1996), it has received unprecedented coverage in relation to the publicity surrounding The Ridings School in Halifax, where teachers demanded the exclusion of sixty disruptive pupils, the headteacher was removed from post, and the Ofsted inspectors called in. The then secretary of state for education promised new legislation to combat indiscipline in schools, involving the prescribing of home–school contracts and giving schools more powers to exclude disruptive pupils. Another response to the current moral panic created by extensive media coverage of incidents is to 'cobble together' statements about the moral and social values schools should inculcate in students. Yet, as I indicated in Chapter 2, the state-controlled National Curriculum is shaped by an ideology of *possessive individualism* which, in spite of its espoused aims of developing students *personally*, *morally* and *spiritually*, ignores their development as social beings and the value-issues they will need to confront in the process. What the state appears to be incapable of entertaining is the possibility that many students are alienated from the curriculum 'reforms' it has engineered in schools because they disconnect learning from their needs as social beings. In 1988, I predicted that 'the proposed national curriculum will unwittingly alienate young people from their own natural powers, which will nevertheless manifest themselves on a massive scale in ever new and sophisticated forms of human destructiveness'. This possibility is not only ignored by the state but unvoiced in the media. If such a possibility were entertained and publicly debated, it would throw the claim that the 1989 reforms are working into doubt and therefore threaten to destabilize a discourse which legitimates the power of the state to socially engineer worthwhile curriculum change. To what extent does research and analytic commentary on the causes of student disaffection provide us with reasons and evidence for believing that the curriculum is a significant factor? The inquiry which follows addresses this question and is therefore biased by 'a search for instabilities' (Lyotard 1979) in current curriculum provision.

'Disaffection': Perspectives on the problem

Deviance theories of disaffection

The 'problem' of disaffected students in schools appears to be one thing policy-makers, the general public and the teaching profession agree about. As a recent NFER report (Kinder *et al.* 1995) points out, the government White Paper *Choice and Diversity* (DFE 1992) 'acknowledged the serious problem of disaffection in schools' and enabled large numbers of LEAs to apply successfully for GEST 20 funding to tackle the problem. The search for solutions has largely focused on two particular manifestations of disaffection; namely, 'truancy' (increasingly redefined as persistent non-attendance from school) and disruptive behaviour. They establish the boundaries of the discourse about causes. Hence, it is hardly surprising to discover that most of the research and analytic commentary on disaffection over the last ten years has focused on these behavioural indicators (see Tattum 1986; Booth and Coulby 1987; Reid 1987; Rogers 1990; Schostak 1991; Carlen *et al.* 1992; Dyson 1992; Cooper 1993; O'Keefe 1993; Irving and Parker-Jenkins 1995; Kinder *et al.* 1995; O'Keefe and Stoll 1995; Dorn 1996). This literature reflects a marked shift away from an earlier individual *psychology* perspective, that sought explanations for disaffection in pathological states of mind and personality traits. The dominant perspective represented in this literature is a *social psychological* one that seeks explanations in theories of social deviance, and matches the current tendency to base strategies for managing truancy and disruption in schools on the assumption that they constitute *deficit* behaviours, often parentally condoned, on the part of a minority of pupils who require separate treatment of a remedial nature from students who conform to the normal requirements of schooling.

Deviance theories therefore tend to underpin strategies which treat truanting and disruptive pupils as a sub-category of those with special educational needs (e.g. Tattum 1986). They imply that the problem of disaffection can be 'contained' in ways which do not destabilize the system of mainstream schooling as a whole and the basic norms and values which underlay it. Such theories tend structurally to confine the problem to largely working-class and black adolescent males in secondary schools, and leave the rest of the system intact. Moreover, they frame the problem as a difficult one for teachers possessing the normal range of skills to resolve without resort to 'exclusion' from school or additional specialist help from educational psychologists and trained SEN teachers. Deviance theories also legitimate decisions by government to address the problem by targeting the use of scarce public resources towards particular schools rather than others.

The use of social deviance theories to frame research and analytic commentary is often implicit and unexplicated. Two major theoretical perspectives appear to frame the current discourse (for accounts of such theories, see Hargreaves *et al.* 1975; Schostak 1991). The first, *cultural transmission theory* stems from the belief that faulty socialization into 'impoverished' local and family cultures is a major cause of disaffection. Such a theory is embedded in accounts of persistent non-attendance as 'parentally condoned absence'. Interestingly, there has been little research on how the parents of 'deviants' viewed their children's conduct. In a rare example of such research, Brown (1987) challenged the cultural transmission theory in a rare example of research into the attitudes of parents with non-attending children. He found that many neither condoned their children's absence from school or held negative attitudes to schooling, and concluded that students' 'views of their schooling are formed independently of their parents' opinions'. The destabilizing potential of his findings is evidenced by the reaction of one major commentator in the field (see Reid 1987), who found them puzzling, surprising and 'difficult to accept', and felt that the problem lay in the sampling or the questions asked.

The second type of social deviance theories used, often tacitly, to frame research and analytic commentary are *process theories* (e.g. strain theory, sub-cultural theory and labelling theory), which seek explanations for disaffection within the students' experience of schooling. For example, Tattum (1986) appears to use a combination of strain and labelling theory to interpret data gathered from semi-structured interviews with students. He argues that the inconsistent behaviour of teachers, when they react differently towards students who break the same rules, is generally perceived by disruptive students as unfair and the major reason for their behaviour. Such differential treatment, Tattum argues, is based on labelling students according to either the reputations they have acquired in school or organizationally defined attributes. It implies a preference for students who conform to some stereotypical image of the ideal student role. Those who find it difficult ('a strain') to conform to the stereotype will tend to react to differential treatment by becoming disruptive.

Schostak (1991), drawing on Hargreaves *et al.* (1975), has argued that different ways of explaining behaviour construed as 'deviant' are by no means ideologically or value-neutral. Different theoretical perspectives 'are founded upon, and lock into' different 'hidden moral and political discourses', which permit certain questions to be asked but not others. Commentators and researchers may differ in their causal explanations (e.g. with respect to the significance of home background compared with school factors) because what they take to count as causal evidence reflects different ideological biases.

However, the findings of school effectiveness researchers (see Rutter *et al.* 1979; Reynolds 1994) that schools can make a difference to students' performance and compensate for social and economic disadvantage are being increasingly used to reconcile the two explanatory frameworks cited above. Both Reid (1987) and Cooper (1993) appear to share the view of school effectiveness researchers that schools can compensate for faulty socialization in the home and neighbourhood. In other words, schools can either reinforce or ameliorate culturally transmitted attitudes to schooling. What is at stake here is whether schools are simply implicated in the production of deviant behaviour or its root cause. If the former, then they can view themselves as having to solve a problem which originates from an external source. Hence the common view expressed in a lot of the literature and current policy pronouncements on disaffection that solutions depend on securing the collaboration of parents. Also, if the schools are not the root problem, then it is sensible for them to entertain exclusion as a last resort strategy. If, however, they are the root cause, then it is difficult for them to find an excuse for failing to solve it, and they will be expected to find solutions which are inclusive.

Cooper (1993) claims that his descriptive analysis of students' experience in two residential schools for students with emotional and behavioural problems, constitutes phenomenological evidence to support the findings of school effect-iveness research. The students' accounts are grouped into three categories: respite from harmful influences in the home, neighbourhood or mainstream school; therapeutic and supportive relationships with teachers and peers in the school; opportunities for developing themselves as individuals. According to Cooper, the analysis is supported by Reynolds and Sullivan's (1979) finding that 'incorporative' as opposed to 'coercive' schools achieve higher rates of academic success and attendance, and lower rates of delinquency. The incor-porative in contrast to the coercive school secures compliance to its norms and values by rewards rather than punishments, by tolerating a measure of deviance and dissent, by giving pupils responsibility within the organization, and generally enhancing their feelings of self-worth.

In a note on his research methods, Cooper claims that his data-gathering and analysis was unbiased and purely concerned with generating a pheno-menological description of students' experience of schooling. However, after close inspection, I would suggest that his descriptive analysis is saturated with implicit theories of deviance that are as much imposed on the data as derived from it (see Cooper 1993: 131–50). Moreover, I would argue that similar theories underpin the school effectiveness finding he believes supports his analysis. As a solution to the problem of deviance, the idea of the incorporative school itself implies process theories which fit the biases that tacitly underpin Cooper's descriptive analysis. First, there is a sub-cultural theory which ex-plains deviant behaviour as something which is learned through membership of oppositional groups within a coercive social organization. Since the incor-porative school is one which secures compliance by co-option rather than coercion, it leaves little social space for oppositional groups to emerge in. Secondly, there is a labelling theory which explains student deviance as the product of stereotyping those who break the rules. In the incorporative school, compliance is secured by rewarding rather than punishing students and thereby reducing the need to define them as deviants.

One can therefore argue that, given the theories of deviance which framed the data-gathering and analysis in the first place, a certain theory of effective schooling inevitably follows. It is not so much the evidence which supports Cooper's theoretical conclusions as the assumptions he makes from the start about what constitutes evidence about the causes of disaffection.

The claims of school effectiveness researchers to have discovered the mech-anism by which schools can make a difference in student attitudes to school-ing is very seductive to those who construe disaffection in terms of deviant behaviours. School effectiveness research provides a quantitative complement to so-called 'phenomenological' studies of school disaffection based on stud-ent interviews, and thereby lends the authority of an 'objective' quantitative science to qualitative analyses of subjective data. In performing this function, school effectiveness research can blinker 'disaffection' research to the issue of theoretical bias.

In this respect, it is interesting to note how Cooper reads interview data about the value students place on their development as individuals in the light of the co-option strategies employed in the incorporative school for securing compliance. Whereas Cooper appears to see no inconsistency between the students' values and securing compliance through co-option, an alternative reading of the student data might be that their individuality is best respected in a school which accommodates their values by negotiating norms. However, such a reading is inconsistent with the assumption that disaffection is a form of social deviance and that its solution involves devising effective strategies for securing compliance to pre-established norms.

For Schostak (1991: ch. 10), an educational strategy for handling disaffection must be founded on a respect for students as persons capable of reflexively and imaginatively transforming the conditions which shape their lives. Educational responses to the problem of student disaffection are not based on a strategic concern to modify behaviour understood as deviant, but on a concern to make schooling more educational for all students by establishing curriculum and pedagogical conditions which respect their individuality as persons. This educational perspective on the problem of student disaffection places questions of curriculum and pedagogy at the centre of any search for solutions.

Cooper's and others' preference or bias towards explaining disaffection in terms of social deviance theories, which also happen to underpin much school effectiveness research, result in a neglect of considerations of the purposes and functions of schooling as these are manifested in the curriculum and its associated pedagogy. As Schostak (1991) has argued, social deviance theories offer 'no effective critique of the structure and purposes of schooling, merely an exhortation to be a "deviance insulative" teacher'.

Disaffection as rational choice

Over the last decade, an alternative understanding of disaffection has begun to emerge in the literature from a few rather disparate studies, with the result that it has been given less 'voice' in the political and public discourse about education. Non-attendance and disruptive behaviour are understood as *rational* rather than *deviant* behaviours (see Sayer 1987; Schostak 1991; Carlen, *et al.* 1992; O'Keefe 1994; O'Keefe and Stoll 1995; Dorn 1996).

On this view, the roots of the problem lie not so much in a 'pathology of absence' as in a 'pathology of presence' (see Sayer 1987). It lies in curricular practices – the ways in which schools organize and transact formal learning – whose aims, purposes and norms have failed to keep pace with social change. For Sayer, the world outside of school has changed beyond recognition and no longer needs to be accessed through books and dependence on the memory store of teachers in an age of mass media and home computers. Why, he asks, should students prolong their dependence on adult authority through an organization invented for the ignorant and untravelled masses when they have been the first to learn the use of the information networks which proliferate around us, and bring the world to their fingertips? What needs to be explained is why so many students attend school and conform to its requirements rather than why some don't? Sayer suggests that many students turn up at school for reasons which have little to do with the formal curriculum provision, although they good naturedly conform to its requirements, but have a lot to do with finding school an unthreatening environment in which they can find space for self-discovery and development through relationships with their peers.

Both Sayer and Schostak call for an *educational* response to this informal curriculum, not by colonizing and subordinating it to the established curriculum structures and thereby spreading the tedium (a strategy evidenced in the establishment of cross-curricular life themes within the National Curriculum). The educational response constructs the formal curriculum from the agendas of the students, to support the development of their capacities for reflexively shaping the conditions of their lives. The unit for organizing learning needs to shift from the 'classroom' to the students' experience of life outside the school. If there is anything special about schools, any value they can add to students' learning outside them, it must be about their contribution to education for 'autonomy, democratic decision-making, releasing potential, giving opportunities for initiative, opening up windows, looking and linking outwards: some would call it truancy' (Sayer 1987).

Disaffection as lack of engagement

One implication of Sayer's and Schostak's analyses is a redefinition of disaffection beyond the boundaries of truancy and disruption to include those who are *present* but have made their disaffection from the formal curriculum *invisible*. Research by Rudduck, Chaplain and Wallace (1996) into students' experiences of teaching and learning in secondary schools, suggests that significant numbers of students have low levels of engagement in learning tasks, and that this is related to a perceived lack of connectedness with the things that matter to them in the world outside school, a perceived lack of control over the planning and execution of their work, and a perceived lack of opportunity to locate their learning in real experiences of the things they are 'learning' about. Wallace argues that students do not have to be engaged in learning tasks to carry them through. They may comply with learning requirements that they find boring or dislike for the sake of enjoying the company of others, even that of a friendly teacher, for strategic reasons, such as winning approval or avoiding punishment, or for instrumental reasons, such as passing exams and getting a job. The student interviews suggested that low levels of engagement are related to highly routinized and institutionalized tasks over which students have little pro-active control. In these respects, Wallace echoes Sayer's 'pathology of presence', and in my view is articulating a form of student disaffection which is as manifest in low achievement as in non-attendance and disruptive behaviour.

If one defines disaffection as a lack of subjective engagement in learning tasks, and not simply in terms of overt behaviour, then its solution for both the *present* and many of the absent will primarily focus on the way these tasks are shaped through both curriculum and pedagogy.

Disaffection and the school curriculum

A number of researchers and analysts, on the basis of student interviews, have identified the formal curriculum requirements in schools, particularly since the inception of a nationally prescribed and subject-based curriculum, as a major source of non-attendance and disruptive behaviour. However, some have tended to be blinkered in their search for solutions by the assumption that the problem essentially lies in the processes by which deviance is constructed in schools (see Booth and Coulby 1987; Irving and Parker-Jenkins 1995). This assumption tends to the conclusion that what is needed is a dual curriculum in schools, one for the disaffected deviants and one for the academically motivated. If Sayer, Schostak and Rudduck *et al.* are right, then the solution rests on a false diagnosis and may mask the scale of the problem in our schools.

This is indeed the position of O'Keefe and Stoll (1995), following O'Keefe's (1994) questionnaire study of students' reasons for truancy. They argue that seeing truancy as a form of deviant rather than rational behaviour focuses attention on blanket truancy and ignores post-registration truancy, where students absent themselves at particular times from lessons in particular subjects. They claim that overall 30 per cent of students are truanting from school in years 10 and 11 and that many of these are disaffected from particular subjects. Only one in ten truants expressed the traditional view of the truant as 'alienated from the whole process of schooling'. The reasons they gave for curriculum disaffection echo Wallace's interviews with disengaged pupils and include 'not relevant to their lives' (36 per cent), 'teacher not making lessons attractive' (29 per cent), and 'unappealing subject matter' (22 per cent).

Kinder *et al.* (1995), in their survey of educational professionals' perceptions of the major causes of disaffection, also highlight the significance of curriculum factors, particularly with respect to the National Curriculum and assessment arrangements cited by teachers with a major responsibility for handling the disaffected at Key Stage 4. The perceived irrelevance to their lives outside school of some prescribed national curriculum subjects, changes in examination and curriculum procedures (e.g. league tables emphasizing GCSE grades A–C and the decline of coursework-based assessment), a sense of failure stemming from curriculum experiences structured in terms of targets and attainment levels, curriculum pressure resulting in a reduction in time for pastoral care, and inappropriate pedagogy were all frequently cited curriculum factors.

Shifting the analysis of the problem of disaffection away from the organizational construction of deviance to focus on the structure and content of the curriculum and the ways it is interpreted in the pedagogical transactions between teachers and students, raises the question of whether schools have the power to effect solutions to the problem. The structure and content of the curriculum embody conceptions of the ends of schooling which are constructed in the socio-political discourses operating in the wider society. It therefore follows that if the causes of disaffection lie primarily in a curriculum and pedagogy shaped by discourses operating in the socio-political sphere, then the schools alone cannot be held accountable for effecting solutions as both current school inspection procedures and school effectiveness research tend to assume.

We find that researchers who agree that disaffection cannot be explained in terms of deviance theory alone, and identify the curriculum as a major cause instead, may nevertheless disagree about why the subject-based curriculum is a source of disaffection. At stake here are questions about the ends of schooling.

O'Keefe's understanding of the curriculum factors which cause disaffection are clearly shaped by the ideological discourse of the 'free market' and appear to shape the way he constructed his questionnaire for students and his interpretation of their responses. He is not in favour of a state-controlled curriculum and clearly understands the link between disaffection and a curriculum structured around subjects in terms of the latter's symbolic and ideological significance for such control. He wants a more deregulated curriculum that is shaped by labour markets and therefore more vocationally relevant. He believes that it will lead to a more socially inclusive educational system. His research reinforces the 'new right' predilection for allowing students at Key Stage 4 to opt out of the National Curriculum in the non-core subjects in favour of prolonged periods of work experience.

On the other hand, Schostak, Sayer and Rudduck *et al.* understand the link between curriculum and disaffection in terms which go beyond a perceived lack of vocational relevance to embrace all that matters to pupils personally and socially.

Understanding disaffection as a problem about the aims, purposes and normative basis of formal schooling in the late twentieth century: (a) brings the curriculum structures in schools into focus in a way that understanding disaffection as a form of social deviance does not; (b) recasts the boundaries of the concept of 'disaffection' to include those students who, for instrumental reasons, outwardly conform to the requirements of the formal curriculum but find few intrinsic reasons for doing so; and (c) gives it a central place on the agenda of curriculum studies as an interdisciplinary field of inquiry and research in education, and treats it as no longer the exclusive preserve of research into special educational needs by specialists in the field.

Disaffection, the purposes of schooling and socio-economic change

Relatively few recent studies of disaffection have employed socio-historical analysis to understand its contemporary manifestations. The ESRC-sponsored study of truancy by Carlen *et al.* (1992) and the institutional and social history of school failure and drop-out in the USA by Dorn (1996) are notable in this respect. Carlen and co-workers' socio-historical account questions certain 'prevailing myths regarding the links between compulsory education and school non-attendance: that truancy is necessarily school-related, an easy option or a feature of faulty working-class socialisation'. The authors argue that most of 'the flaws' currently being attributed to our educational system, including truancy and indiscipline, originate in historical and structural contradictions that 'have always characterised the beleaguered relations between state, family, education and the economy'. The standards debate is nothing new and has persistently recurred since the introduction of compulsory schooling. At the source of such debates is the problem of normalizing schooling as something which is self-evidently good for everyone. Carlen *et al.* argue that ever since the introduction of compulsory schooling, a substantial section of society have remained unconvinced of its benefits. Schooling in this context takes on a major function of containment and control, but they find little historical evidence for believing that efforts to compel students to attend and legal threats will significantly influence attendance, which is essentially shaped, they argue, by students', parents' and families' experience of the changing relations between schooling, the economy and the labour market.

Carlen *et al.* (1992) argue that non-attendance is currently being perceived by policy-makers as an important issue because it is the other side of the coin to the issue of attendance posed by the twin pillars of the 1988 Educational Reforms, namely, the National Curriculum and Local Financial Management in Schools (LMS). They locate both in the ideological project of the government; namely, the creation of a deregulated and highly differentiated education market operating through the mechanism of parental choice, and in which schools compete for parents' custom on the basis of information they provide about the quality of their products (students). Competition is accentuated through LMS, which links funding to the number and type of students enrolled. Within this deregulated market, the purpose of the National Curriculum, with its subjects focus, minimum standardized benchmarks and its accompanying key stage system of assessment, is to serve as a guarantor of diversity and choice. Its social function is to legitimate the deregulated education market by 'driving up' standards. The structure of the National Curriculum reflects its 'mechanistic' function as a means of social control over the learning process. Schools are expected to turn on the 'social control' screw more tightly with respect to student behaviour, under the guise of becoming 'effective schools'. In the name of raising standards, such a control strategy will, Carlen *et al.* prophetically conclude, increase rather than reduce the incidence of school-located problems.

There is little evidence, Carlen *et al.* (1992) argue, that the subject-based National Curriculum is actually linked to corresponding changes in the labour market, job opportunities, the transition between school and work, and thereby to the occupational aspirations of students which influence their motivation, discipline and school attendance. This lack of a motivating relationship between the National Curriculum and productive labour means that non-attenders are unlikely to opt into a process of schooling whose social function will largely appear to be one of containment and control; a strategy for delaying rather than equipping students for entrance into the labour market and the responsibilities of active citizenship.

Carlen *et al.* (1992) point out the contradiction in the English educational reform between the market mechanisms for extending choice and the claim to provide universality of educational provision through the National Curriculum. They argue that mechanisms like local financial management, open enrolment and opting out of local government control do not provide a basis for universal choice because the relationships between family, education and society do not in reality operate under conditions of perfect competition. The lines between producer, consumer and product are mediated by social relations across schools, community, family and work, and overlaid by relations of class, race and gender. In this social context, the market principle of extending choice and diversity is largely an illusory one.

In reality, Carlen *et al.* (1992) argue, the subject-based National Curriculum and key stage assessments serve the interests of sectionalized elites in society, and are socially and economically divisive inasmuch as they function to legitimate unequal distributions of wealth and other social goods. This is at odds with their overt aim of driving up standards universally, for the education market in effect produces winners and losers. What is not clear is how the reforms can achieve their aims of creating both universality of choice and uniformity of standards within a social context where schools become increasingly differentiated according to the ability of their students.

Carlen *et al.* (1992) do not see the solution to non-attendance to lie in curriculum provision which is *differentiated* within or between schools on the basis of academic aptitude, vocational ability, or social class or gender characteristics. Such differentiation, they argue, is neither an effective or efficient means of distributing talent in society and can never carry parity of esteem.

What are required are changes in the form, content, control and social context of schooling for all students, which emphasize their 'active involvement in, rather than separation from mainstream society'. Such changes would transform the experience of schooling as a system of containment and control into the experience of an active learning system linking the school, community and workplace. Learning would transcend the boundaries between school and the world outside to make it 'a more relevant, critical and meaningful' process for all students. Such a process implies a flexible curriculum, which is both responsive to the individual needs and interests of *all* students and to the corporate needs of society. This curriculum would not be differentiated according to categories of ability like 'academic', 'technical', 'vocational', *etc.*

Dorn's (1996) recent socio-historical analysis of the 'drop-out' problem in the USA draws similar conclusions to Carlen *et al.* He locates the problem in the success of the American high school at the turn of the century as a 'warehouse' for unemployed youth. The emergence of the modern wage-labour market in the nineteenth century pushed 'succeeding generations of adolescents' out of full-time employment and increasingly into high schools, which by the early twentieth century were becoming more successful in warehousing them than other adolescent institutions such as private youth associations. By the middle of the twentieth century, they had become 'the dominant institution for youth'. According to Dorn, the competitive advantage of the high school lay in the fact that it both kept youth out of the labour market while at the same time accumulating value for them as future workers. This was made possible by the traditional award of the high school graduate diploma. During the first half of the twentieth century, businesses increasingly used graduation at eighteen as a screening device for entry into many jobs. Hence attendance at high school and the award of its diploma on graduation successfully empowered youth to compete successfully in wage-labour markets. Once the majority of adolescents were earning high school diplomas, the expectation that all should graduate became established.

However, for Dorn (1996), the 'credentialing' function of the high school in the employment sector was not the only factor that made attendance at high school a normal expectation. Most of the institutions for youth in the late nineteenth and early twentieth centuries were expected to have a strong socializing function. This was bequeathed to the high school, which took on the role of ensuring that adolescents removed from the labour market accomplished a smooth transition from the dependency of childhood to the responsibilities of the adult by learning appropriate behaviour for entry into adult status. The opportunities for 'idle' adolescents, particularly those from poverty-stricken backgrounds, to engage in extreme or delinquent behaviour and to perpetuate them into adulthood, concerned a number of social reformers who came to see schooling as a mechanism of containment and control. Hence, the rise in expectations that high schools would fulfil both a credentialing and socializing function for all the youth in society, resulted in compulsory secondary schooling after the Second World War and a great deal of social significance being given to school attendance. It was in this social context, Dorn contends, that the 'drop-out' emerged as a 'pressing social problem'.

At the heart of the problem, Dorn argues, lay a contradiction between the sorting and credentialing function of the high schools and their socializing function, which became apparent as high school enrolment expanded in the early part of the twentieth century and in attempts to resolve it through the differentiation of the curriculum. Sorting at the point of entry became replaced by sorting within the schools and the development of differentiated curricula. When selection on entry ended, the 'comprehensive' high school curriculum maintained the power and status of an academic track and the value and prestige of the credential associated with it. The other tracks, like vocational and 'life-skills' education, didn't possess parity of esteem. The contradiction between the credentialing and socializing functions remained unresolved in spite of the rhetoric of inclusive schooling.

Dorn argues that we perceive drop-out as a problem because it carries an economic and social stigma. Most of that stigma he contends stems not so much from skill and information deficiencies that could have been prevented if the drop-outs had remained in school, but from the practice of employers who will hire a high school graduate before hiring a drop-out and of colleges who require a diploma as a condition of entry. The problem stems from the value placed on academic credentials in society. Dorn's socio-historical analysis of the problem does not support the current tendency to see the resolution in maximizing the number of students graduating with a high school diploma or some alternative set of credentials, because the social value of a credential doesn't necessarily lie in the knowledge and skills developed in the process of acquiring it, but rather in its relative rarity and difficulty of acquisition.

From this perspective, the US Goals 2000 target of getting 75 per cent of drop-outs to drop back into education to successfully complete a high school diploma or its 'equivalent' – a GED – expresses a shallow analysis of the drop-out problem. Meeting the target would not resolve the problem because it would depend on alternative credentials that had little value in the labour market compared to the diploma and would mean giving many students largely worthless bits of paper. Dorn claims that the target of Goals 2000 is quite arbitrary, since there is no evidence that merely increasing the numbers of graduates will meet the production needs of society. It is what students learn that is important and many alternative credentialing programmes are based on a very limited and narrow curriculum. He suggests that the importance of the high school diploma could be reduced by eliminating it as an entrance requirement for public colleges. Potential students without this credential would then not have to waste their time acquiring a GED or other alternative, and spend their time more valuably by attending classes. This might make it easier for drop-outs to drop back into the high school.

For Dorn, a genuine concern for drop-outs is inconsistent with making it more difficult for them to re-enter schooling by demanding a high school diploma or its equivalent. The drop-out problem was created by the success of the high school as a warehouse which not only removed many youth from the labour market but returned them after four years with a marketable credential. This made it possible to criticize high schools for failing to graduate everyone at eighteen.

However, Dorn claims, changes in the labour market are eroding age-related institutions like high schools and forcing a redefinition of dependency. Continuing labour market segmentation means that unemployment and under-employment have become a fact of life for all ages. This fact can no longer be masked by vocational education programmes as a remedy for youth un-employment. Such programmes, Dorn argues, rarely matched students to jobs well and express a tension between training for specific jobs, which may not exist after training, and giving general education some vague vocational ori-entation. Why, he asks, should students remain in school on such programmes when part-time jobs exist for them? Those that carry graduate equivalent credentials may prove attractive to some students but it is, Dorn contends, impossible to disentangle the value of the skills acquired from the value attri-buted to the level of difficulty in obtaining the credential. He believes that 'supported employment' or training following employment is likely to be a more effective investment than vocational education, which assumes that skills are sufficient to ensure employability. The former penetrate the job environ-ment and are sensitive to changes in labour market conditions. Whereas vocational education programmes see individuals rather than the job market as problematic, employer-based training may see the latter as, if not more, problematic. Four years of youth, from fourteen to eighteen, in a state of social dependency on schooling, can no longer be rationalized as preparation for the job market, when jobs for high school graduates are no longer in plentiful supply and the market has expanded at the periphery in terms of an expansion of low-wage, part-time and temporary jobs which are attractive to youth in search of disposable income.

Dorn concludes that schooling cannot solve the problem of poverty and needs something more than overcoming poverty as its purpose. Underlying this expectation is the illusion that schooling for all to eighteen will eliminate dependency on society by guaranteeing employability, whereas the reality is that it promotes dependency by preventing youth from gaining employment in peripheral jobs, part-time and temporary, and thereby beginning to penetrate the job environment.

Both Carlen *et al.* and Dorn tend to the conclusion that the major business of schooling is to honour everyone's right to a general education, the purpose of which is neither the reproduction of an academic elite or the instrumental acquisition of vocational skills. Rather, they link it to an induction into active citizenship within a democratic society, and therefore with the development of capacities for shaping the conditions of their existence in society. The purpose of schooling is to enable students to play an active role in the construction of their own futures rather than to allocate and distribute futures for them.

The kind of change Dorn and Carlen *et al.* call for is grounded in an analysis of the causes of non-attendance in the historical and structural conditions which have shaped the complex transactions between schooling, the family, the economy and the state. Their analyses reveal a 'pathology of presence' which identifies the factors that explain Rudduck and her co-workers' (1996) picture of schooling, as a process which disconnects learning from students' experience of contemporary living in order to prepare them for futures many have difficulty envisioning for themselves and have had little say in determining. Both Carlen *et al.*'s (1992) socio-historical analysis of the roots of this pathological state of schooling, accentuated rather than diminished by the Education Reform Act, and Dorn's (1996) analysis suggests that schools alone cannot carry the burden of responsibility for resolving the problem of disaffection. Trying to make themselves more effective as systems of containment and control will not address the roots of the problem. Solutions need to be generated in a wider social and political process in which fundamental questions about the content, control and context of schooling are publicly debated.

However, this does not imply that schools have no generative role to play in facilitating such a process at local and national levels by shaping the terms of the debate, the evidence it can draw on and the direction in which solutions are sought. At the present time in the UK, politicians, inspectors and media people appear to be controlling the terms of a public debate that is shaping the ways schools respond to the problem of disaffection. It is an agenda framed almost entirely by theories of deviance, which limit and restrict the range of solutions that can be officially entertained in schools by ruling out alternative ways of understanding the problem.

Concluding remarks: Disaffection as a problem about the relationship between curriculum, schooling and society

This review of research and analytic commentary in the field of student disaffection from schooling began as a search for a destabilizing account of state-engineered curriculum change in the UK. It has ended as a critique of the social purposes and functions of secondary schooling as these have evolved historically. Large-scale student disaffection, in all its manifestations, signals the collapse of the warehousing, credentialing and allocative functions of schooling and of containment and control as its primary purposes in the final years of the twentieth century, a period of unprecedented societal change in which most of the old certainties reflected in relatively stable moral, social and economic orders, and sustained by the authority of institutions, are fast disappearing.

These functions and purposes did not simply shape the form and content of the curriculum. They were as much shaped by the curriculum as they shaped it. The social prestige associated with the cultivation of the intellect through the acquisition of academic knowledge, and its perceived disconnection from the passions and prejudices which govern people's lives, appears to require a vision of schooling as a warehouse which detaches individuals from society to credential them for important roles and positions in society. Changing the functions and purposes of schooling therefore involves raising fundamental issues about the form and content of the curriculum.

Confronting the problem of student disaffection from schooling in advanced societies will involve resolving some fundamental issues about the functions and purposes of schooling and entail radically rethinking the form and content of the curriculum. Current research into school effectiveness and improvement in the UK, as I indicated earlier in discussing its relationship to deviance theories of disaffection, tends to neglect the curriculum dimension because it fails to problematize the functions and purposes of schooling presupposed by the form and content of the National Curriculum. I shall try to demonstrate in the next chapter how contemporary school effectiveness research, and its recommendations for school development, simply reinforce the warehousing and credentialing functions and a view of schools as systems of containment and control.

If I am correct, then such research is, like the National Curriculum, operating in the 'time warp' exposed by the mass disengagement of students from contemporary schooling. This problem will not be resolved by separating issues about school development from questions about the nature of education and its relationship to the form and content of the curriculum. The challenge of contemporary social change requires policy-makers to accept that there can be no school development without fundamental curriculum change in which teachers play a major generative role in the transformation of their students' experiences of schooling. Such an acceptance entails that they come to see education policy as something which empowers teachers to undertake imaginative curriculum experiments rather than an instrument of social engineering which transfers the power to effect change from teachers to the state.

4

Social Complexity, Subsidiarity and Curriculum Policy-making

Introduction

As the UK Government moved from a decentralized into a highly centralized system of curriculum decision-making, other advanced modern societies, particularly in Europe, appeared to be moving in the reverse direction. It is my contention that both movements – the centralizing and the decentralizing tendencies – are different responses to profound transformations occurring in the social and economic context of schooling in advanced societies. However, in some countries, curriculum policies reflect a 'reconciliation' between these opposing tendencies.

In the UK, the experience of social and economic change has resulted in a very high degree of centralized control over the curriculum. Goodson (1994) argues that the increasing globalization of economic and social life – of markets, information and technology – provides a context for centralizing curriculum decisions when the nation-state experiences both economic decline and threats to 'national identity' occasioned by a decreasing control over transactions across national boundaries. According to Goodson, the centralization of curriculum control is the response of a nation that goes into a state of 'moral panic' when it experiences itself to be economically and socially 'at risk'. He argues that the 'English' National Curriculum is constituted as an instrument for both economic regeneration and the maintenance of national identity in response to European integration. Moreover, the framework in which the content is reconstituted for these purposes is that of the traditional school subjects, which Goodson claims are class-based and 'evoke a past "golden age" when schooling was selective and people "knew their station"'. If he is correct, and I believe he is in this respect, then the national curriculum framework, as presently constituted within England and Wales, will promote the interests of an elite group in maintaining control over the conditions of access to the economic and cultural 'goods' of society. I will return to the relationship between academic subjects and social class at some length in a later chapter, when discussing Stenhouse's theory of general education and the principles of distributive justice.

In the light of Goodson's (1994) analysis, one might interpret the development of a highly prescriptive National Curriculum in England and Wales – in which content is organized in terms of the traditional 'grammar school' subjects and hierarchically structured by 'objectives' – as an attempt to construct a 'straight-jacket' which prevents teachers and schools from responding to social change by engaging in 'innovations' which undermine the established curriculum framework of academic subjects and the view of nationhood they are used to transmit.

Issues surrounding 'national identity' were clearly at stake in the debates surrounding the introduction of a literary canon of set texts in English, and the construction of national curricula in geography and history. Reflecting on my own experience of schooling, I am very aware of what I learned in geography in spite of my inability to recall the facts in any detail. What I do remember are those coloured maps of the world in which the British Empire appeared in red. I continually recall an impression of sitting in my primary school classroom, in the years immediately following the Second World War, gazing at a largely red world and the feelings of pride in my country it evoked. In this respect, my life since has been one of slow and progressive disillusionment with the vision of Britain as a nation which I acquired at school, a vision of 'fair-play', 'cultural tolerance', 'personal integrity' and 'moral courage'.

In the rest of this chapter, I will examine contemporary curriculum policy-making in the light of the social and economic changes occurring in advanced modern societies. If such changes lead some countries to develop a highly prescriptive national curriculum, then why do they also lead other countries to devolve more responsibility for curriculum decisions to the schools and their local communities? The explanation may enable us to understand Stenhouse's view of the curriculum as an innovative social experiment. I will draw on policy-making trends indicated in the July 1995 version of the OECD (CERI) report on 'Teachers and Curriculum Reform in Basic Schooling' (OECD 1995a) and the recent work of two prophetic authors: the British organizational theorist and economist, Charles Handy, and the German social theorist, Ulrich Beck.

Taken together, Handy and Beck provide a comprehensive, complementary and reasonably coherent account of the major issues emerging in advanced economies, issues which basic education will increasingly need to address. Both depict the increasing complexities of life in modern societies, arising from the contradictions and paradoxes of technology-driven economic growth. Governments, faced by such complexities, are discovering the limits of their capacity to centralize social change. Both writers show how complexity changes the relationship between individuals and social structures, creating more social space for people to take charge of their own lives. The growth of complexity in advanced modern societies has important implications for appropriate levels of curriculum decision-making in educational systems.

Also, both writers provide significant insights for me into a question I have been asking over the last ten years; namely, why are environmental issues emerging as a central object of social concern? Their social analysis has led me to conclude that the development of 'environmental awareness' should constitute a central goal of curriculum provision in the schools of the twenty-first century. In subsequent chapters, I will focus on the potential of a particular curriculum innovation in environmental education and the problems of accommodating it to the prevailing education policy context in the UK.

In spite of a great deal of consensus between Handy and Beck on the nature of the modernization process and its consequences, their accounts are in contention in one important respect. They appear to differ over the extent to which issues surrounding the distribution of socially produced wealth will become overshadowed by a preoccupation with the distribution of the environmental risks and hazards that accompany techno-economic development. Beck argues that they will, whereas Handy's account of social change implies that both environmental risk issues and issues of wealth distribution will be salient, with neither overshadowing the other. I will argue later that this difference in their analysis of contemporary social change stems from their different social locations.

The turbulent society and the logic of economic productivity

The OECD (CERI) report on 'Teachers and Curriculum Reform in Basic Schooling' (OECD 1995a) summarizes recent trends in curriculum policy-making in member countries as follows:

> In most Western European countries there is a recent tendency to increase the rate of autonomy at the school level. In the past too often the results of central, top-down innovations appeared to be disappointing because of problems of implementation.
> . . . completely decentralised systems are not present in the countries we describe in this study. In most cases there is tension between participants on the different levels about responsibilities and accountability. In times of economic recession there is mostly a request for a stronger central control and less autonomy for individual schools.
> (OECD 1995a: 74)

These extracts express a dilemma all the 'advanced' western states are wrestling with. States feel they need to steer the curriculum in ways which are consistent with their economic goals but find that the context of policy implementation is too complex to handle from the centre. The dilemma is well illustrated by attempts at the state level to establish national educational standards through the idea of a core curriculum which will command a public consensus and the pressure on schools at the local level to respond to the complex changes taking place in their social environment.

> Information is changing quickly. Nevertheless most countries try to establish a kind of stable core curriculum ... knowledge is no longer a closed or bounded area we all agree on, which is necessary to acquire for a future role in society. In a core curriculum national governments try to arrange a mutual agreement about content. There are educational reasons for such a pursuit ... Nevertheless, in spite of the efforts to develop national standards, schools are confronted with the demands of society and the actualities of every day. Children have their own interests and capabilities. Tension has grown between learning and teaching. There is a growing need for differentiation and adaptive teaching.
>
> The main source for data is not the teacher anymore ... Media like E-mail and Internet enable children to gain information from far outside the school.
>
> (OECD 1995a: 70)

I shall return to this dilemma in educational policy-making at the end of this section. In the meantime, I want to examine the paradoxical nature of the social change process from which it arises.

Increasing complexity in society, according to Charles Handy (1995a) in the *The Empty Raincoat*, is itself an unintended consequence of economic progress. Rich societies are experiencing unprecedented turbulence and chaos. The pursuit of economic goals – increased productivity and profit – has resulted in a dramatic decline in 'proper jobs'. Handy illustrates the logic of economic productivity with the formula '1/2 times 2 times $3 = P$', used by the chairman of a large pharmaceutical company to summarize his policy. His policy was to get half as many people in the core of the business within five years, to pay them twice as well and get them to produce three times as much. That is what equals productivity and profit. Handy argues that 'Productivity means ever more and ever better work from ever fewer people' and that many do not want these seventy hours a week jobs and the risk of 'burn out' which goes with them, but people will be doing them for thirty rather than the traditional forty-seven years, retiring in their fifties and posing the issue of what they do with another twenty-five years of life-expectancy.

Outside the core of well-paid jobs, Handy (1995a) points out that organizations are increasingly replacing full-time employees with part-time and temporary workers on lower wages. This is also part of the logic of productivity. It implies that organizations want more work for less money. Surplus labour and skills are exported onto the peripheral labour market and pulled back in when necessary. In these circumstances, people pay the costs of their unused time rather than the employing organizations. In theory, Handy claims, the exported workers will create new work for themselves to keep themselves busy and in cash, but 'conditioned to life as employees' they 'lack the kinds of intelligence and inclinations which would allow them to be independent'. Moreover, the logic of productivity, Handy argues, implies that more and more work will be meaningless. It implies infinite consumption that decreasingly matches what people need. He writes: 'What work there will be in future will, for many, be non-essential work, selling goods and services which we could happily do without, building yellow-page economies of glitz and extras, hardly the stuff of real life' (p. 14).

The social turbulence unintentionally created by the unremitting pursuit of productivity and profit dispels, according to Handy (1995a), certain assumptions about economic progress; namely, that it will create more jobs, which in turn will lead to a more equitable distribution of wealth. He cites the 1992 Report of the US Congressional Budget Office, which shows that two-thirds of the growth in personal income between 1977 and 1989 went to the wealthiest one per cent of families, while the middle classes gained 'a miserly 4 per cent over this period while 40 per cent of all families actually ended up worse off in real terms at the end of this decade of affluence'. Wealth, Handy argues, did not trickle down in the USA or elsewhere. In Britain, a 1993 government report revealed that the bottom 10 per cent saw their income fall by 14 per cent, whereas the average household income increased by 36 per cent. The rich got richer and the poor, relatively speaking, got poorer.

Handy links these inequalities with 'the wasteland of many inner cities', where 'there are mindless murders of tiny children, rapes of old ladies, burglaries and thefts every thirty seconds in some places, a total disregard for human life and property, senseless anonymous violence' (p. 13).

> What held it all together was only the hope among the poor that, maybe, in a world of constant growth there would be room for some of them, too, amid the rich. It is beginning to seem a rather forlorn hope.
> (Handy 1995a: 12)

Handy argues that the social legitimation of capitalism has rested on a certain view of distributive justice; namely, that 'those who achieve most should get most'. Such a principle justifies inequalities in society, some doing better than others. However, he argues that this principle 'will only be acceptable in the long term in a democracy if most people have an equal chance to aspire to that inequality'. The social consequences of the pursuit of productivity in the face of increasing international competitiveness with the the opening up of global markets are, according to Handy, constituting conditions where significant numbers of the citizenry are in danger of loosing their loyalty and commitment to society because they perceive it as unfair.

The unremitting pursuit of economic productivity, for Handy, is ultimately a self-contradictory social goal, because the inequalities it creates prevents significant numbers of people from consuming the goods on offer. It is also self-contradictory because it puts our environment at risk. In *Beyond Certainty* he writes:

> It is a strange irony, just one of many which itch away at our modern state. To give our people the necessities of modern life we have to spend more of our money and more of their time on . . . the junk of life. Worse to produce these things we consume the world's resources, pollute its environment, muck up its country side and dirty its towns and cities. This was not the brave new world that capitalism promised with its freedom of choice in the markets of the world.
>
> (Handy 1995b: 2)

From wealth to risk distribution?

Environmental problems are a significant consequence of what Ulrich Beck, in his book *Risk Society*, calls techno-economic development:

> In advanced modernity the social production of wealth is systematically accompanied by the social production of risks. Accordingly, the problems and conflicts relating to distribution in a society of scarcity overlap with the problems and conflicts that arise from the production, definition and distribution of techno-scientifically produced risks.
>
> (Beck 1992: 19)

For Beck, the problem of how socially produced wealth is to be distributed, which Handy depicts as an increasingly complex one, now overlaps with the equally complex one of how the environmental 'risks' created by the techno-scientific 'productive forces' driving the modernization process 'be prevented, minimised, dramatized, or channelled?' Beck describes the emergence in 'advanced societies' of the problem of 'sustainable development'. In relation to the social production of risks and hazards societies are deliberating on, he asks: 'how can they be limited and distributed in a way so that they neither hamper the modernization process nor exceed the limits of that which is "tolerable" – ecologically, medically, psychologically and socially?' (p. 19).

For Beck, the emergence of this problem is indicative of a new phase in the modernization process, the transition from 'modernity' to 'advanced modernity'. Other social and cultural analysts use the terms 'post-modernity' or 'high modernity' (Giddens) to depict this phase of social evolution. In spite of these various labels, the analysts using them appear to agree that they refer to societies in which the modernization process has become self-reflexive, as their members increasingly critique the scientific and technological basis of the social production of wealth.

According to Beck, we are moving in advanced modern societies from a preoccupation with the distribution of socially produced wealth towards a preoccupation with environmental risk distribution. One 'paradigm of inequality' is being replaced by another as the 'struggle for one's "daily bread" loses its urgency'. Both paradigms he argues are related to 'different periods of modernization'. Issues about the distribution of socially produced wealth occupy 'the thought and action of people' when the resources for meeting material needs are scarce. But once those needs are largely satisfied, the modernization process begins to lose its legitimation basis. The negative side-effects of techno-economic development on the environment form the basis of a growing critique of this process, and concern with wealth distribution becomes subordinated to concern with the distribution of environmental risks and hazards. Beck argues that we are currently in a transitional stage between the two paradigms of inequality in the 'welfare states of the west', where issues of wealth distribution are being joined by issues of risk distribution as public knowledge spreads about the polluting side-effects of techno-economic development. He writes:

> We do not yet live in a risk society, but we also no longer live only within the distribution conflicts of scarcity societies. To the extent that this transition occurs, there will be a real transformation of society which will lead us out of the previous modes of thought and action.
>
> (Beck 1992: 20)

Handy's analysis of the social inequalities which are being generated by the technologically driven quest for economic productivity in advanced modern societies suggests that the transition Beck predicts may be a difficult one to accomplish. Western societies may not be scarcity societies in the sense that Third World societies are, but in spite of their relative economic wealth, problems of wealth distribution paradoxically persist. Beck argues that the promise of 'emancipation from undeserved poverty and dependence' underlies the modernization process. But according to Handy, the promise is increasingly coming to be seen by many citizens as an illusion, in which case issues of wealth distribution are unlikely to be overshadowed in the foreseeable future by issues of environmental risk distribution. We are, perhaps, going to have to grapple in 'advanced societies' with both sets of issues, giving them equal consideration and priority in policy- and decision-making processes in society. Such a state of affairs will present policy-makers with an unprecedented level of social complexity to handle.

However, the discourse about wealth distribution will operate at a different level. It will no longer be framed by the assumption that the problem is essentially about the distribution of socially produced wealth. The means of production and their technological and scientific basis will become increasingly the object of critique, as Handy's work amply illustrates, not simply because of the environmental risks and hazards they bring, but also because of the way they shape and condition the way the wealth they produce gets distributed. We are learning that the means of wealth creation are far from neutral with respect to its social distribution. One can agree with Beck that the modernization process is moving into a new self-reflexive phase, without agreeing that the issues surrounding the social production of environmental risks and hazards will overshadow the socio-economic issues of wealth distribution. This is because, in spite of the benefits technological and scientific developments have brought to many, people are increasingly aware of their negative side-effects on the social distribution of wealth and of inequalities of access to the social goods wealth buys. Advanced modern societies are not so much characterized by environmental issues overshadowing socio-economic ones, but by the emergence of a process of reflexive modernization in which the citizenry examine, debate and critique the means by which wealth is socially produced in the light of both their socio-economic and environmental consequences. However, I shall argue later that this generalization may need to be qualified in favour of Beck's position with respect to modernizing societies that resist adopting Anglo-American attitudes towards the labour market.

Social transformation and the liberation of the individual

According to Handy (1995a), the paradoxical consequences of techno-economic development – it has brought enormous benefits to more people in the form of material goods and better health and housing, as well as the negative consequences depicted above – have to be lived with rather than unambiguously resolved. This is no recommendation for a fatalistic attitude and passive inaction. Handy argues that we can do something to 'reduce the starkness of some of the contradictions, minimise the inconsistencies, understand the puzzles in the paradoxes', but we can't resolve them completely, make them go away, or escape from them. What should be done, however, will be far from clear. For Handy, life will 'be best understood backwards' and lived forwards, although such retrospective understandings will offer 'clues' about possible future directions.

The intelligent response to the complexities and paradoxes of living in advanced modern societies is one of imaginative experimentation based on a tolerance of ambiguity and risk. Increasing complexity and paradox in a society enlarges the social space in which its members can participate in the construction of their own and their society's future. Lash and Wynne, in the introduction to *Risk Society* (Beck 1992), commenting on Beck's theory of reflexive modernization, note that it implies more than structural change but a changing relationship between social structures and social agents. When the modernization process reaches the self-reflexive level, 'agents tend to become more individualised, that is, decreasingly constrained by structures' and able to 'release themselves from structural constraint and actively shape the modernisation process' (p. 2).

Beck himself is quite explicit about the changing relationship between social structure and agency which is constitutive of reflexive modernization. He argues that we are eye-witnesses to a social transformation which is freeing people from the social forms of industrial society, such as class-, family- and gender-based roles, and creating 'a social surge of individualisation' where people 'have to refer to themselves in planning their individual labour market biographies' (Beck 1992: 87). The mechanism that 'liberates' individuals from traditional social ties is a labour market which requires 'individual mobility and the mobile individual' (p. 88), and a welfare state which protects people against the harsher consequences of mass unemployment and deskilling.

The individualization of the forms and conditions of existence wrought by dynamic labour markets and cushioned by social welfare implies for Beck (1992: 88) 'the variation and differentiation of life-styles and forms of life, opposing the thinking behind the traditional categories of large-group societies'. Individuals become the units for reproducing society rather than social classes, family groups and gender roles. In the words of Beck, they become 'the agents of their educational and market-mediated subsistence and the related life planning and organisation' (p. 90). However, he is concerned to point out that individualization must not be equated with the emancipation of individuals from all forms of social control. The process of individualization does not necessarily mean that individuals are empowered to create and shape the conditions of their existence, their social life-world. Liberation from traditional ties is accompanied by increasing dependency on the labour market and the institutionalized and standardized ways of life that support its operation; namely, 'education, consumption, regulations and support from social laws, traffic planning, product offers, possibilities and fashions in medical, psychological and pedagogical counselling and care' (p. 90). In this context, the idea of individuals as centres of choice and planning arises from the operation of social power which stands over and against the individual: the social power of a labour market which requires people to become units capable of infinite consumption.

However, Beck (1992: 90) argues that the process of liberation from traditional ties also raises expectations for a 'life of one's own' free from 'industrial and administrative' interference in the personal/private sphere. Inasmuch as the individualization process is self-contradictory, by creating new dependencies while at the same time raising expectations of empowerment, it provides a social space in which individuals can collectively form social movements to resist various forms of dependency on the power of the labour market to shape their lives, and to support their self-chosen experiments in personal and social living. Beck believes that the emergence of such social movements 'are expressions of the new risk situations in the risk society', namely ecology, feminism and peace.

Although the individualization process does little to resolve inequalities in the distribution of wealth – 'the hierarchy of income and the fundamental conditions of wage labour have remained the same' – Beck does not apparently view them as especially significant for the development of personal and social experiments in which people attempt to create and shape their life-worlds. This is because of the cushioning effects 'of a comparatively high material standard of living and advanced social security systems'.

As we have seen, his analysis of social change in this respect differs from that of Handy, who sees people becoming increasingly disillusioned with traditional legitimations for the unequal distribution of wealth as they become more aware of the self-contradictions inherent in its social production. One reason for this difference of perspective is suggested by Handy himself, although his work makes no reference to Beck (and vice versa). Beck is a German sociologist and Handy an Anglo-Irish economist and organizational theorist living largely in England. Their different origins and locations may give a clue to their rather different views of the significance of wealth distribution issues in advanced modern societies. Handy contrasts attitudes towards the labour market in the USA and Britain with those that prevail in some European countries, including Germany:

> Britain and the US have the most open labour markets and, therefore, the highest number of people in work, but their workers are the least protected and often the worst paid . . . Over the last twenty years the numbers of people in paid work have grown by 30 million in America but only by 10 million in the European Community. But the Americans and British have to work longer and odder hours, accept more part-time and self-employment and enjoy less protection. Fifteen per cent of British workers put in more than 48 hours a week and 20 per cent regularly work on Sundays. The Continentals think this is mad. Britain and America add on less than 30 per cent to the wage or salary to take care of social security and pensions. Italy, France and Germany add 50 per cent.
>
> (Handy 1995a: 27–8)

The issue at stake, Handy argues, is whether it is best to have fewer workers who are better paid, better educated and better protected, or whether it is best to have more workers who are less well-paid, less well-educated and less well-protected? The continentals believe, says Handy, that only good work is 'tolerable in this modern age' and that no work is better than bad work. On the other hand, the British and Americans, according to Handy (1995a: 28), believe that 'any work is better than no work, even if the result is a progressively down skilled workforce'. He argues that the consequence of American and British policy is a more divided society, illustrating this with the facts that the top 10 per cent of earners in America are paid six times as much as the bottom 10 per cent, while in Germany 'the ratio is just over two'.

I conclude that Beck's view of social transformation in modern societies – the movement from a concern with wealth distribution to a concern with risk distribution – assumes a continental perspective on the labour market and the role of the welfare state and social security. On the other hand, Handy's analysis of the self-contradictions in the social production of wealth stems largely, if not exclusively, from his knowledge and experience of the British and American labour markets. Both views have merit in their respective socio-political contexts. However, in the foreseeable future I would argue that, in the UK and USA at least, wealth distribution issues will be coupled with, rather than overshadowed by, issues of risk distribution. In my view, both kinds of issues will be important in supplying the motivation for people to resist the power of the labour market and to take responsibility for their lives by engaging in innovative personal and social experiments. The wealth distribution issues may well, contrary to Beck's thesis, resurface in continental societies, since in many one can discern a trend towards the American and British view of the labour market as they struggle for competitive advantage in global markets and find themselves hampered by high levels of investment in social security and protection. The heat surrounding Britain's reluctance in the past to accept a common European currency, 'the minimum wage' and other aspects of the EEC's Social Charter, is perhaps an indication of a crisis of attitude in many continental countries. The British Government certainly claimed that its own attitude to the labour market was more widely shared in Europe than was apparent in Brussels.

It is Handy's contention that transformations in the labour market are paradoxical. On the one hand, business organizations are getting smaller and employing fewer people in proper jobs for shorter periods in their life span, while increasing their use of temporary and part-time labour, whether skilled or unskilled. Hence the problems of mass unemployment, increasing inequities in pay, deskilling of the workforce and the black economy. On the other hand, because businesses are getting smaller by getting rid of slack, they are exercising less control over people's lives and presenting them with emancipatory possibilities; opportunities for people to resist the culture of conspicuous consumption and exercise some control over the conditions of their existence, including the conditions which shape their work.

Handy (1995a) called one of his books *The Empty Raincoat* after visiting the open-air sculpture garden in Minneapolis. One of the sculptures, by Judith Shea, was of 'a bronze raincoat, standing upright, but empty, with no one inside it'. It symbolized for him a 'pressing paradox' of our times:

> We were not destined to be empty raincoats, nameless numbers on a payroll, role occupants, the raw material of economics or sociology, statistics in some government report. If that is to be its price then economic progress is an empty promise. There must be more to life than to be a cog in someone else's great machine hurtling God knows where. The challenge must be to prove that the paradox can be managed and that we each one of us, can fill that empty raincoat.
>
> (Handy 1995a: 1–2)

The 'do-it-yourself' economy

More people in the future, argues Handy, will be 'outside' the employing organizations that drive economic growth and the culture of conspicuous consumption. This need not mean that they have to see themselves as 'out of work', because there are more kinds of work than jobs in employing organizations. The new growth sector for work will reside in the 'do-it-yourself' economy. Some of this work will be paid for and counted when people employ themselves and sell their knowledge and skills directly to the customer. Among the customers of self-employed work will be the new 'slimmed down' business organizations, which prefer to hire in knowledge and skills as and when required rather than stock-pile their slack. Increasingly, their skilled workers will be on the outside of the organization working in, and this gives these workers greater flexibility, independence and control over their working conditions.

In *Beyond Certainty*, Handy relates advice he gave his own children on leaving college:

> 'I hope you won't go looking for a job', I said. I was not advocating the indolent life or a marginal one. What I meant was that rather than scurrying about looking for a corporate ladder to climb or a professional trajectory to follow, they ought to develop a product, skill, or service, assemble a portfolio that illustrates these assets, and then go out and find customers for them.
>
> (Handy 1995b: 26)

The curriculum structures in British schools and even in universities, with their emphasis on traditional academic subjects, have not made it easy for students to develop their particular talents through formal education, although some 'curricular space' has appeared at the level of higher education, particularly within the 'new universities'.

However, for Handy, the 'do-it-yourself' economy covers more than self-employment, and includes unpaid work people do in their own time rather than paying others to do it (e.g. caring for their old and sick, doing their own repairs, growing their own food). Handy (1995a: 30) argues that:

> As more and more people get pushed out or leave organisations, it makes good economic sense for them to do for themselves what they used to pay others to do for them . . . Why pay others to do or make what you can do or make yourself, if now, you have more time than money on your hands? Because this new growth sector is invisible, productivity does not seem to be producing the output increases, nor the conventional jobs, which we would have expected.

One might add that unpaid work of this kind also makes good economic sense for the self-employed who have never 'spent time' inside an employing organization, since they are more in control over the use of the time they spend in paid work. Handy coins the phrase 'portfolio living' to depict the life of those who choose to participate in a 'do-it-yourself' economy. A portfolio life will contain a mix of paid and unpaid work, the balance varying at different times depending on personal choice and circumstances. Handy (1995b) suggests that portfolio living involves thinking of life in terms of a circle rather than a line. Abandoning the metaphor of the line 'as the organising design of our autobiographies' means no longer thinking of their line of work up a career ladder or their family line from son/daughter to marriage to parenthood to grandparent. Instead, argues Handy, a portfolio life is like a pie chart:

> with different segments marked off for different occupations, each coloured for kind and degree of remuneration. Some occupations will be paid in money, some in other kinds of reward: love, creative satisfaction, power, joy, and the like. And of course the chart will be constantly changing, the dimensions of the occupation segments expanding or contracting according to the time invested, the remuneration colours fading or brightening according to the returns on the investment, and this not only over the years of one's life but from week to week, even day to day.
>
> (Handy 1995b: 27)

If policy-makers are to take the 'well-being' of their citizens seriously, they may have to give up assuming that progress equals economic 'growth and efficiency' in a formal economy where productivity is controlled by employing organizations. As Handy (1995a: 1) argues:

> Part of the confusion stems from our pursuit of efficiency and economic growth, in the conviction that these are the necessary ingredients of progress . . . It is easy to lose ourselves in efficiency, to treat that efficiency as an end in itself and not a means to other ends.

Basic education in societies with rapidly growing 'do-it-yourself' economies will, in terms of content and outcomes, need in some respects to be more flexible and differentiated, to support the development of the various and diverse interests, talents and capacities individuals possess. It will also, in terms of learning processes, need to foster the more active and dynamic qualities which enable people to take charge of their own lives and see themselves as creators of innovative experiments in living. The scale of the educational problem is indicated by the large numbers of people cast onto the peripheral labour market who passively suffer their fate and appear to be incapable of seizing control over their futures.

Knowledge work

It is not only a growing 'do-it-yourself' economy which begins to put people rather than organizations in control of the economic and social conditions of their lives. Handy (1995a) points out that even proper jobs are of a kind that empowers the employees in relation to the organizations they work in. Technology-driven production is resulting in a reduced need for many kinds of work, except 'knowledge work'. 'Clever workers with clever machines', says Handy (1995a: 23), 'have put to an end the mass organisation'. The 'means of production' are now, he argues, in the hands of the workers in ways Marx couldn't have imagined. 'Focused intelligence', or the ability to acquire and apply knowledge and know-how, is, according to Handy, the new source of wealth and it is not the kind of property which can be owned by the organization. It cannot take intelligence away from someone or own it. It is not a property whose possession can be controlled by those who own the organization. Therefore, says Handy, 'it is hard to prevent the brains walking out of the door if they want to' (p. 24).

The inability of organizations to redistribute intelligence implies that they cannot stop people developing it and using it in ways they determine. If they do not like the way the organization treats their knowledge, individuals can sell it to another, perhaps rival, 'business' or establish their own. It is, according to Handy (1995a: 25), 'a low-cost entry market-place' that makes 'for a more open society'. He argues that it's unfortunate that 'intelligence goes where intelligence is'. The well-educated give their children good education and thereby secure their access to power and wealth. The most likely outcome of this new kind of property, intellectual property, is, according to Handy, an increasingly divided society unless 'we can transform the whole of society into a permanent learning culture where every one pursues a higher intelligence quotient as avidly as they look for homes of their own' (p. 25). Handy is not very clear what he means by 'focused intelligence' but the concept appears to be similar in some respects to Dreyfus's (1981) idea of 'situational understanding' (see also Elliott 1993), which picks out a cluster of cognitive abilities exercised in making intelligent judgements in particular practical situations.

This kind of practical intelligence is not necessarily best developed through a curriculum organized in terms of the traditional academic subjects which tend to reinforce the passive acquisition of knowledge rather than its use in the practical contexts of living. Such a curriculum may well constitute an obstacle to the equitable distribution of opportunities in society for people to develop their capacities for situational understanding. Traditional standards of academic excellence may provide the criteria for allocating individuals to the best jobs, thereby giving them access to power and wealth, but they may not be the appropriate criteria. As Goodson (1994) argues, a major function of a subject-based 'academic' curriculum could simply be to reproduce a social elite, since only a few may be capable of mastering the bodies of decontextualized and abstract propositions which define school subjects, in comparison with the number of people who could be capable of developing an intelligence which focuses on the problems and issues that arise in concrete human situations. One of the attractions of a subject-based curriculum is that it enables policy-makers to standardize learning outcomes in a way an issues-focused curriculum, aimed at developing capacities for understanding 'human situations', does not.

One implication of Handy's concept of 'focused intelligence', if I have understood his meaning in the terms outlined above, is that it is a form of intelligence that will not only be increasingly exercised in 'proper jobs' inside organizations. A great deal of work in the 'do-it-yourself' economy will also constitute knowledge-work, in which case we will not need to plan a different kind of education for separate categories of workers (i.e. knowledge workers inside organizations and the self-employed portfolio people).

Implications for the curriculum

A curriculum which prepares students for life in the kind of societies described above will look very different to one dominated by nationally standardized learning outcomes that constitute a basis for allocating people to 'proper jobs' in employing organizations that will subsequently control their futures, and are deemed to constitute the essential knowledge and skills required for economic growth. Currently, mainly national curricula specify such knowledge and skills as 'core curriculum' objectives. Priority is therefore given to the *economic ends* of the society as these are conceived in terms of a 'state-steered formal economy'. In the context of an economy increasingly shaped by individual citizens, operating on a 'do-it-yourself' basis or as knowledge-workers or both, priority will need to be given in basic education to enabling all pupils to begin to construct for themselves a positive vision of their own futures in an increasingly complex, less structured and more open and dynamic society. Basic education will need to prioritize the development of those dynamic capacities – cognitive, interpersonal and motivational – associated with the ability to continuously shape and reshape the conditions of one's existence in the light of an unfolding vision of the 'good life' and of how one's natural talents can be developed to realize it.

The curriculum implications of this are two-fold. First, there is a need for a common general education which enables students to use the cultural resources available in society to construct their own vision of the good life and the values they wish to live by. Secondly, there is a need for a more differentiated 'vocational education', in the broad sense of an education which enables individual students to identify and develop their particular talents in ways which reflect their vision of the good life. In this latter respect, students will need access to a curriculum which is more open and responsive to their self-defined learning needs, with respect to both conditions of access and content. This kind of flexible and 'vocationally' orientated curriculum provision will not segregate life and work. It would match the life-concerns of individual students, and while transcending their need to 'earn a living' would not discount it. Such a curriculum would locate their economic well-being in the context of their development as persons capable of constructing their own future in an increasingly dynamic and complex society.

In this book, I am primarily concerned with the implications of social change for the idea of a 'common general education', rather than on its implications for the development of what Rawls (1971: 107) has called 'productive trained abilities', or Stenhouse (1967: 113) calls an education for 'productive enterprise'. The latter requires a separate book to be written. However, the critique of planning by objectives which runs through this book should be seen in this context. I am critical of its use as a basis for planning the curriculum for general education. It may well be appropriate, and this is acknowledged by Stenhouse (1975: 80–81), as a basis for developing productive trained abilities, in a context where students exercise control over which abilities they wish to acquire.

The principle of subsidiarity

The complex problems of wealth distribution and environmental protection which advanced modern societies face, depicted by both Handy and Beck, render governments powerless to effect solutions through centralized planning.

> The road we have been on, throughout this century, has been the road of management, planning and control. Those who stood on top of society's mountains could most clearly see the way ahead; they could and should plan the route for the rest and make sure that they follow it . . .
> We applied this approach to our organisations. We thought this way in government. Even when we said that government should get off the backs of the people we did not really mean it, because the people would not then be managed to their best advantage. We have tried to plan and control world trade and world finance and to make a greener world. There should be a rational response to everything, we thought; it should be possible to make a better world.
> It hasn't worked. Management and control are breaking down everywhere. The new world order looks very likely to end in disorder . . . Scientists call this sort of time the edge of chaos, the time of turbulence and creativity out of which a new order may jell.
>
> (Handy 1995a: 15–16)

Governments in advanced modern societies, faced with their powerlessness to handle the complex social problems which have arisen, are tending to delegate more responsibility for decision-making to groups and organizations at the local level who are more in touch with, and more able to respond to, the needs of those most affected by social change at the grassroots in society.

Handy (1995a) uses the term 'subsidiarity', made fashionable by Jacques Delors to characterize the desired relationship between nation-states and the European Community, to describe this process of reverse delegation. Within the context of a particular nation-state, the state delegates discretionary powers closer to the grassroots while retaining responsibility for quality control at the centre by reserving powers to set, monitor and enforce standards. The principle of subsidiarity says:

> find the optimum level of subsidiarity and then collapse as much into that as possible so that the group or team or individual have the means at their direct disposal to do what they are responsible for . . . it is the team which is closest to the action that is the appropriate level of subsidiarity. That done it is the job of the centre to set standards but not necessarily to specify how they should be delivered. The unit is then judged, after the event, by its performance against those objective standards.
>
> (Handy 1995a: 117)

The Finnish Government is very explicit about its view of the implications of increasing complexity in society for the location of curriculum decision-making. It resolves the dilemma in favour of a radical reduction of centralized administrative regulation, and more decision-making powers for schools who are to construct the curriculum by networking with local agencies rather than planning in isolation.

> What is typical of development in society, says the report, is the reduction of centralised administration and the networking of various functions. This is manifest in the decision making powers being delegated more and more to schools and the schools' increasing cooperation and collaboration with their surroundings and other institutes of learning. Latitude in the national distribution of lesson hours and in the curriculum guidelines as well as resource conditions in the schools themselves allow greater variations in curricula. As far as the future is concerned, we are faced with a more and more open situation, say the Finns, in all fields of human endeavour. Consequently schools now have a chance to play a great role in trailblazing and effecting changes.
>
> (OECD 1995a: 73)

This trend away from a centrally administered curriculum towards curriculum subsidiarity is also evidenced in many other OECD countries in Europe:

> In lieu of earlier centralised models, the development of education is, at least in Finland but in other OECD countries too, now based on curricula drafted in the schools themselves with the view that the teacher is to develop his or her work and that we can identify certain strengths in the school community . . . Research shows that teachers' participation

in the writing of the curriculum is an important prerequisite for any real changes in the inner work of the school. Curricula made by others remain something external, and there is no commitment to implement them.

(OECD 1995a: 74)

The policy dilemma, depicted at the beginning of this section – between national governments feeling a need to steer educational outcomes at the centre and its inability to do so in the face of growing social complexity – is being resolved in some countries by a less tightly prescribed core curriculum which leaves space for schools to construct specific learning experiences for pupils through local networking:

> Interaction between the school and agencies outside the school is a vital point of interest. Just as people acquire many of their experiences from the local community, so must the school obtain subject matter for teaching from this source. The pupils will be able then to build upon experiences that they bring to school, and seek new experiences after inspiration from the school. The teaching will become more active and close to life, and a bridge will be built between the common national content of education and the pupil's own environment.

(OECD 1995a: 69)

I wish to highlight three elements referred to in these accounts of emerging policy trends:

1 The reduction of centralized administrative regulation and the delegation of responsibility for curriculum decisions to schools. It is clear that governments are not decentralizing in the sense of abandoning any central agency. What appears to be emerging is a federal structure consisting of a network of units (schools) coordinated through a central agency which is very much reduced in size when compared with the centralized administrative systems that regulated teachers work in schools. Within a federal system of education, schools are not accountable to the centre in the same way that they are within a bureaucratic system.
2 The construction by schools of social networks with agencies, groups and individuals in the local community.
3 Increasingly differentiated and diverse provision of curricula within and between educational institutions to cater for a range and variety of individually and locally determined learning needs, but located within a framework of shared educational goals and values – a common vision.

However, these policy trends may not resolve all aspects of the dilemma governments face in reconciling their steering function with increasing social complexity. The aim of delegating many curriculum decisions to the local level may be highly ambiguous. Decentralization can constitute a strategy for increasing the power of the labour market to shape the conditions of teaching and learning in educational organizations. It does so by opening up the educational process to the operational requirements of a dynamic labour market and the institutionalized and standardized range of lifestyles associated with it. By promoting networking between schools and local employing organizations at the local level, by involving more representatives of local business interests in school management, and by encouraging schools to negotiate curricula through their local networks, central governments can 'steer' the educational system in ways which empower the labour market to shape an educational process that produces those flexible and socially mobile units of 'choice' depicted by Beck.

Alternatively, decentralization can constitute a strategy for empowering teachers and students to shape educational processes by moving responsibility for curriculum decision-making closer to their lives. When decentralization is legitimated in terms of the subsidiarity principle, it raises expectations that the strategy has an emancipatorary aim. In practice, however, decentralization may be used to empower the labour market but be rationalized, in terms of the subsidiarity principle, as the devolution of decision-making powers from the state to schools. However, such a strategy will not resolve the state's dilemma about how to steer the economy in the face of growing social complexity.

As Beck points out, the individualization process effected by the labour market is a paradoxical one. In liberating the individual from traditional ties, it not only establishes the conditions for new dependencies on institutions, and lifestyles shaped by the 'market economy' and the culture of conspicuous consumption, it also sustains but at the same time raises 'emancipatory' expectations in individuals; namely, of being able to shape the conditions of their human existence. The rapid development of technology to replace labour in the production of wealth paradoxically establishes the social spaces in which individuals can exercise initiatives in shaping their 'life-world'. This is because it transforms the labour market in ways which give that market less power to control the individualized lives it created in the first place, and it accelerates the production of environmental risks/hazards which leads to the formation of social movements in which citizens attempt to reduce the power of 'market forces' to shape their environment.

One might therefore conclude that decentralizing policy trends in the curriculum field may well manifest tensions and conflicts between central steering agencies at government level and schools concerning curriculum aims and content. These can become constructive tensions if they lead policy-makers to acknowledge the desirability of enabling society's future citizens to play a more active role in shaping both the economic and environmental (natural, physical and social) conditions which govern their existence.

5

School Effectiveness Research and its Critics: Alternative Visions of Schooling

Introduction

In this chapter, I examine in detail the 'findings' and methodology of school effectiveness research and its assumptions about what makes an effective school and what is involved in improving the quality of schooling. This kind of research aspires to influence educational policy, but has been criticized for neglecting the curriculum and pedagogy as significant dimensions of school effectiveness. I will try to clarify further what is at stake here, and begin to establish links between the conception of education which underpins the critiques of school effectiveness research and the conception embedded in the idea of curriculum change as an innovative experiment in which teachers play a major generative role. In conclusion, I will argue that the profound changes occurring in the social context of schooling will require schools to become more self-reflexive, and by implication 'experimental' institutions, if they are to avoid being trapped in a time-warp alongside the school effectiveness research paradigm.

The findings of school effectiveness research have indeed been music to the ears of politicians and government officials. Currently, for example, they are being used to politically justify a refusal to respond to teachers' anxieties about the increasing size of the classes they teach, the use of traditional teaching methods such as whole-class instruction, and a tendency to blame headteachers for 'failing schools' on the grounds that they lack a capacity for strong leadership.

As they seek to win friends and exercise influence in the political arena, school effectiveness researchers rarely present their findings as controversial within the educational research community. I remember sitting in a meeting a few years ago of the advisory group to the shadow secretary of state for education, listening to a school effectiveness researcher trying to persuade the latter that educational researchers agreed on what an effective school was. He was evidently persuaded because when a subsequent policy document came to the group for discussion, it asserted such a consensus. My attempts to persuade him that no such consensus existed had little influence on the final draft of the document; it was amended by substituting 'largely agreed' instead of 'agreed'.

This kind of misrepresentation of the views of the educational research community continues. In their report on the 'The Key Characteristics of Effective Schools' to the UK Office for Standards in Education (Ofsted), a London Institute of Education group of researchers claim that:

> there is now a much greater degree of agreement amongst school researchers concerning appropriate methodology for such studies, about the need to focus explicitly on student outcomes and, in particular, on the concept of the 'value added', by the school.
>
> (Sammons *et al.* 1995: 3)

If the report had claimed greater agreement between school effectiveness researchers, then one might not object. But there are many of us engaged in school research who describe ourselves as school researchers, and aspire to make a contribution to practitioners' and the public's understanding of what goes on in them and how it might be improved, but who do not accept the central assumptions of the school effectiveness research paradigm; namely, a mechanistic methodology, an instrumentalist view of educational processes, and the belief that educational outcomes can and should be described independently of such processes. What the claim of the London Institute research group amounts to is an attempt to redefine the field of school research in a way which denies the legitimacy of dissenting voices.

These dissenting voices within the educational research community invite, in my opinion, a particular form of response from school effectiveness researchers; namely, to participate in a moral discourse about the concept of education that underpins their findings and the values which frame it. But the nature of this invitation is made less than clear by the critics. The few school effectiveness researchers who have made an effort to respond to external criticism, and to his credit Reynolds is one of them, tend to see it as simply a critique of their methodology in favour of more qualitative and naturalistic methods. The critics often reinforce this impression because, although they explicate the values they perceive to underpin the methodology of school effectiveness research, they are not so explicit about their own educational values, which are nevertheless implicit in their critiques. As we shall see, they accuse school effectiveness researchers of neglecting certain aspects which they believe to be important for education, and of failing to gather the relevant data by appropriate methods, but why are these neglected aspects educationally significant?

In the next section, I examine the 'findings' of school effectiveness research. In doing so, I argue that their status as research findings, which have nothing original and interesting to say about schools, is highly questionable, and that they are best viewed as ideological legitimations of a socially coercive view of schooling. I also indicate how these 'findings' rule out an alternative vision of schooling as an educational process. In the subsequent two sections of the chapter, I examine a number of critiques of school effectiveness research with a view to explicating what is at issue; namely, alternative conceptions of the educational process and of the values which define it. I hope to show that these critiques share a common vision of education. It is indeed the one that the school effectiveness research 'findings' appear to claim little 'rational foundation' for. It should become clear that what is at issue between school effectiveness researchers and their critics are fundamental questions about the nature of education and its central values. I shall argue that the collaboration some of the former are seeking from researchers operating within the so-called 'school improvement paradigm', to get their 'findings' implemented in schools, is unlikely to materialize. The majority of school effectiveness research's external critics are school improvement researchers operating with a completely different vision or 'theory' of education. What would be worthwhile is greater dialogue between these two groups of researchers with a view to examining the value-issues at stake between them. In the final section, I argue that school effectiveness research is already becoming outmoded as a paradigm capable of addressing the challenges which the process of social change in advanced modern societies are presenting to schools.

Defining the effective school: A problem about the facts or a question of values?

We have now seen nearly two decades of school effectiveness research in both the USA and Britain. It has aspired to discover the 'mechanism' (see Hamilton 1994) that enables schools to control and shape pupils' achievements and thereby refute the findings of Colman *et al.* (1966) and Jenks *et al.* (1972): that differences in such achievements are largely correlated with socio-economic background factors and that schooling has little effect on their distribution. The researchers involved hoped thereby to provide policy-makers with a rational foundation for educational reforms aimed at improving the effectiveness of schools. The hope remains and school effectiveness researchers on both sides of the Atlantic continue to claim that early studies by Edmonds (1979) in the USA and Rutter *et al.* (1979) in Britain substantially refuted Colman and Jencks by discovering that schools can make a difference to pupils' achievements, and that later studies have largely confirmed, albeit refined and elaborated, the depiction by these early studies of the key characteristics of effective schools.

Edmonds (1979) came up with six factors, while Rutter *et al.* (1979) came up with seven. It is interesting to compare the images of the effective school they portray. First, Edmonds:

(a) They have strong administrative leadership without which the disparate elements of good schooling can neither be brought together nor kept together; (b) Schools that are instructionally effective for poor children have a climate of expectation in which no children are permitted to fall below minimum but efficacious levels of achievement; (c) The school's atmosphere is orderly without being rigid, quiet without being oppressive, and generally conducive to the instructional business at hand; (d) Effective schools get that way partly by making it clear that pupil acquisition of basic school skills takes precedence over all other school activities; (e) When necessary school energy and resources can be diverted from other business in furtherance of the fundamental objectives; and (f) There must be some means by which pupil progress can be frequently monitored . . . some means must exist in the school by which the principal and the teachers remain constantly aware of pupil progress in relationship to instructional objectives.

(Edmonds 1979: 15–24)

The seven factors cited by Rutter *et al.* (1979) in their UK study, entitled *Fifteen Thousand Hours*, are summarized by Reynolds (1994: 19) as follows:

- *the pupil control system*, with effective schools using rewards, praise, encouragement and appreciation more than punishments;
- *the school environment provided for pupils*, good working conditions for pupils and teachers, responsive to pupils' needs, well cared for buildings;
- *the involvement of pupils*, opportunities to participate in running of the school and in educational activities in classrooms;
- *the academic development of pupils*, positive use of homework, setting clear and explicit academic goals, high teacher expectations of pupils' capabilities;
- *the behaviour of teachers*, providing good models of behaviour such as good time-keeping and willingness to deal with pupils' personal/social problems;
- *classroom management*, prepared lessons in advance, kept attention of whole class, maintained discipline unobtrusively, focussed on rewarding good behaviour, acted swiftly to deal with disruptive behaviour.
- *the management structure*, firm leadership by head combined with decision-making processes in which all teachers felt represented.

Firm or strong leadership, setting clear and explicit learning goals, high teacher expectations of pupils in relation to these goals, a primary focus on the activities of teaching and learning, and the maintenance of a pupil control system based on positive reinforcement are common characteristics identified by both Edmonds and Rutter *et al.* As for differences, we find Edmonds stressing the setting of minimum standards in the areas of basic literacy and numeracy, and the monitoring of pupil progress in relation to them through the use of standardized tests, while Rutter *et al.* include in their list of factors the quality of the pupils' working environment, teachers who act as models of good behaviour, and pupils' active involvement in school and classroom activities.

In spite of the slight differences reflected by the findings from the early school effectiveness studies, perhaps reflecting cross-cultural differences in the research context, some critics have argued that they are underpinned by common values. These are rarely made explicit by the researchers involved, who have tended to portray their findings as objective and unbiased truths. Perrone (1989) claims that the findings reported by both Edmonds and Rutter *et al.* stress the values of 'orderliness, uniformity, and adherence – values viewed by many as paramount to societal progress', and they reassert the 'importance of hierarchical leadership'. We shall return to this issue of the value perspective underpinning school effectiveness research later when we address the problem of practitioners using its findings to improve their schools.

Ten years following the publication of the two early studies cited above, school effectiveness researchers in the USA and Britain were feeling confident that they had identified a comparable set of core components of effective schools. For example, Reynolds (1994: 20–21) reports that:

> Corcoran and Wilson's (1989) study of exceptionally successful second-ary schools generated a list of common elements in their effective schools that has distinct similarities with findings from the British secondary school studies. Their common elements were:
> + a positive attitude towards the students by teachers and the principal;
> + strong and competent leadership;
> + highly committed teaching staff;
> + high expectations and standards;
> + an emphasis upon high achievement in academic subjects;
> + intensive and personal support services for at-risk students;
> + stable leadership and public support in the catchment area of the school for a period of years sufficient to implement new policies.

The first five factors are all reflected in the findings of Edmonds and Rutter *et al.* What we have here are modest refinements and additions to the early findings.

According to Reynolds (1994), 'the certainties that are reflected in the above international account of "what works" are now, however, increasingly being replaced by uncertainty, controversy and disagreements as to what the "core" beliefs of the school effectiveness paradigm are'. The claims of school effect-iveness researchers, according to Reynolds, are being somewhat tempered by recent studies using new statistical methods such as multi-level modelling. He argues that they are problematizing the earlier findings in the following ways:

1 *The size of school effects*: early beliefs were misplaced since recent research shows only 8–15 per cent of variations in pupil outcomes are due to differences between schools.
2 *The causes of school effects*: early beliefs that school effects were distinct from teacher or classroom influences were misplaced. A large number of studies using multi-level modelling show that 'the great majority of variation between schools is in fact due to classroom variation and that the unique variance due to the influence of the school, and not the classroom, shrinks to very small levels' (Reynolds 1994).
3 *Consistency of school effects over time*: school performance can significantly vary over a period of two to three years.
4 *Consistency across a range of outcome measures*: there is much evidence that schools need not be effective 'across the board'. Academic effectiveness is not necessarily linked with social or 'affective' effectiveness. 'Indeed', Reynolds (1994) argues, 'recent evidence from the "ALIS" project of Fitz-Gibbon and colleagues (1989) suggests that it is unwise even to talk about a school's academic effectiveness only, since there is a substantial range of effectiveness across subject departments'.
5 *Differential school effects*: 'there can be different school effects for children of different ethnic groups, ability ranges and socio-economic status within the *same* school' (e.g. Nuttall *et al.* 1989).
6 *No school improvement blueprint*: independent of school history and context or personnel. Even similar characteristics across contexts may be generated in different ways appropriate to local context, stage of development of school and the personalities involved.
7 *No cross-cultural agreement*: on what makes schools effective, for example assertive leadership and frequent monitoring of pupil performance. These may work in the USA but not in The Netherlands (the former) or Britain (the latter).

In spite of these problems, Reynolds (1994: 23–4) remains confident about the enduring usefulness of school effectiveness research and its findings. First, he claims, it has destroyed the home background or social disadvantage alibi of teachers and others, and 'that consequently little can be done to change things'. The school is held more accountable today because it is seen to be responsible for pupil success and failure. He claims this without qualification, and yet earlier in his paper he reported that in certain societies (e.g. Sweden) the amount of variation in achievement due to school influence 'is virtually zero' and that the capacity of schools to effect change may well depend on the policy context they operate in.

Secondly, Reynolds (1994) claims that school effectiveness research has developed 'value-added' approaches to assessing school performance as opposed to the use of raw scores. Thirdly, its great contribution is a concern for pupils 'and their academic and social outcomes from education'. Such concern he assumes to be synonymous with a concern for learning defined in terms of pre-specified and standardized outcomes: 'School effectiveness researchers "back map" from the outcomes of education to the processes and only count as effective those processes where there is definitive proof that the processes actually worked' (1994: 24).

Fourthly, he argues it is likely that there are some enduring truths in the processes that have been found to be effective within countries. For example, high teacher expectations of pupils; pupil involvement in lessons, extracurricular activities and the running of their school; providing incentives for behaviour based on rewards rather than punishment; organizational cohesion, consistency and constancy (the big C's), 'which in the end will generate control'.

The reader might understandably wonder whether at the end of all this costly research and debate anything interesting or original has been discovered, for surely the so-called 'enduring truths' that remain are nothing but a set of platitudes? I will return to this question shortly.

Reynolds displays a considerable capacity for publicly acknowledging the growing internal critique of previous 'findings' without losing too much confidence in them. In the light of the internal critique they are qualified and then boldly reasserted as a rational foundation for school improvement. He is not alone among school effectiveness researchers in this respect. In a recent report from the University of London Institute of Education by Sammons *et al.* (1995) to Ofsted, we find its authors reporting and acknowledging the same problems as those cited by Reynolds, and then confidently moving on to cull a list of 11 key characteristics of effective schools from the research literature. They argue that, given the reservations they expressed, it has nonetheless been possible for them and other reviewers of the literature to identify a consistent core of 'common features concerning the processes and characteristics of effective schools'. The eleven key characteristics they identify are as follows:

1 *Professional leadership* – firm and purposeful, participative approach, the leading professional.
2 *Shared vision and goals* – unity of purpose, consistency of practice, collegiality and co-operation.
3 *A learning environment* – an orderly atmosphere, an attractive learning environment.
4 *Concentration on teaching and learning* – maximisation of learning time, academic emphasis, focus on achievement.
5 *Purposeful teaching* – efficient organisation, clarity of purpose, structured lessons, adaptive practice.
6 *High expectations all round* – communicating expectations, providing intellectual challenge.
7 *Positive reinforcement* – clear and fair discipline, feed-back.

8 *Monitoring progress* – monitoring pupil performance, evaluating school performance.
9 *Pupil rights and responsibilities* – raising self-esteem, positions of responsibility, control of work.
10 *Home–school partnership* – parental involvement in their children's learning.
11 A *learning organisation* – school-based staff development.

(Sammons *et al.* 1995: 8)

One can see the continuities with the findings of the early foundation studies and how, with the exception of the odd addition (e.g. item 11), the list as a whole constitutes an elaboration and refinement of them. As a school researcher, but not one of those committed to the aspiration of school effectiveness research or its methodology and therefore an outsider, I wonder why those who are so committed are able to accommodate, and even assimilate, the internal critical debate about the findings, without acknowledging their 'death by a thousand qualifications'. The kind of critical issues cited by Reynolds and the London Institute Group simply confirmed my initial impression, nearly two decades ago, that the quest for the mechanism of school effectiveness was misconceived. That initial impression stemmed from my view of education. I felt that the school effectiveness research model of schooling was underpinned by values that were anti-educational. I did not view school effectiveness research to be consistent with my own understanding of *educational values*.

My response, however, does suggest an answer to my question, about why the increasing problematization of school effectiveness research findings from within does not fundamentally undermine the researchers' commitment to them. It is surely because their findings reflect the values which define their conception of schooling and indeed of education.

When I first read the list produced by Sammons *et al.* (1995), I was struck by the number of platitudes it contained. It appeared to be stating the obvious. I read some of them out (e.g. items 1–4 and 6) to an audience of Austrian teachers in Vienna, presenting them – admittedly in a rather 'tongue in cheek' manner – as 'original findings'. I obtained the desired response – a great deal of laughter. For example, the initial description of items 4 and 5 embodies *a priori* truths which we do not need empirical research to discover. Most of us would find it conceptually odd if definitions of 'good schools' made no reference to a focus on teaching and learning (item 4), and anyone who has done an elementary course in the philosophy of education will have learned that 'the intention to bring about learning' is a logically necessary condition of teaching. So we don't need school effectiveness research to inform us about 'truths' that are essentially conceptual ones.

However, these 'findings' may not be as obviously true and innocuous as they at first sight appear. When we look carefully at the factors listed beside each of the initial descriptions, we begin to realize that we are being given information that is not simply an elaboration of things that are obviously true. Schools might well give priority to improving the quality of teaching and learning without maximizing learning time, emphasizing academic goals, or focusing on achievement. The classroom practices in these schools may express the beliefs that the quality of learning is more important than the amount of time pupils spend 'on task', that the acquisition of systematically organized academic knowledge is not the main aim of education, and that the latter requires teachers to focus on the quality of the teaching–learning process rather than its outcomes, since if the former is right then the pupils themselves will take care of the latter. Such beliefs are negated by the factors cited in item 4. They are recognizable as beliefs which belong to the tradition of 'progressive education', and indeed when one scrutinizes the factors listed beside item 5, and other items, one gets the impression that the 'findings' constitute a negation of this tradition in defence of the established mainstream European tradition of education: one that emphasizes the transmission of systematically organized academic knowledge (i.e. knowledge organized through the academic disciplines). In Britain, it is, of course, the tradition enshrined in the 'grammar school'.

This raises the issue of whether the factors cited in Sammons and co-workers' (1995) list can in any way be regarded as 'objective findings' or a 'rational basis' for policy, because they appear to be shaped by a particular educational ideology, however well-established and taken-for-granted it may be in the national culture. If one rejects the beliefs and values this ideology consists of, then one will dismiss these 'findings'. Indeed, one may question whether many of the factors cited required research to produce them at all. Can they not be read as the kind of things anyone who subscribes to the ideology will inevitably produce as a characterization of effective schooling? Are they not products of an ideological commitment rather than research, which merely provides a legitimating gloss to mask this fact?

To maintain their values, school effectiveness researchers have continuously to reassert the validity and usefulness of their findings, and therefore to accommodate or assimilate their internal critique to their convictions. The mechanism they believe they have unearthed may not work as well as they expected, its performance now appears to be unstable over time, some of its components don't work in certain contexts, and it works better for some people than others. Moreover, it is less powerful than originally claimed. Nevertheless, they believe it works after a fashion and this is nothing 'to sneeze at'. What this enthusiastic band of researchers tend not to question on the basis of their internal discussions is whether this rather 'wonky mechanism' they have discovered does more harm than good. To do so would be to call the values they are committed to into question. So what are these values?

Earlier I referred to Perrone's (1989) claim that underpinning the early school effectiveness studies are the values of orderliness, uniformity, adherence and hierarchy. If we look at the 'consistent core' of characteristics distilled by

Sammons *et al.* (1995) from their recent review of school effectiveness research to date, such values 'stare one in the face'. Underpinning the findings are a set of values that appear to be a constituent of a social control ideology. Occasionally, school effectiveness researchers say as much without, I suspect, comprehending that many would take issue with them, not simply with their findings but with the values and ideology they proclaim in promoting them. For example, in a statement cited earlier, Reynolds argued for the enduring nature of certain findings, claiming that the factors they identify 'in the end will generate control'. Of course, all education involves the exercise of some form of intervention with the intention of influencing learning, but their are different ways of exercising such influence as we shall see later. The values that Perrone picks out might be characterized as a structure of 'coercive control', inasmuch as they appear to leave little room for the exercise of self-directed and autonomous thinking on the part of pupils within the learning process.

However, control values do not simply underpin the findings, they also shape the methodology of school effectiveness research and the conceptualization of the basic research question or problem. The use of sophisticated statistical methods, like multi-level modelling and multiple-regression analysis, in recent school effectiveness research may have stimulated the internal problematizing of earlier findings, but they are underpinned by the same control values. As Brown *et al.* (1995: 8) point out, such methods imply a model of the school as consisting of 'nested layers' of hierarchically organized systems and sub-systems. Hence, classrooms as teaching–learning systems are seen as sub-systems nested within subject departments, which in turn are seen as sub-systems nested within schools. They go on to argue that:

> The model does, of course, have a common-sense logic if the way one sees the world of education is essentially one of top-down management, and a common feature of writing on school effectiveness is the clear implication that it is necessary for a subject department to be nested within a school that is managed effectively if it is to be effective.
>
> (Brown *et al.* 1995: 8)

In other words, the model of the school implied by the research methodology embodies a view of education defined in terms of control values, and Brown *et al.* clearly don't like it. They also point out that, even when the use of multi-level modelling methods has led researchers to conclude that 'the greater part of the variance among pupils' achievements' can be explained 'by differences at classroom rather than school level' (p. 9), the researchers invariably continue to focus on the school. I would suggest that they do so on the assumption that the achievements in 'effective classrooms' would be even better if they were more nested within an effective system of managerial control. Hence, the response to this finding would be to continue with the quest to identify the key components of such a control system. Brown and her co-workers' response is quite different. It is to focus on how classroom teachers 'make sense of their educational world' and 'which variables are most salient in their thinking' (ibid.).

This difference of response can only be explained in terms of different views of schooling shaped by different sets of values. One might conclude therefore that, however sophisticated, the methodology employed by school effectiveness research will never generate findings that require the researchers involved to conclude that their is no such thing as an effective school in their terms, no mechanism which can make such organizations work in the way desired. And this is because the methodology employed is grounded in the assumption that such a mechanism exists, which in turn is grounded in the researchers' shared commitment to an ideology of social control. It is the latter which shapes the research question – 'What is the mechanism that makes schools effective?' – and determines the selection of a methodology for arriving at the answer.

Throughout this chapter, I have employed the term 'mechanism' to describe the quest of school effectiveness researchers, drawing on the view of Hamilton (1994) that their research practice stems from a group of sixteenth- and seventeenth-century philosopher-scientists, from Galileo to Newton, who projected a new world view; namely, that the natural world 'operates like clockwork'. In the light of such a world view, this group of theorists, argues Hamilton, set themselves three tasks:

> First, to identify mathematical functions that represent the periodic . . . motion of the universe; secondly, to use these functions to predict future states of the world; and finally, to identify imperfections in the world that could be eliminated by reference to the idealisations inscribed in the laws of nature.
>
> These assumptions became the bedrock of the scientific revolution . . . nature was to be interrogated. Prescriptions were to be read off from the resultant revelations; and, in turn, these prescriptions were to be read into the conduct of human affairs. New knowledge, therefore, was the key that unlocked both the workings and the intentions of the hand of god.
>
> (Hamilton 1994: 4–5)

What I take Hamilton to be saying here is that once events in the world came to be viewed as the work of an underlying mechanism, it opened up the possibility of discovering how the mechanism works to produce those events, in the form of general laws. On the basis of such knowledge, it then becomes possible to predict future events, formerly believed to be known only to God. Hence, a knowledge of the laws governing the workings of the mechanism which controlled the future offered the promise of knowing 'the mind of God', and therefore of human beings taking control over the future states of the world. Imperfections in the world could then be ironed out in the name of progress. Such was the promise of modernity.

Hamilton (1994) points out that a science which offered the prospect of discovering the 'intentions of the hand of god' in the universal laws that governed events in the world proved to be very attractive to those with responsibility for government, and cites the one-time Lord Chancellor of England, Francis Bacon, as an early example. Bacon perceived, in his own words, 'a great affinity and consent between the rules of nature and the true rules of policy'.

The extension of the mechanistic world view to cover the social as well as the physical/material world, as the basis of a new social science, offered governments the prospect of a rational basis for extending their control over the organization of society through large-scale social planning and 'engineering'. Now it can be argued that, although policy-makers may find a social science attractive in extending government control over the organization of individuals in society, the findings of such a science do not entail these 'use values'. They are introduced by a particular policy perspective but in no way shape the research methodology, which on the contrary is developed to overcome researcher bias and ensure the production of objective truths. To the contrary, I would argue that the mechanistic world view that frames the research questions and shapes the use of a particular numbers-based methodology, embodies a very clear value-position. The *Fontana Dictionary of Modern Thought* (p. 514) is instructive in this respect when it defines 'mechanism' as the theory that all causation is *efficient*; that is, 'That for an event to be caused is for its occurrence to be deducible from the antecedent (in some cases contemporaneous) condition in which it occurs, together with the relevant universal laws of nature'.

However, it is possible to have a very different view of causation. I may, for example, view learning as a possible outcome of teaching without also viewing that outcome as deducible and therefore predictable from a statement about its antecedent pedagogical conditions. As I shall argue, we can specify what would count as the pedagogical conditions for effecting worthwhile learning without being able to deduce what precisely their effects or outcomes will be. In which case we will not require those conditions to be an *efficient cause*, because to do so will be inconsistent with the values that define our understanding of what is involved in effecting worthwhile learning; for example, that it should enable pupils to appropriate content in a personally significant form. Different theories of causation in relation to our social practices reflect different conceptions of what it means to influence other people's thoughts and conduct and of the quality of the transactions involved. Such theories of causation are shaped by values. The search for the mechanism, the efficient *cause*, which enables one to predict the outcomes of schooling is shaped by a set of control values which define schooling as a coercive process of social induction. On the other hand, the search for the pedagogical conditions which effect worthwhile learning, without predetermining its precise outcomes, is shaped by a concern to respect pupils' capacities for constructing personal meanings, for critical and imaginative thinking, and for self-directing and self-evaluating their learning. Such values are inconsistent with the idea of schooling as an efficient cause of learning and a process of social control.

The above analysis of the social control values embedded in the theory of causation, which underpins the quest for the mechanism of school effectiveness, enables us to understand the affinity between school effectiveness research and a view of policy-making as a process of 'social engineering'. It helps us to understand the concern of school effectiveness researchers like Reynolds to influence policy-making in a way which makes it more 'rational', and why they appear to be more concerned with influencing policy than with listening to oppositional voices from within the educational research community. I am referring here not to the internal critiques so ably summarized by Reynolds, but to external critiques, like those of Perrone, Brown *et al.* and Hamilton, which stem from school researchers operating outside the school effectiveness research paradigm.

Dissenting voices: The alternative vision of schooling

Perrone (1989), in his critique of some of the early school effectiveness studies, passionately represents what he takes to be the teachers' perspective on teaching and learning, and argues that the values which underpin it are inconsistent with the findings of such studies:

> The variables that did not relate to school effectiveness as determined by test-score measurements are, among others, the size of the school, variations in class size, age and experience of teachers, internal forms of organisation, amount of teacher preparation time, staying with the same children for more than a year, and level of parental participation. One cannot spend a lot of time in schools and really believe that these are not qualitatively significant. One also has to know that such conclusions are likely to work against many of our more valued commitments.
> (Perrone 1989: 45)

Implicit in this passage is a very different vision of education and the values which frame it to one shaped by the values of 'orderliness', 'uniformity' and 'adherence', which he claims to underpin school effectiveness research findings. It is a vision of education as a highly personal transaction between teacher and pupil in collaboration with the parents. This is why the findings he cites work against 'our valued commitments'. They are inconsistent with the values which define the qualities of an educative personal relation between teacher and pupil.

Perrone goes onto argue that school effectiveness research 'ignores the complexities of practice in schools' and as a result, while 'potent in its assertions', such research is 'weak in its descriptive qualities'. He believes that the control values which underpin the research findings shape the research process in a way which makes the researchers blind to such complexities and therefore to the teacher's perspective. For Perrone, the significance of describing practice as a complex affair is that, in doing so, researchers may discover what he and many other school researchers and practitioners believe to be important about the process of education. This is clear when he illustrates the contention that school effectiveness findings give us poor-quality descriptions of educational processes in schools. For example, he argues that Rutter and co-workers' (1979) 'finding' that 'the provision of school outings' is significantly correlated with exam success, neglects to produce any description of:

> the circumstances, purposes, or length of the outings; likewise, he does not mention whether they related to what was being studied or whether they were followed up. It is as if the content did not matter. Seldom in this literature do we learn about the content of curriculum. Further, we receive little acknowledgement of the complexity of schools, communities, teaching and learning, an oversight that I fear encourages too many educators to view school improvement as little more than the application of a five-step model that usually begins with a 'strong principal'.
> (Perrone 1989: 43)

By failing to describe practices from the practitioner's perspective – the perspective of one who is required to realize an educative personal relation with their pupils – the aims and content of curriculum activities, the pedagogical conditions which govern pupils' experience of them, and the community context in which they are developed, all get ignored by school effectiveness research. Perrone implies that they cannot be ignored by a teacher wanting to establish an educative personal relation with pupils, and are important dimensions for evaluating the quality of education in schools.

I have inferred from Perrone's (1989) critique a view of education as a complex personal transaction between teachers and their pupils, the quality of which requires teachers to consider and make decisions about, among other things, the aims and content of the curriculum and the pedagogical conditions under which it is appropriated by pupils. Perrone sees classroom teachers, rather than 'the system', as the source of quality in education. However, his critique is more obscure on the question: 'What educational values should define the quality of teachers' transactions with pupils and inform their deliberations about curriculum and pedagogy?' We can reasonably infer from it certain things about the nature of these values: (1) that they are best characterized as moral values, since we largely assess the quality of 'personal' transactions in these terms; and (2) that as moral values they will not define the quality of education primarily in terms of 'technical efficiency'. This explains Perrone's critical stance towards the values he perceives to underpin the findings on school effectiveness. From his evaluative perspective, the control values which underpin these findings entail a view of 'teachers as technical operatives' in a technological system of pupil surveillance and control. They are values related to a vision of schools as technically efficient machines. For Perrone, such values are inconsistent with the moral nature of the educative personal relation between teachers and their pupils.

Perrone's (1989) critique is not an idiosyncratic one by any means. Most of the external critiques reflect a view of the educational process which has much in common with his, as I hope to show. In doing so, I want to clarify the fundamental issues at stake between them and school effectiveness researchers.

Silver (1994) cites a number of critiques of the findings of Rutter *et al.* (1979) which perceive similar underlying values and neglected aspects of practice in schools to those cited by Perrone (1989), and imply a shared moral vision of education.

> *Fifteen Thousand Hours* was the subject of widespread critical comment . . . Burgess, for example, accused it of 'diverting attention from questions we should be asking about inner city schools . . . the focus of *Fifteen Thousand Hours* is almost exclusively managerial'. He considered the study to have mistakenly taken public examinations as 'the single, measured outcome of academic achievement'. It ignored curriculum and pedagogy, and had no 'sense of history, both a broad and more local framework within which the achievement of these schools can be placed and evaluated', and it had no sense of the 'actual texture' of the schools.
>
> (Silver 1994: 92)

Here we get the same criticism about the neglect of curriculum and pedagogy, and the emphasis on predetermined outcome measures as indicators of pupils' achievements in school.

Of a critique by Stephen Ball, Silver (1994: 99) reports that:

> He considered management to be a form of organisation which 'reduces the autonomy of teachers and attempts to minimise their influence over policy making; it is also couched in an ideology of neutrality'. For these reasons he believed 'the school effectiveness movement' to have been 'thoroughly implicated in the formation of and establishing of the conditions for the discourse of management'.

Once again, we get a critique of the control values underpinning school effectiveness research in the light of a view of education which gives teachers a major generative role in quality development.

Silver also reports a review of Rutter's *Fifteen Thousand Hours* by Barry Holz, a researcher at the Jewish Theological Seminary in New York:

> He broadly welcomed it, including the way it worked for the reduction of teachers' 'sense of powerlessness in the face of debilitating realities beyond their control'. And yet he felt something was missing, something

of the 'vision' that was often overstated and romanticised in the 1960s, but which saw education as something bigger than improved reading scores and behaviour'. Holz concluded: '. . . it maybe worth our while to remember that we once hoped that schools would create new models of community, encourage new commitments toward meaningful vocations, end racial discrimination, and open up new avenues out of poverty and unhappiness. Right now it seems we rejoice if children can be taught to read'.

(Silver 1994: 102)

Here we appear to have a fairly clear articulation of a set of values. Rather than focusing on aspects of the educational process which school effectiveness research neglects – curriculum, pedagogy and the generative role of teachers – this criticism asserts a neglect of certain social ends of schooling, such as the construction of new forms of social solidarity or community, equality of respect for all citizens regardless of race, and equality of opportunity. The reference to 'meaningful vocations' might in the context of the other values mentioned be reasonably interpreted as a 'commitment to the common good'. Moreover, it should be noted that Holz is, in articulating these values, seeing schools as agents of social change, a change in the direction of a more 'liberal-egalitarian' society (see Rawls 1971).

School effectiveness researchers might well accept Holz's criticism, arguing as many do that they have focused on 'academic outcomes' and need to take more account of social outcomes. However, for me, Holz's remarks raise questions about the relationship between the social ends of schooling and its educational ends, between social and educational values; a relationship which school effectiveness researchers might draw in terms of a distinction between 'academic' and 'social outcomes', but one their critics might see as informing their understanding of the processes of schooling as opposed to its outcomes.

One of the consistent themes which runs through Silver's own historical analysis of the quest to discover the basic ingredients of effective schooling, is that its reductionist and fundamentalist nature leads it to confuse the idea of an *effective* school with that of a *good* school. He cites the argument that a good school might be an effective one but the reverse is not necessarily the case. There are two ways of understanding the difference, I would argue. First, an effective school might not be an educationally good one because its outcomes are either regarded as undesirable or too limited to adequately satisfy the criteria of educational desirability. Secondly, an effective school might not be a good one because its level of technical efficiency might be educationally undesirable. In the light of this distinction, let us revisit Holz's reported criticism of school effectiveness research. His remarks could be read to imply that the effective schools identified through such research are not good schools, because in neglecting social ends their outcomes are too restricted. I have suggested already that school effectiveness researchers will read them in this light. But his remarks can be read from a different perspective; namely, that the schools identified as effective are not good schools because, although they are technically effective in teaching children certain skills, they are not effective agents of social change directed towards the ends cited by Holz. The implication here is that technical efficiency is not sufficient in judging what constitutes a good school, and that it would be inappropriate to assess the relationship between the process of education and its social goals in these terms. This reading would assume a rather different theory of causation to the one which underpins school effectiveness research, one framed by values other than control values. I would suggest that such a theory is framed by the values which are embedded in the idea of education as a 'complex personal transaction' (see Perrone 1989, above) between teachers and pupils, in which case we can argue that the causal relationship between the process of education and its social ends is not so much one of technical efficiency and control as one which respects and accommodates the educational values that can be derived from a certain vision of a 'just society'.

School effectiveness research and its 'theory into practice' problem

Some of the recent critiques of school effectiveness research in Britain broaden the focus of criticism to take into account increasing attempts to ground school development processes in its findings, thereby addressing a problem that has emerged as a major concern for the researchers; namely, that teachers don't use their findings to improve their schools. Reynolds in particular has addressed this problem at some length and proposed a solution to it. The solution involves bringing educational researchers working in what he calls the school improvement paradigm into a form of collaboration with school effectiveness researchers.

The core beliefs of the school improvement paradigm are characterized by Reynolds (1994) as:

1 An emphasis on teachers inner mental states rather than on quantifiable organizational and behavioural variables.
2 Support for 'bottom-up' rather than 'top-down' change initiatives.
3 The use of qualitative and naturalistic methodologies for evaluating/ self-evaluating school improvement initiatives as opposed to quantitative approaches.

I will now examine Reynolds' 'solution' in the light of an alternative account of the problem, expressed in recent critiques by Brown *et al.* (1995) and Hamilton (1994). We shall see how Reynolds' proposal is based on a profound misunderstanding of the issues at stake.

Reynolds (1994: 24), in attempting to explain the theory–practice problem, notes that: 'The focal concerns of most practitioners – the curriculum and their instructional practices within classrooms – are not areas that most school effectiveness researchers have been much interested in'. Here lies the heart of the problem as far as school effectiveness research is concerned. It is not that the findings of such research make no reference to the curriculum or instructional processes, but they treat them as manifestations of the operation of systems variables. They assume that the major determinants of the quality of pupils' curriculum and pedagogical experiences are systems rather than teachers. The vast majority of the external critiques of school effectiveness research assume the contrary, and in doing so take sides with the practitioners.

Like earlier critics, Brown *et al.* (1995) find the 'top-down' model of school effectiveness problematic because it results in findings which ignore the perspective of classroom teachers and the complexities of teaching in them. But why is it important not to ignore them? They argue that 'any serious attempt to innovate in classrooms has to start from where teachers are and how they construe their own teaching, their pupils and what they are trying to achieve' (p. 9), and:

> The effectiveness correlates have taken little account of the variables that are most salient for those in schools and classrooms who have the responsibility for making the schools effective and whose implicit theories (no matter how misguided they may appear) will provide the basis for understanding why things turn out as they do.
>
> (Brown *et al.* 1995: 10)

Brown and co-workers' first argument above is a response to the suggestion of Gray and Wilcox (1994: 14) that qualitative data on teachers' (and pupils') views of the findings of school effectiveness research need to be gathered and treated as seriously as those of external reviewers. Brown *et al.* point out that this suggestion was tempered by increasing evidence from studies using new statistical techniques, that the greater part of the variance in pupils' achievements stems from differences at classroom rather than school level. However, they argue that it is an inadequate response to such evidence because the questions asked of teachers reflect the researchers' constructs of potentially significant variables and 'reveal nothing about how the teachers make sense of their educational world, nor about which variables are most salient in their thinking' (Brown *et al.* 1995: 9). What is required, they argue, are 'detailed phenomenological studies of classrooms'.

Clearly, Brown *et al.* believe that teachers' subjective theories of effective schooling differ significantly from the 'objective' findings of school effectiveness researchers. And presumably this belief is grounded in the kind of phenomenological studies carried out by Brown and McIntyre (1993), whom they cite. Moreover, these subjective theories are often implicit in teachers' practices rather than operating at the level of conscious self-awareness. This is why understanding such theories must be grounded in the qualitative study of classroom practice, because one cannot simply ask teachers what their theories consist of. Such understandings need to be inferred from observational data, albeit in a context of dialogue with the teachers concerned.

In their first argument above, Brown *et al.* are making the point that teachers' practices won't change without corresponding changes taking place in their implicit theories. They will resist change that does not appear to be consistent with their beliefs. Therefore, the starting point for change is with classroom teachers and their understandings of teaching and learning, rather than with the organization as such. However, as it stands, this conclusion doesn't necessarily follow from the fact that teachers' practices contain implicit theories. A 'hard' behaviourist would treat such theories as mere epiphenomena and argue that changes in practice do not depend upon changes in teachers' beliefs. Rather, changes in behaviour can bring about changes in belief. A 'softer' sort of behaviourist might agree with Brown and her co-workers' conclusion that the starting point for change is the teachers, and suggest that their behaviour can be modified in conformity with the findings of school effectiveness research by techniques that get them to replace their implicit theories with these scientifically validated findings. Teachers may resist changing their beliefs but such resistance can be 'dissolved'. On the basis of qualitative information about how teachers make sense of their life and work in classrooms, school managers, assisted by external school development consultants, would devise 'techniques' for getting teachers to change their commonsense theories of teaching and learning in ways which are more consistent with the findings of school effectiveness research. Such 'techniques of persuasion' might well include 'structured discussions', in which teachers are encouraged to debate their commonsense understandings in the light of the 'scientific evidence' about school effectiveness. A 'soft' behaviourist might agree that, in the short term, one can change teachers' behaviour without changing their beliefs through the provision of extrinsic motivation, but in the longer term behavioural change may depend on the consistency between behaviour and beliefs.

Brown and her co-workers' second argument above suggests that they would object to both 'hard' and 'soft' behaviourism. It makes more explicit a hidden presumption of their first argument; namely, that teachers ought to have the major responsibility for determining the quality of education. However, they appear to be ambiguous about why this should be so. Is it because top-down change strategies for making schools effective simply won't work because they bypass teachers' generative capacities, such as a capacity for constructing their own understandings of the processes they are engaged in? Or, is it because strategies which bypass teachers' generative capacities are intrinsically wrong regardless of their 'effectiveness'? Brown *et al.* seem to adopt the latter point of view when they object to Reynolds' initial short-term strategy for sorting out teachers operating ineffectively in schools. Reynolds (1994) argues that 'we would need to be directive with them, and would need to tell them what to do, independent of whether they agree or not'. Brown *et al.* object to the strategy, not simply because it won't work, but because it is inconsistent with teachers 'having a sense of ownership and responsibility for decision-making'. I would suggest that their argument is not as ambiguous as it appears. In objecting to Reynolds' strategy, they are perhaps saying that it may work in changing teachers' behaviour in the desired direction but it will not *work for education*, because autonomous teachers are a necessary condition for providing pupils with learning experiences that are *educationally worthwhile*.

This kind of argument is less ambiguously presented by Hamilton (1994), whose critique further illuminates what is at issue between the two educational research paradigms. He argues that two models of science emerged in the nineteenth century: (1) the natural/physical and social sciences and (2) the Baconian and Kantian:

> The extrapolation from knowledge to action was seen to be mediated – on the one hand by explanation and prediction . . . or, on the other hand, by consciousness and understanding . . . In the first case knowledge is linked to action via the algorithmic process of 'reading off' information and 'reading into' action. In the second case, the evidence is never mathematically compelling: action arises from the exercise of prudent choice among moral alternatives.
>
> (Hamilton 1994: 10)

He goes on to cite Dewey's advocacy of this second view of the relationship between knowledge and action: 'unless the professional information enlightens (the teacher's) own perception of the situation and what to do about it, it becomes either a purely mechanical device or else a load of undigested material' (p. 10).

Hamilton argues that school effectiveness research operates in the Baconian tradition, on the assumption that *knowledge is information*, from which practitioners can just read off a set of rules and then read them into practice. He concludes that it won't work as an implicit theory of the relationship between theory and practice because it ignores the practitioner's perception of the situation. It is a similar conclusion to the one drawn by Brown *et al.* In citing Dewey in support of his argument, Hamilton is rather more explicit than Brown *et al.* about the sense in which change strategies based on school effectiveness findings won't work. They might change teachers' behaviour and in that sense work, but it will be behaviour of a mechanical kind, and this is undesirable as a basis for professional action in the teaching role. In effect, Hamilton is saying that mechanical behaviour in teachers doesn't work for education.

Hamilton's (1994) paper identifies a radical difference in the theories of the theory–practice relationship that underpin the two paradigms of school research that Reynolds wants to bring together. If the theory embedded in school effectiveness research can be located in a Baconian social science, then the theory embedded in the 'school improvement paradigm' can be located in a Kantian social science. Also, the vast majority of the external academic critiques of school effectiveness research, such as those I have cited, can be located in the latter tradition. From this standpoint as Hamilton argues, the rendering of knowledge as information is never compelling for action. If behaviour does result in conformity with it, this is because the force of compulsion arises from the context of transmission rather than the information given. We may reasonably interpret the kind of school improvement programmes currently being mounted – which aspire to get knowledge about school effects fed into a managed process of whole-school development planning, implementation and evaluation – as the construction of such a transmission context. As a solution to the pedagogical problem of how one gets teachers to learn and apply knowledge about school effects, it will not appeal to self-reflective teacher-researchers operating within, what Hamilton calls, the Kantian tradition of social science.

Hamilton's (1994) account of the theory of action which underpins that tradition – that action arises out of the practitioner's exercise of 'prudent choice', defined as a careful and sound judgement between moral alternatives – gives us a clue towards understanding what the educational significance of teacher autonomy might be. To understand a situation as requiring good judgement between moral alternatives is to experience it as morally complex and dilemma-ridden in the sense that the right course of action is not a clear-cut matter. Each alternative appears to satisfy some of the moral requirements of the situation. It is not as if the moral ends are clear and all that is left is a decision about the most technically efficient means of satisfying them. Prudent choice therefore implies a process of deliberation about what constitutes the right course of action in a morally complex and dilemma-ridden situation; a process in which reflection about right action (about means) is inseparable from reflection about its moral ends.

This theory of human action provides an explanation for why Brown and her co-workers' critique of school effectiveness research is so critical about its disregard of classrooms as the place 'where the crucial decision making occurs' and of the ways the teachers who work in them make sense of their educational world. I would suggest that the criticism stems from an understanding of education, which we have seen they share with the other critics cited, as a morally complex affair involving a careful consideration of both the curriculum and pedagogy by teachers. From this perspective, the quality of education depends on the quality of teachers' deliberation and judgement in classrooms.

A theory of action as prudent choice also explains why Brown *et al.* think that policy-makers who think they can use school effectiveness findings to tell schools how to improve are being simple-minded. They argue that such a notion:

fails to address the issue of how the findings are to be integrated into the thinking and practice of those who are seen as needing to improve. The involvement and commitment of teachers, with a sense of ownership and responsibility for decision making, is an essential element for innovation. In those circumstances, it cannot be assumed that teachers will be ready to accept the findings as an agenda handed down from on high.

(Brown *et al.* 1995: 9)

These remarks clearly imply a 'Kantian' rather than a 'Baconian' theory of action, inasmuch as they suggest that the practical usefulness of research findings will depend upon the extent to which they illuminate teachers' thinking and judgement at the level of the classroom. Brown *et al.* are not suggesting that research findings must confirm teachers' prevailing understandings of classroom situations. They point out that these tend to be 'implicit' theories that will need to be developed for practice to be improved. Research findings are useful not when they confirm existing understandings, but when they support the development by the teacher of new ones. Thus one can argue that Brown *et al.* are implying a context of teachers self-consciously deliberating about their practical situations as a condition for determining the utility of research findings. Becoming aware of existing tacit understandings is a necessary starting point for this process, because it is only when a teacher reflexively examines the understandings which shape his or her practice that he or she is able to reconstruct them as a basis for improving that practice.

From this it follows that the usefulness of school effectiveness findings, for the purposes of school improvement, can only be deliberatively determined by teachers at the classroom level, in which case the priority for school improvement at the level of management is how to support and encourage a process of deliberative reflection – often called 'action research' – on the part of teachers at the classroom level. Given such conditions, we could ask whether the introduction of school effectiveness findings is likely to provide teachers with a useful resource for developing new insights into classroom situations. The answer provided by the critiques we have looked at may appear to be 'no', because these findings do not conceptualize education as a morally complex process which requires teachers to exercise prudent choice. However, they may constitute an important resource for helping teachers to reflect about the relationship between factors in the organizational context and the teaching–learning process. The practical outcomes of such reflection may be less than desirable from the standpoint of school effectiveness research, for they may constitute strategies for reducing the influence of factors cited in this research as characteristics of effective schools. From this standpoint, the theory–practice problem will remain unsolved by such strategies, and policymakers will have 'wasted' an awful lot of money supporting a certain model of school improvement.

A 'soft' behaviourist approach appears to be what Reynolds (1994) is advocating as a solution to the theory–practice problem. He assumes that teachers seeing things differently constitutes a problem about getting them to use school effectiveness findings but not a problem about their validity. The use of qualitative methodologies, like the phenomenological studies of class-rooms advocated by Brown *et al.* for eliciting teachers' 'inner states of mind', might, from Reynolds' standpoint, provide school developers with the infor-mation they need to get teachers to use school effectiveness findings effect-ively. Hence his argument that there is a need to create links between school effectiveness researchers and researchers and developers working in the school improvement paradigm, which operates from rather different 'core beliefs' to school effectiveness research. According to Reynolds, this 'paradigm' should be more closely aligned with school effectiveness research to provide the latter with 'an effective "delivery mechanism"' (p. 27). This proposal that the school developers and researchers operating from within the alternative paradigm should become the 'midwives' for school effectiveness researchers is based on the view that:

> From school effectiveness we have an emerging sense of the factors associated with effective schooling, and from school improvement we have a set of delivery mechanisms that may prove useful in implanting the knowledge into school programmes.
>
> (Reynolds 1994: 28)

The phase 'implanting the knowledge into school programmes' supports my contention that Reynolds is a 'soft behaviourist' wanting to co-opt school improvement researchers as 'agents of persuasion'. However, he is pessimistic about the feasibility of shifting from 'conflict to cohesion' between the two paradigms in the way he proposes, not because of their intrinsic incommen-surability, but rather because of factors operating in the academic context that are to do with professional territoriality. He concludes with the follow-ing political argument for the form of collaboration he proposes:

> The absence of a valid knowledge base on effectiveness and improve-ment plays into the hands of those who have already highly developed, but unfortunately non-rational, policy schemes for further market-based reforms of educational practice. One hopes that persons involved in the continued disciplinary problems at the 'cutting edge' where effectiveness and improvement interact will remember this.
>
> (Reynolds 1994: 29)

In other words, researchers from the two paradigms need to join forces to generate a 'rational' basis for policy-making in opposition to the growth of 'non-rational' market-based reforms. This argument is far too simple-minded. Academia is full of 'New Right' libertarian intellectuals who have been only too willing to enunciate what they believe to be the rational basis of a market-based distribution of social goods like 'education' (see, for example, Nozick 1974; Tooley 1995). From their point of view, social goods are justly distributed in society through the operations of markets. They might argue that what is at stake between them and school effectiveness researchers are different theories of distributive justice, and that a libertarian theory can be rationally defended against any theory which legitimates a distributive role for the state.

The reason why many school improvement researchers won't collaborate – although Hopkins (1994) may disagree – is this. The concept of education which underpins their research, and the values which frame it, are entirely inconsistent with the concept of education and values that underpin school effectiveness research findings. Since the idea of teacher autonomy is linked to this concept of education, school improvement researchers are unlikely to collaborate in an enterprise which implies the idea of 'teachers as technicians'. Moreover, school improvement researchers operate with a similar view of the educational process, and the teacher's role in it, to that of many classroom teachers. This explains why the latter appear reluctant to use the findings of school effectiveness research. What is at stake in the theory–practice problem is the concept of education.

Reynolds is, in a sense, right to cite 'professional territoriality' as a problem in bringing the two paradigms together, but he fails to understand that at the root of the problem lies a conflict about the nature of education and its relationship to schooling. School improvement researchers have traditionally been concerned with how schools can change to become more *educative* institutions, and from their point of view this is a very different enterprise to making them more *effective* as production systems.

I have argued that the external critiques are informed by a view of education which is very different from the view of schooling implicit in school effectiveness research. These critiques have highlighted the control values which frame school effectiveness research, but are less than explicit about their own. However, those critics who have addressed what I have called the pedagogical problem for school effectiveness researchers – that is, the problem of getting teachers to use their findings – do provide us with an indication of where their values lie. They lie in their conception of the capacities of human beings to form their own judgements about the right course of action in morally complex situations. These are capacities for 'situational understanding', 'deliberative reflection' and 'autonomous action'. Hamilton's critique of the Baconian theory of the theory–practice relation, implicit in school effectiveness research, is framed by such values. The same can be said of the critique of Brown *et al.*

I conclude that a similar set of values informs the critiques of the view of schooling conveyed by school effectiveness research findings. As we have seen, this view implies that schooling is a passive process for pupils, in which knowledge is represented as information to be acquired, and is framed by the control values associated with 'technical efficiency'. In contrast, the critics present a vision of education as a set of highly personal transactions between teachers and learners, involving complex considerations of curriculum and pedagogy. It is the vision which school effectiveness research 'findings' not only neglects but also negates.

In my view, curriculum and pedagogical decision-making only becomes a complex affair when teachers value their pupils as self-determining agents of their learning. This implies that learning is a dynamic and unpredictable process whose outcomes are not something the teacher can confidently predict or control. His or her responsibility is to establish the curriculum and pedagogical conditions which enable pupils to generate personally significant and meaningful learning outcomes for themselves. This is a very complex affair indeed and very context-bound. It explains why teachers should play a major generative role in determining the quality of the educational process.

School effectiveness research: 'Time warped' in modernity?

Reynolds, towards the end of his review of school effectiveness research, argues that it is in a 'time warp':

> In Britain and internationally, there is a sense in which the entire enterprise of school effectiveness appears in a 'time warp'. The studies that have been conducted are all aging rapidly and are of less and less use in the educational world of the 1990s. This world has new needs at the level of pupil outcomes from schools – the skills to access information and to work collaboratively in groups, and the social outcomes of being able to cope in a highly complex world are just three new educational goals which are never used as outcomes in the school effectiveness literature. Will the schools that generate high test score performance in the 1970s and 1980s be the schools that also generate these new social and academic achievements? It seems rather unlikely.
>
> (Reynolds 1994: 23)

I certainly agree that school effectiveness research findings are in a 'time warp', but disagree with Reynolds' assumption that the paradigm itself will be able to generate a rational foundation for school improvement programmes in the future, even when the world of schooling will look very different. Will the dominance of outcomes-based schooling resist the fundamental changes taking place in advanced modern (or post-modern) societies?

I very much doubt if any educational research paradigm will be able to claim that it has a premium on objective knowledge. The educational discourse of the future will require researchers in education to be much more self-reflexive about their research practices, and to make more explicit the value assumptions which condition their methodologies and shape their findings.

Schools will also need to become much more self-reflexive institutions. In Chapter 3, I sympathetically explored the view that the problem of student disaffection from schooling can be explained in terms of profound social changes, occurring in the occupational and social structures of advanced societies, which are creating conditions that make it difficult for schools to maintain their traditional function of allocating people to 'destination groups' – to careers, roles and positions – in a socially and occupationally stratified society. In Chapter 4, I analysed the social context of contemporary schooling in greater detail. For the purposes of my present argument, the following points are relevant. Large hierarchical employing organizations are flattening out and slimming down; professional expertise is fragmenting and bursting out of its traditional role and status containers, and is increasingly contracted into organizations on a temporary and even part-time basis; the new technologies are rapidly replacing unskilled and even skilled jobs and the main work in the new organizations is 'knowledge work' involving competence in information processing, analysis and problem-solving. In the social sphere, people's lives are being decreasingly shaped by traditional authority-based institutions like the family and the church. Society is becoming increasingly individualized in both the social and occupational spheres, and people are becoming what Charles Handy has called 'portfolio people'.

The implications of all this for schools are profound. Their future as traditional bounded organizations is doubtful. They may have to reconstruct their role in society as the coordinating centres of electronically-based learning systems and networks which are flexible and open to inputs from learners faced with the task of constructing their own futures. The idea that the outputs of learning can be determined independently of pupil inputs and pre-specified in terms of clusters of trained abilities linked to a stable and unchanging set of productive enterprises is already becoming obsolete as a basis for curriculum design, and is gradually being replaced by the idea of transferable skills and of a core of generic personal abilities – cognitive, interpersonal and motivational – which constitute capacities for exercising intelligent judgements in complex and unstructured situations.

The school of the future, as I hope to demonstrate in Chapter 7 through my accounts of school initiatives in community-focused environmental education (ENSI), is likely to be a much more flexible organization with highly permeable boundaries. Personally, I can't imagine a highly reductionist research paradigm, which searches for a 'mechanism of effectiveness' among all this complexity, having much of a future. However, I can imagine that the project of constructing a vision for general education as opposed to a more specialized and increasingly individualized vocational education – in the broadest sense of discovering and developing one's natural talents – will become increasingly urgent. The individualization process in advanced societies challenges schools to develop an education which enables pupils to take active responsibility for shaping the conditions of their existence in society. In learning to take such responsibility, they need to be able to locate the development of their natural talents within a personally constructed vision of a life worth living. Involving teachers in the development of a form of mass education, which gives all pupils equal access to the cultural resources of society is, in my view, the major challenge for school improvement in the future. Let's hope the teaching profession is not kept so busy producing, implementing and evaluating their school development plans in the National Curriculum dominated schools of today that they fail to notice that they are working in a 'time warp', and hence fail to rise to the challenge.

6

Culture, Education and Distributive Justice

Culture and education: The curriculum theory of Lawrence Stenhouse

In this chapter, I re-examine a curriculum theory, already extensively referred to in this book, which the critics of school effectiveness research and school researchers who share their assumption that curriculum and pedagogy are central to school improvement strategies like action research and self-evaluation, might appeal to in justifying their position. I will show how this theory constitutes a different interpretation of *equality* as a social end of education to the one embedded in school effectiveness research. Since this is what fundamentally divides the effectiveness researchers and their critics, there can be no productive discourse until both parties are prepared to appeal to, and together reflect about, the different understandings of *equality* implicit in their educational theories. The theory I shall examine is that of Lawrence Stenhouse, a theory which has been passionately reaffirmed and reinterpreted in the contemporary context of government-prescribed educational reform by Richard Pring (1995) in his 1993 Stenhouse Memorial Lecture, 'The Community of Educated People'.

Recalling a conversation with Stenhouse in 1967, as he took up the directorship of the Schools Council's Humanities Project, Pring argues that he saw the educational problem to be addressed by the project as follows:

> How can we seriously address the aspiration of secondary education for all, irrespective of age ability and aptitude, where we are deeply rooted in a tradition of liberal education which seems accessible only to an academic few? How can the best that has been thought and said be made available to young people whose interest in, and talent for, literature and the arts and history seem so limited? How can they be invited into the house and made to feel at home, not simply being forced to press

their noses against the window, without the whole educational enterprise being trivialised.

(Pring 1995: 127)

The problem for secondary schools as Stenhouse understood it, and having worked closely with Stenhouse on the Humanities Project I would confirm Pring's account, was a problem of equality of access to the cultural resources of society regardless of what one might call a young person's natural assets – special talents, abilities and potentials – and age. How can everyone be made to feel at home in the house of culture? Behind Stenhouse's question, as Pring points out, there is a vision of society as a 'community of educated people' and a view of schooling as the modelling of that vision.

It is a very topical question today as I write. The *Independent* newspaper (8 February 1996) I read over lunch carries a report by Judith Judd on Nick Tate's talk to a conference on 'Culture and Curriculum'. The chief executive of the School Curriculum and Assessment Authority, a descendant of the old Schools Council, was reported as saying that 'The curriculum needs to be firmly based on a cultural heritage' and that it should give young people a sense of past achievements and help them to see the relevance of those to the present day.

This is a familiar line from Nick Tate and Stenhouse would have applauded. He believed that the humanities curriculum should provide all pupils with equal access to the best that has been thought and written, and that this access involved helping them to see its relevance for their lives. However, Stenhouse stressed the critical significance of the latter and it became the focus of the Humanities Project. For him, the crucial questions were about the curriculum and pedagogical conditions which enabled pupils to make connections between the cultural heritage and the things that concerned and mattered to them in their lives. I would argue that what made Stenhouse equally concerned with curriculum processes, perhaps more so than Tate appears to be, was a passion that all pupils should have *equal access*, regardless of ability and aptitude.

Would Stenhouse also have applauded another familiar line of Tate's, the assertion of our cultural heritage as so-called high culture, a pre-nineteenth-century canon which includes Schubert and Mozart but not Blur's latest hit, and Shakespeare and Jane Austin but not Mills and Boon, and forms of representation which include books but not television, video or computers? I very much doubt if Stenhouse would have welcomed a state-prescribed canon. It undermines what he saw as a primary responsibility of teachers; namely, to select from the best that has been thought and written a curriculum for their pupils in the light of their knowledge of the things that matter to them. If this responsibility is removed, it not only signifies mistrust of teachers, but for Stenhouse would restrict their judgement of how best to establish connections between the cultural heritage and the life experiences of pupils. In other words, it would make the task of establishing the pedagogical conditions for securing equality of access more difficult, and Stenhouse regarded it difficult enough anyway. From the standpoint of his commitment to equality of access, it is undesirable to segregate teachers' responsibility for pedagogical conditions from responsibility for curriculum decisions.

However, reading Stenhouse's (1967) *Culture and Education*, it is clear that, like Tate, he had reservations about the educational value of much of what passes as mass culture and its representation in forms of mass communication. His reservations flowed from his view of the relationship between 'culture' and 'individuality'. We need to understand this view and its relationship to his concept of education in order to understand his reservations about mass culture.

Stenhouse (1967: 16) argued that although culture defines limits, it must do so in order to extend the individual's range of thought and feeling: 'Culture provides the disciplined and ordered experience without which freedom and creativity can only be pathetically rudimentary. It is the framework of creative innovation'. He was only too aware of a static view of culture which implied a more deterministic relationship to the thought and action of individuals, and left little room for the expression of individuality. He rejected the idea that induction into a culture necessarily involves, as a condition of access, a total conformity of belief and behaviour to the complex of shared understandings and norms a culture consists of.

To illustrate the difference between a *passive* and an *active* relationship to culture, Stenhouse uses the analogy of a man on a punt on the river (presumably an Oxbridge type). If he drifts with the current, we may say that the punt moves because of the current, but if he takes control of the situation and punts upstream, he must make allowances for the current. It becomes a dynamic medium for purposeful action. Culture is like the current. Stenhouse (1967: 28–9) argued:

> Culture is in some sense given a causal force when we submit ourselves passively to it; but when we wish to become purposeful and active, it is still culture which we must handle actively. And when we wish to work actively upon culture, we require symbols as tools. One aspect of culture, its symbol systems and particularly language, provides a medium through which man can reflect; and to reflect means to gain control over culture rather than to be controlled by it. The embodiment of culture in language does not shackle man, but liberates him. Language opens up culture as a resource . . . Words rooted in common meanings and learned in communication are manipulated in reflection to produce unique personal meaning.

For Stenhouse, our cultural heritage can be viewed as a resource which individuals can use to reflect about the things which matter to them in life, and this is made possible by language. The use of language enables individuals to use culture as a medium for reflecting about the conditions of their existence and thereby take more control of their lives. Hence the significance for Stenhouse of the role of discussion in establishing and maintaining an active relationship between the individual and the culture. It is by sharing understandings of the meaning of cultural products with others, and conversing about their significance for living, that individuals learn to think creatively and critically about them, and thereby reflectively extend and elaborate their understanding of the things that matter. As Pring (1995) remarks, Stenhouse believed that 'the group is prior to the individual, that individuals are well educated because they take part in groups and share experiences which have an educative quality'. The development of individuality and personal autonomy depends upon the quality of reflection a group or community of individuals establishes in relation to the culture it views as a resource.

Stenhouse viewed education as a dynamic and discursive process of cultural induction. In *Culture and Education* he argued that the primary value in education is 'the development of individuality and creativity in relation to the culture', and that the central purpose of education is 'to transmit culture through the symbols which make it accessible to criticism and creative thinking' (Stenhouse 1967: 58).

Pring's exposition of the 'logic' which underpinned the design of the Humanities Project illustrates very clearly how Stenhouse's view of 'culture as a resource' differs from a view of 'culture as objective text' and how the former is embedded in his educational theory.

> The humanities could be seen as a series of objects – commodities to be delivered, in present day parlance, or texts to be remembered – but they could and should be seen as the public recordings of the best of the conversations about those very matters which concern all young people, and thus the resources upon which the learner might draw. In that way the curriculum was a rendering of the impersonal into that which was personally significant.
>
> (Pring 1995: 128–9)

When culture is viewed as 'objective text', the curriculum is selected as an illustration of objective truths and eternal values, and the connection between culture and the personal concerns of pupils is weakened. The latter are assumed to be largely irrelevant to curriculum decisions. This view is succinctly put by Lord Quinton (quoted in Pring 1995: 136):

> Education is the transmitter of culture and the inculcation of values is at the centre of education. Traditionally high culture, as embodied in the canon and more theoretical academic disciplines and made possible by developed linguistic capacity, has been assumed to be the most supremely valuable part of education. Hitherto those who wished to extend education from the few to the many aimed to enlarge the constituency for high culture. In transmitting that culture one does not have

to attend too carefully to the views, speculations or questionings of those to whom it is transmitted.

When culture is viewed as a resource for autonomous thinking, the curriculum constitutes a selection from the culture in terms of its personal significance for pupils. It renders culture, through a process of reflective discussion, accessible to their thinking about the issues that matter in their lives. Pring's account of Stenhouse's vision of the Humanities Project clearly illustrates this view of the curriculum as a resource and the role of group discussion in relation to it.

> It was the job of the teacher to assist in that sharing of experiences by enabling it to benefit from what drama and art and history and literature had to say, and from each other's considered reactions to it. Such an exploration would, therefore, build on that evidence, be shaped through the social interaction by which such evidence was sieved, investigated and discussed. And there would be the gradual dawning of the realisation that, although that exploration could be more or less reasonable, could meet appropriate standards of enquiry, could be illuminating, could withstand the serious criticism of others, it always fell short of the certainties which are wanted. There would be the gradual realisation that, in these crucial matters of value and of how life ought to be lived, there are no infallible authorities and no certainties. And we are as it were, in this uncertain state of mind together – teachers and learners – but we can feel much more confident to act in our uncertainty if our beliefs are subject to the critical scrutiny that only a caring and serious community of enquirers can bring . . . The outcome of the transaction between teacher and learner, between learner and learner, and between learner and text is essentially a personal response – one which should be objectified, certainly, if it is not to be fossilised and if it is to be the basis of further exploration and critical scrutiny, but one which is too important to be the object of public gaze and appraisal or of official assessment and league tables. Personal growth, as opposed to the techniques and skills for growing, is not that kind of thing.
>
> (Pring 1995: 129–30)

Towards the end of this passage, Pring begins to show how Stenhouse's view of the outcomes of education, as a personal and dynamic response which arises from a complex transactional process, is radically different to the view of learning outcomes which informs so much contemporary policy-making in education (i.e. as predetermined and static objectives). Indeed, as we have seen, Stenhouse (1975) produced a considerable critique of the 'objectives model of curriculum planning', arguing that it distorted the nature of knowledge as a medium within which to think about problems. The *ends* of education, according to Stenhouse, cannot be specified independently of the means of realizing them. Conceptions of educational ends, like the development of 'autonomous thinking', cannot be broken down into specific learning objectives, but they do imply principles of procedure which orientate work in classrooms. In support of Stenhouse, Pring (1995: 135) argues:

> The clear distinction between ends and means is one of the most endur-
> ing but pernicious myths of curriculum planners – pernicious because
> it sets the stage for others, beyond the teachers and outside the edu-
> cational traditions, to say what should be the outcomes of teaching, as
> though the curriculum involves no transaction between teacher and
> learner, no struggle to make sense, no making personal that which arrives
> parcelled up in an impersonal way, no social interaction within which
> the learners explore their different, competing meanings, no confronting
> together the uncertainties which, though informed by art and literature,
> will never be solved.

In distinguishing education as a 'dynamic' process of cultural induction from a passive process aimed at securing conformity, Stenhouse saw the teacher's task as 'not to cause learning but to control the direction of learning'. Such control was to be exercised not by defining learning objectives and targets for pupils in relation to a curriculum conceived as an objective text, but by adopting 'principles of procedure' for handling cultural content in classrooms, aimed at protecting and fostering autonomous thinking and reflective discussion among pupils. Such principles specify the pedagogical conditions which enable pupils to access culture as a resource for developing their own understanding of the things that matter to them. For example, in the specific context of the Humanities Project, teachers were asked to handle 'cultural evidence' in the light of such principles as 'discussion rather than instruction should be at the core of classroom activities', 'protect divergence in discussion and ensure minority viewpoints are represented' and 'avoid using the classroom as a platform for promoting your own views on controversial issues'. By establishing such pedagogical conditions for handling cultural resources in 'humanities classrooms', teachers controlled the direction of learning and indeed its quality without predetermining the precise outcomes. In contrasting traditional conformity-compelling teaching with creative teaching, Stenhouse (1967: 75–6) wrote:

> The formal teacher approves the work of his class when he feels they
> are approaching the goal that he has set them. The creative teacher is
> happy when he feels that his pupils are moving in a worthwhile direc-
> tion, and is not concerned to define too closely the result he expects of
> their progress.

Such a view of how teachers provide all young people with equality of access to our cultural heritage is clearly based on a very different concept of education to the one enshrined in the UK National Curriculum, with its

framework of predetermined learning targets and levels of attainment specified for each as measures of progression in learning. It is also clearly contrary
to the concept of education which underpins school effectiveness research, in
particular the assumption that concern for the quality of learning outcomes
is expressed by detailed pre-specification. Although Stenhouse argued that
teachers do not cause learning of the kind he believed to be educationally
worthwhile – the outcome of individual, reflective, critical and creative thinking – he clearly believed that in establishing pedagogical conditions which
fostered these qualities in the process of learning, teachers influenced learning
outcomes. Effective teachers considered from his point of view are those who
enable students to generate learning outcomes which express these qualities
of thinking. What he was rejecting was the idea of teaching as an 'efficient
cause of learning', with its inbuilt control values.

In my view, there is a clear connection between the view of the educational
process embedded in critiques of school effectiveness research and Stenhouse's
concept of education as the development of individuality. However, what
Stenhouse does is to justify his concept in terms of a theory about the relationship between culture and the individual. His explicit educational theory
explains why those who appear to share his concept of education emphasize
that education is a complex process of highly personal pedagogical and curriculum transactions, in which the quality of teachers' judgements are highly
significant for the quality of education.

> But the teachers themselves are in turn deliberating about the appropri-
> ateness of those cultural resources – the selection of them for teaching
> purposes and the values to be attributed to them in the light of particu-
> lar conceptions of the life worth living. Teachers, in other words, are
> part of a wider community of educated people, deliberating about, and
> questioning the values which permeate their teaching in the light of
> their experience of the practice of educating.
>
> (Pring 1995: 132–3, on Stenhouse)

Some may feel that the specification of pedagogical conditions, rather than
learning outcomes, constitutes a greater erosion of teacher autonomy because
they impose limitations on teachers' freedom to choose their own methods.
However, this objection would not worry Stenhouse. He pointed out that
procedural principles did not prescribe what teachers did in classrooms. They
provided criteria to support teachers' judgements about the educational quality of their work with pupils. How they realized these standards in action, in
particular situations, was for them to determine on the basis of studying their
own classroom practices. Principles of procedure, for Stenhouse, supported
deliberation and reflection by teachers on how to realize the values of education in their classroom practices. It is worth remembering that a major
outcome of Stenhouse's curriculum development work with teachers in the

Humanities Project was the emergence of the 'teachers as researchers' movement in Britain.

Stenhouse might well have judged the effective schools identified by the criteria established through school effectiveness research to be anti-educational organizations. He would be sceptical about the extent to which any pupil in these schools, whatever their measurable progress in achieving predetermined learning outcomes, had secured the kind of access to the house of culture that made them feel at home there. To feel at home they would need to feel they were free to develop themselves as individuals. Equality of access for Stenhouse implied equal respect for the individuality of all young people. I would suggest that the critics of school effectiveness research not only tacitly operate with a similar educational theory to the one articulated by Stenhouse nearly thirty years ago, but they also share a similar vision of equality as an end of education.

On former prime minister John Major's reference, at the Centre for Policy Studies, to the mania for equality, 'not of opportunity but of outcome', among progressive educators, Pring writes of Stenhouse:

> Certainly there was a mania for equality. But it was not for equality of outcome. Rather was it an equality of respect, a recognition that all – yes all – had a right to enter the house with the teacher, to be made to feel at home, and not to be left to press their noses at the window. And, in being encouraged to join the community of educated people, irrespective of one's measured ability, so there could be no equality of outcome, because the consequence would always be the personal making sense, that personal resolution of the questions which one was asking.
>
> (Pring 1995: 141)

In the light of the above account of the relationship between culture and education, let us revisit Stenhouse's reservations about what passes as mass culture in contemporary society. He argued that mass culture threatens the values of individuality and creativity because its effects on the individual are to create conformity of thought and action through the construction of stereotypical images of the things that matter in our lives. This is because the techniques by which mass culture is constructed and represented are those of mass communications. Such techniques, he argues, make it difficult for the 'artist' to handle criticism and feedback in the course of a performance and its highly commercialized context, where it becomes more important to 'sell' a performance by appealing to the status quo, imposes constraints on the creation of something original and profound. Stenhouse (1967: 50) wrote:

> The words, symbols and images given to us by the mass communicator are not good tools of discourse and of thought, because they overdetermine our reactions. They prejudice us rather than liberate us. To acquire all the mythology of sex in mass communication is not to be given the

means of thinking more clearly and more creatively about sex, but it is to be trapped within a network of ideas which cannot be handled critically and productively.

Having said this, Stenhouse urged a sense of balance. Not all the products of mass culture are inferior in quality. Artists and producers in the field of mass communications are not powerless in relation to the medium and the context of its use. Some are concerned about the effects of their work on the lives of people in their audiences, and are prepared to take some risks for the sake of quality. While urging teachers to avoid a comfortable optimism, Stenhouse (1967: 51) argued for a sense of balance: 'There is nothing to be gained from a narrow-minded condemnation of all that stems from the mass media. It is sufficient that we should care about the quality of the art that is offered to the greater public'.

Stenhouse would, I suggest, view Tate's reported remarks about popular culture and education to be an example of narrow-minded condemnation. He would leave the question about which 'objects' of mass culture have educative potential for teachers to make a judgement about, under conditions where they are required to justify their selections from the culture in the light of evidence they gather about their use as resources for developing pupils' thinking. If we combine Tate's endorsement of the introduction of a canon of pre-1900 literary works to the English and Welsh National Curriculum with his general remarks about popular culture, we must conclude that, in spite of some points of agreement with Stenhouse, he neither shares his view about the relationship between culture and education or his view of equality as a social end. Indeed, we must conclude that Tate simply endorses the views built into the National Curriculum he has the responsibility for delivering; namely, that 'education' is the means of securing the conformity of the young to understandings which are predetermined by an elite group of 'cultural guardians', anxious to shore up an exclusive sense of national identity. For Stenhouse, the cultural resources for education would not exclude the best that has been thought and written in different cultures. The 'house of culture', in which all pupils are to feel at home among the community of educated people, is an inclusive rather than exclusive house. Unfortunately, the effective school of today in Britain, inasmuch as its outcomes are defined by current national curriculum policies, is not the one which helps all young people to feel equally at home in 'the house of culture', regardless of their class, gender and race, but rather one which extracts the greatest degree of conformity from the greatest number to a restricted and narrow construct of national identity,

The latter point of view is represented by a number of Conservative politicians and intellectuals in Britain, and it can be rationalized in terms of a particular version of 'equality of opportunity', that employed by John Major in the talk to the Centre for Policy Studies (cited above). Major was making a distinction between equality of opportunity and equality of outcome, and rejecting the latter as a social end of education in favour of the former. This view of the social conditions governing access to educational goods is consistent with the view that induction into the culture involves the conformity of the mind to extrinsic standards. Lord Quinton, in a passage from his Victor Cook lecture, begins to make a connection between the curriculum as 'objective text' and 'equality of opportunity'.

> The history of formal education can be looked at from two points of view, one concerned with what is taught, the other with whom it is taught to. The second factor does not have to affect the first. If what has hitherto been taught only to a few is the best there is, why should it not be made available, as numbers expand, to a larger number?
>
> (quoted in Pring 1995: 136)

Lord Quinton is claiming that the personal interests and concerns of pupils are irrelevant to judgements about what is worth teaching. The latter can be defined by reference to objective standards of excellence. Pupils' subjectively determined standards of what constitutes worthwhile content may be significant for judgements about the means but not about the ends of education. However, argues Quinton, the fact that access to 'objectively defined' worthwhile content has in the past been confined to 'the few', is no reason in the future to deny access to many. He appears to be endorsing the principle of 'equality of opportunity' to 'objectively defined' educational goods, but not in a form which implies equality of outcome.

This is a rather different view of equality of opportunity to that of Stenhouse. For the latter, the ends of education refer to the development of individuality and autonomous thinking and imply that educational outcomes, although open to critical appraisal and assessment in retrospect, are personal creations and not susceptible to standardization. Judgements about content should be consistent with such ends. Grounding them in a consideration of the personal interests and concerns of pupils – of the things that matter to them in life – and of their educational needs in the light of these concerns, is clearly consistent with the ends of education cited by Stenhouse. He clearly did not share Quinton's view that concern for what is taught can be separated from concern for whom it is taught to. We find him rejecting much of mass art as curriculum content, not because it doesn't conform to a high cultural canon but because he judged it to be inconsistent with pupils developing their 'individuality' and 'autonomous thinking' in relation to the things that matter to them. However, he qualified this by arguing that such judgements have to be tested 'experimentally' in classrooms. The classroom was not the site for implementing a predefined curriculum, but a laboratory for experimentally constructing one. Hence, the significance for him of the teacher as a researcher. If pupils do not feel their individuality and autonomy of thought are being enhanced, do not feel a sense of well-being or being 'at home in the house of culture', then we have no warrant for claiming that the content presented to them is educationally worthwhile.

For Stenhouse, equality of access to the 'house of culture' implied equal opportunities for self-realization and determination. Unlike Quinton, it implies a dynamic rather than a static conception of the curriculum. The *educational quality* of a learning outcome depended on the extent to which it constituted a personal, original, creative and critical response to the content selected. It is achievements which express their individuality and powers of autonomous thought that enable pupils to feel 'at home' in the culture.

The problem with the traditional academic curriculum, from Stenhouse's point of view, is that its form as an objective text guarantees that many young people will be denied access to the culture it 'guards'. It specifies conditions of access which are linked to a particular form of human association. Academic success has been traditionally associated, in England for example, with entry into certain high-status professional groups who emulate the mores and manners of the upper middle class in society. The extension of the academic curriculum, organized in the form of subjects, from the private to the public sector, primarily functioned as an avenue of organized upward social mobility. Many from the working class refuse to attempt the transition and refuse to conform to the 'academic requirements of entry' into the 'destination groups', while those that attempt it find themselves increasingly alienated from the forms of association in which they were reared (see Stenhouse 1967: 117–18).

Stenhouse drew from this analysis of the limitations of the traditional academic curriculum, in securing equal access to common cultural resources, some implications for successful schooling. The 'successful' school is not so much the school that provides equal access to common cultural goods, as the one that controls access to certain 'destination groups' by aligning its forms of association or ethos with them and having a curriculum which reflects their knowledge and skill requirements. Stenhouse was writing at a time when schools tended to be differentiated according to the 'destination groups' they catered for and the vocational cultures which distinguished them. The public and grammar schools catered for the middle-class professions and occupations through the traditional academic curriculum, while the modern schools tended to cater for 'rude mechanicals'. In other words, they were vocationally specialized institutions. He addressed the question of the relationship between a general and vocational education as follows:

> In the perspective of our view of culture, then, we see vocational education and general education as providing two different bases for human association. On the one hand, one learns to associate for the purposes of productive enterprise with one of the specialised groups created by the division of labour; on the other, one is inducted into a complex of understandings which supports a general social and political intercourse.
> (Stenhouse 1967: 113)

Stenhouse rejected the notion that a traditional academic curriculum, based as it was on a certain hierarchically positioned division of labour in society, could form an appropriate basis for general education. This is precisely what the comprehensive system of schooling that was emerging as he wrote attempted. It was heralded by the Labour government at the time as 'grammar schools for all'. Through the Humanities Project, Stenhouse attempted to realize an alternative conception of general education that equalized the access of all young people to that complex of understandings, of which our general culture exists, in a form which 'supported human associations over a much wider range and enabled people to talk together both about common every-day experiences and about the fundamental issues which underlie human experience' (Stenhouse 1967: 110). The Humanities Project established a beachhead in the innovatory British secondary modern school but failed to make the transition into the grammarized comprehensive system. I would argue that the problem school effectiveness researchers are addressing in Britain is very context-bound. It is the problem which arises in trying to make a vocational education for social elites – represented in the European tradition of an academic education – a basis for a general education of the masses. Stenhouse argued that the enterprise was misconceived. Nearly thirty years after he did so, school effectiveness researchers, aided and abetted by 'New Labour', are now attempting to prop up a system in trouble, because as Stenhouse would have predicted, significant and growing numbers of young people are experiencing alienation even when they are 'achieving'. School effectiveness researchers appear to be recommending an increasingly coercive form of schooling to maximize achievement levels under a smoke-screen of research-speak and techno-talk, like 'rational basis for policy-making', 'objective data', 'value added', 'outcomes based education', etc.

Culture and Education was written prior to the establishment of comprehensive schooling on a national basis. In it, Stenhouse (1967) was attempting to formulate a comprehensive theory of general education that was sadly neglected in the reorganization of secondary schooling. He may well have accepted current developments at post-14 towards a mix of vocational and academic courses, and the learning of a core of techno-scientific knowledge throughout the basic education of pupils. However, he would have regarded such developments as ways of organizing learning for the purposes of productive enterprise. In this context, he may not have objected to the use of the objectives model as a basis for designing certain curriculum elements which focused on the acquisition of necessary technical knowledge and skills. Nor might Stenhouse have disapproved of systematic approaches to teaching basic numeracy and literacy at the core of the primary school curriculum, for this would provide a foundation for both a specialized 'vocational' and general education. Stenhouse, however, wanted to balance curricular designed for the purposes of productive enterprise against a form of general education which gave pupils equal access to the cultural resources (including science and technology viewed as 'cultures' rather than sources of technical knowledge and skills), which enabled them to make sense of their lives. From his point of view, the latter should have at least equal priority in planning the curriculum experiences of all pupils in basic education, and it is in this area that his curriculum theory should be located.

Curriculum theory and Rawls' principles of justice

I have attempted to show how the curriculum theory of Stenhouse, a theory that also appears to underpin the critiques of school effectiveness research, implies a particular conception of equality of educational opportunity. In my view, it is highly consistent with the liberal egalitarian theory of social justice provided by Rawls, and published some four years after the publication of *Culture and Education*, coincidentally with the launching of the Humanities Project. To my knowledge, Stenhouse was not familiar with Rawls' book as he developed this project in schools across Britain.

Rawls' (1971) *A Theory of Justice* has perhaps been the most seminal contribution to political philosophy in the twentieth century. Ever since its publication, our public discourse about social justice has to a considerable extent been shaped by the debates surrounding Rawls' theory. It provides an excellent example of Stenhouse's view that ideas are resources for thinking about the problems of living rather than objects of mastery. There is probably a general consensus among political philosophers at this point in time, twenty-five years later, that Rawls did not succeed in providing a rational foundation for the liberal-egalitarian principles of justice he formulated. They would argue that the search for 'rational foundations' is a misconceived enterprise (school effectiveness researchers take note), a thoroughly modernist project, and we should now be learning in the terminal years of the twentieth century to think and live without them, as post-modernists. Regardless of this critique, Rawls articulated a vision of the values that he believed liberal democracies should represent, which regardless of the question of its 'rational foundations' will continue to provide an important resource for thinking about the problems of justice in post-modern societies.

As Kymlicka (1990: 303) has pointed out, Rawls' central conception of justice consists of one idea, namely that 'All social primary goods – liberty and opportunity, income and wealth, and the bases of self-respect – are to be distributed equally unless an unequal distribution of any or all of these goods is to the advantage of the least favoured'. Hence, for Rawls, justice balances the twin principles of equity and difference. It involves the equal distribution of social goods unless unequal distribution benefits the underprivileged. This is why it is characterized as the 'liberal-egalitarian theory' of justice and contrasted with utilitarian and libertarian theories.

Rawls (1971) discusses the relationship between his principle of difference and the egalitarian principle of 'redress', namely that 'since inequalities of birth and natural endowment are undeserved, these inequalities are to be somehow compensated for' *by* 'giving more attention to those with fewer natural assets and to those born into the less favourable positions' (p. 100). In pursuit of this principle alone, argues Rawls, more resources might be spent 'on the education of the less rather than the more intelligent, at least over a certain time of life, say the earlier years of school' (p. 101). However, he points out that the principle of redress is only plausible as a prima facie principle which needs to be weighed against others in the pursuit of justice. For Rawls, the principle of difference, while not the same as the principle of redress – it doesn't require society to even out handicaps as if everyone were competing in the same race on an equal basis – does give some weight to the considerations addressed by the latter. He illustrates how it does this with a reference to education:

> the difference principle would allocate resources in education, say, so as to improve the long-term expectation of the least favoured. If this end is attained by giving more attention to the better endowed, it is permissible, otherwise not. And in making this decision, the value of education should not be assessed only in terms of economic efficiency and social welfare. Equally if not more important is the role of education in enabling a person to enjoy the culture of his society and to take part in its affairs, and in this way to provide for each individual a secure sense of his own worth.
>
> (Rawls 1971: 101)

For Rawls, the difference principle also offers an interpretation of another prima facie social principle, namely that of 'fraternity'. It represents equality of self-esteem and respect which entails in itself no specific social requirement. However, when this principle is viewed in the light of the difference principle, it implies that the 'better circumstanced are willing to have their greater advantages only under a scheme in which this works out for the benefit of the less fortunate' (Rawls 1971: 105).

Central to this idea of benefit for the less fortunate is enhanced self-respect. Inequalities in achievements and rewards are to be justified in terms of their contribution to the enhancement of 'self-respect': a primary good which all individuals equally need. Rawls (1971) argues that the equality of self-respect implied by the principle of fraternity is a value manifest in a genuinely democratic form of social life by an 'absence of manners of deference and servility'. Enhancing feelings of self-respect among the least favoured in society implies limits on 'the forms of hierarchy and the degrees of inequality that justice permits' (p. 107). Hence, educational resources, Rawls argues, are:

> not to be allotted solely or necessarily mainly according to their return as estimated in productive trained abilities, but also according to their worth in enriching the personal and social life of citizens, including here

the less favoured. As a society progresses the latter consideration becomes increasingly more important.

(Rawls 1971: 107)

It is not difficult to see the connection between Rawls' account of the implications of his difference principle for education and the educational theory of Stenhouse with its vision of the school as a microcosm of society conceived as the 'community of educated people'. This might be summarized as follows:

1 Stenhouse's emphasis on providing all pupils with equal access to culture regardless of ability and aptitude and in a form that enhances their individuality and autonomy, can be linked to Rawls' view that the value of education, in part and perhaps most importantly, lies in enabling all pupils to enjoy their culture and to take part in its affairs regardless of their natural endowments and social circumstances. For both Rawls and Stenhouse, equality of access to the culture implies a form of induction into a fraternal community which enhances the self-respect and self-esteem of all pupils. Any distribution of educational resources in favour of the well-endowed should not deprive the less well-endowed of an opportunity to appropriate their culture in a form which enhances their self-respect.

2 Rawls argues that educational resources should not solely, or even mainly, be distributed on the basis of returns in estimated productive trained abilities that are of instrumental value for the economy or the welfare of social institutions, but should also be allocated to enrich the personal and social life of the individual. This links with Stenhouse's opposition to the dominance in schools of learning organized largely for the purposes of productive enterprise and to the use of an objectives model of curriculum planning which renders culture an instrument for the production of knowledge and skills required by certain 'destination groups', rather than a resource for individuals to use in constructing their personal and social identities more broadly as members of society. Stenhouse, as I suggested above, did not dismiss the need for objectives in some areas of the curriculum, but objected to their use as a basis for planning all pupils' learning experiences on the grounds that, in the field of culture, they distort the nature of knowledge as a medium for critical and creative thinking about the human condition.

In summary, I would argue that Rawls' difference principle supports Stenhouse's argument for a balance, between a curriculum which provides all pupils with equal access to cultural goods, and a curriculum organized for the purposes of productive enterprise in which those with natural abilities suited to these purposes will achieve more than the less well-endowed but may well benefit the latter in the longer term. Rawls' principle, allied to the interpretation it provides of the principle of fraternity, basically rules that arrangements in the educational system which distribute rewards and benefits unequally but justifiably in favour of the well-endowed should not disadvantage the less well-endowed's equal access to the general cultural. Such access is a condition of acquiring self-esteem as a member of society – an essential primary good.

School effectiveness research, equity and justice

Let us now look at school effectiveness research in the light of Rawls' theory of justice. The report on school effectiveness research to Ofsted by Sammons *et al.* (1995) claims that a shift in the concerns of recent school effectiveness research, at least in Britain, has occurred:

> Early school effectiveness research incorporated explicit aims and goals concerned with equity and excellence. Three important features were:
>
> ◆ clientele (poor/ethnic minority children);
> ◆ subject matter (basic skills in reading and maths);
> ◆ equity (children of the urban poor should achieve at the same level as those of the middle class).
>
> ... such research was often dominated by the perspectives of school improvers and providers of external support to schools. More recent research, especially in the UK context, has moved away from an explicit equity definition towards a focus on the achievements of all students and a concern with the concept of progress over time rather than cross-sectional 'snapshots' of achievement at a given point in time. This broadens the clientele to include all students, not just the disadvantaged, and a wider range of outcomes (academic and social). As in the US, however, the majority of UK studies have also been conducted in inner city schools.
>
> (Sammons *et al.* 1995: 3)

Since most of the early school effectiveness studies were carried out in the USA, this passage appears to be indicating to British policy-makers a shift of concern with respect to the social ends of education. Whereas researchers in the USA were seeking an understanding of how educational goods could be distributed more equitably by focusing on the conditions for equalizing the achievements of the poor in relation to the middle class, it seems that British researchers have been more concerned that all children should achieve more, however unequal their progress. Former prime minister John Major will no doubt be delighted that British researchers lack the mania for equality of outcomes that prevailed across the Atlantic. However, let's examine what, if anything, is at stake in this shift before claiming that school effectiveness research is underpinned by the same ideology as the educational policies of the Major government.

In the early US school effectiveness studies, interestingly carried out in the wake of the debate surrounding Rawls' theory of justice, the concern for equity was interpreted, in a context of scarce public resources, as making the enhancement of life-chances for the children of the poor and ethnic minorities a primary goal of public schooling. This was to be accomplished by equalizing their achievements in basic literacy and numeracy in relation to the population as a whole. Such studies appear to have been motivated by the egalitarian principle of redress, which Rawls' principle of difference accommodates but balances against inequalities in the distribution of goods which have the effect of benefiting the disadvantaged in the longer term. Looked at in the social context of public education in the USA, the focus on basic skill acquisition, seen as a means of redressing inequalities in life opportunities in the society, appears to be consistent with Rawls' liberal-egalitarianism. The focus on basic skills fits Howe's (1995) account of liberal-egalitarianism as a principle of distributive justice:

> liberal-egalitarianism identifies the disadvantaged in terms of the relatively low share of social goods they possess. It then sets about the task of eliminating identified disadvantages by implementing various compensatory social programs, educational and otherwise.
>
> (Howe 1995: 348)

However, as we have seen, Rawls linked his principle of difference with that of fraternity and the idea of equality of esteem for the individual as a morally autonomous person. In this respect, the interpretation of the liberal-egalitarian theory of justice, which underpinned school effectiveness research in the USA, appears to dissociate a concern for redressing disadvantage from the need of young people to develop as morally autonomous persons, the foundation of their self-esteem and self-respect.

This may explain why attempts at the policy level to redistribute social goods on a liberal-egalitarian basis are sometimes viewed, as Howe has pointed out, to be inconsistent with democratic values. Of such redistributions, Howe (1995: 348) writes:

> All of this is conceived so as to require little or no input from those most affected. In this it is profoundly undemocratic, for it assumes that the social goods to be distributed, as well as the procedures by which this is to occur, are uncontroverted. In fact they reflect the interests of those who have been and continue to be in charge.

The early school effectiveness research appears to have been biased by the interests of liberal-egalitarian policy-makers who dissociated the egalitarian principle of redress from the principle of equality of esteem for the disadvantaged. Hence, the factors it identified did not characterize effective schools as places that are effectively preparing pupils to shape the conditions of their existence in a democratic social order. Rather, they are characterized as effect-ively preparing them for passive citizenship. For example, Howe's point about the undemocratic nature of liberal-egalitarian redistributions of social goods helps us to understand a US research finding cited by Perrone (1989: 44):

> Donald Medley (1979) reports that effective teachers of lower socio-economic status children ask more low level questions – facts, names, dates; are less likely to pick up and amplify students responses; have fewer student initiated questions and comments and give less feedback on student questions. He claims further that effective teachers devote most of their time to large group or whole group instruction.

What characterizes such instruction is that it is fundamentally undemocratic in its assumptions about the pedagogical conditions under which children are to secure access to the subject matter.

So far, then, we might argue that school effectiveness research is biased by a narrow and authoritarian concept of liberal-egalitarian justice. Let's now look at the recent British studies to see how they shape up in relation to that of Rawls. These studies, at least according to Sammons *et al.* (1995), imply no explicit equalizing intention. It is sufficient if all pupils make progress in learning, with the implication that none are disadvantaged, across a wide range of outcomes (academic and social), however unequal the levels of suc-cess attained. Such a concern would be consistent with Rawls' 'difference principle' if (a) inequalities in learning outcomes are to the benefit of the 'least able' pupils in the longer term, and (b) the latter have equal access to cultural resources in a form which will enhance their self-respect and enrich their lives. One cannot help feeling that underlying the view that the effect-ive school is the one which improves the progress of all children, however unequal, is the assumption that schooling is largely about the organization of learning for the purposes of productive enterprise. Again, if (a) applies but not (b), we have a research process blinkered by a rather limited and author-itarian vision of liberal-egalitarian justice.

Can we therefore conclude that school effectiveness research in Britain tends to fit a liberal-egalitarian view of distributive justice in spite of the dif-ferences of emphasis between the early US studies and the more recent British ones? If we can, and in some respects the emphasis on 'progress for all' does fit an aspect of Rawls' difference principle, then the difference of emphasis with the early US studies might be understood and explained in the following terms.

The difference consists in the US studies tacitly emphasizing the egalitar-ian principle of redress (equity), while the British studies tacitly emphasize the 'difference principle', but both principles are simply two aspects of the liberal-egalitarian conception of justice. The different emphases between the two groups of studies may best be explained in terms of their different social and curriculum contexts rather than in terms of any fundamental conceptual disagreement. The US researchers tended to select schools where pupil intakes largely consisted of the urban poor demonstrating low levels of basic skill acquisition. The problem they addressed was how these schools could improve the achievements of their pupils to the same levels of achievement as those attained by middle-class pupils, and thereby establish the conditions of access to 'a good life'. The British studies, on the other hand, have operated in the context of comprehensive schools, which aspired to socially inclusive intakes and an elaborate national curriculum covering a broader range of goals than basic skill acquisition. Whereas schools may be able to effect greater equality in educational outcomes with respect to a basic skills curriculum, this may not be possible with respect to academic subject knowledge, where mastery may be dependent on unequal distributions in the population of certain natural abilities.

In the light of the above, we might understand school effectiveness studies as an attempt to provide policy-makers with a basis for state interventions shaped by a liberal-egalitarian view of the just distribution of educational goods. However, according to Kymlicka (1990: 55), the prevailing justification for the distribution of economic goods (and I would add goods like education) in our society is that of 'equality of opportunity', and he argues that it conflicts in certain respects with Rawls' liberal-egalitarianism. This explains why I feel that the conception of justice which underpins current British research into school effectiveness retains an element of ambiguity and is rather unclear. In their search for patronage in the 'corridors of power', the researchers may well have reason not to confront the ideological biases which shape the research process. However, some school effectiveness researchers in Britain have been critical of certain aspects of the recent Conservative government's market-based reforms in education. So I am content to describe their concept of justice as crudely liberal-egalitarian. It is far less sophisticated than Rawls' conception of distributive justice and that entailed in Stenhouse's theory about the relationship between culture, education and the individual. As we have seen, both conceptions are highly congruent with each other. Brown *et al.* (1995) have argued that what school effectiveness research lacks is a decent educational theory. I would agree and add that it also lacks a decent theory of distributive justice, for as we have seen from the discussion of Stenhouse and Rawls, the two are not unconnected. Different theories of distributive justice imply different educational and, more particularly, curriculum theories.

Equality of opportunity, libertarianism and market-based education

What is at stake between a liberal-egalitarian theory of distributive justice and the conception of equality of opportunity that dominates current policy-making in our society? The principle of 'equality of opportunity' asserts that people's success or failure in life should be determined by fair competition rather than social circumstances, in which everyone has an opportunity to demonstrate competence. Success is distributed fairly if it is deserved (i.e. earned or merited) by performance (see Kymlicka 1990: 56). As Kymlicka points out, those who share this ideological perspective may disagree on the means of ensuring equality of opportunity. Some believe that legal non-discrimination in education and employment is sufficient, while others believe that affirmative action programmes for socially and culturally disadvantaged groups are also required. Nevertheless, in spite of such disagreement over policy, there is a shared conception of equality of opportunity operating:

> it is fair for individuals to have unequal shares of social goods if those inequalities are earned and deserved by the individual . . . But it is unfair for individuals to be disadvantaged or privileged by arbitrary or unde-served differences in their social circumstances.
>
> (Kymlicka 1990: 56)

The key justificatory idea underpinning the ideology of equality of opportunity is that of 'desert' and it appears to be a fair basis for distributing social goods because 'it ensures that people's fate is determined by their *choices* rather than their circumstances' (Kymlicka 1990). Let's now examine how this ideology differs from Rawls' liberal-egalitarian theory of justice. For Rawls, inequalities in 'natural abilities' are as morally arbitrary as social inequalities. Just as distributions of social goods on the latter basis are morally undeserved, so are distributions based on inequalities in natural abilities. The natural tal-ents a person does or doesn't possess is, like his or her social circumstances, a matter of chance and therefore no basis for making morally just distribu-tions of social goods. However, the difference principle in Rawls' theory of justice enables him to argue that, although no-one deserves a greater share of social goods than others by virtue of inequalities in natural talent, it might be just and fair to distribute goods on this basis if, and only if, those with the least natural ability also benefit from the distributive arrangements. Rawls accommodates certain aspects of the 'equality of opportunity' ideology while rejecting its justificatory grounding in the idea of 'just deserts'.

Given the liberal-egalitarian outlook of school effectiveness studies, they are at tension with an ideology of equality of opportunity, since the latter is open to the verdict that, once the conditions of equal opportunities have been satisfied, some do not deserve by virtue of their performance to benefit. What then might be the relationship between an equality of opportunity ideology and recent market reforms?

Reynolds (1994: 29) clearly sees school effectiveness research findings to be in conflict with market-orientated reforms and to provide a more 'rational basis' for policy-making in education. What he doesn't appear to understand is that the knowledge it generates as a 'rational basis' for policy-making is not politically neutral. It is shaped by a conception of distributive justice which is at variance with one which is often used to defend market-based educational policies; namely, a *libertarian theory* of justice. I want to show how the principle of equality of opportunity operates within this theory.

Libertarians defend market-freedoms on the grounds that they are inherently just. Hence, they oppose any strong role for the state in the distribution of social goods like education (see Kymlicka 1990). The key idea employed to demonstrate the justice of free markets is that of self-ownership. The individual is viewed as the owner of his or her natural talents and the fruits of their use: wealth and property. Hence, individuals have a natural right to dispose of such fruits – their just deserts – as they choose, free from interference from the state. The libertarian theorist, Robert Nozick (1974), argues that a just distribution is that which results from people's free exchanges: 'From each as they choose, to each as they are chosen' (cited by Kymlicka 1990: 97). According to Nozick, society should respect these rights because they reflect the Kantian moral imperative that people should be treated as ends in themselves and not be used for achieving other ends without consent. Hence, as bearers of these rights of ownership, society must treat individuals with equal respect, and this implies limits on the extent to which individuals can be expected by society to make sacrifices on behalf of others. From such a libertarian perspective, the just distribution of social goods should be largely determined by people's choices and the resources at *their* command, rather than by the state.

As Kymlicka argues, both Nozick and Rawls appeal to the abstract Kantian principle that individuals should command equal respect by being treated as ends rather than means, and this sets limits on the extent to which one person can be used for the benefit of others. However, they significantly differ about the nature of individuals' moral claims on others and society. Kymlicka (1990: 105) sees this difference as follows: 'for Rawls one of the most important rights is a right to a certain share of society's resources. For Norzick, on the other hand, the most important rights are rights over oneself'. Kymlicka points out (p. 106) that for Norzick, the naturally disadvantaged and the untalented have no legitimate moral claims over the resources of the talented, whereas for Rawls and other liberal thinkers, although the freedom of individuals to develop and use their talents in self-chosen projects should be respected, their possession of talent is a matter of luck rather than desert. Individuals do not have a moral right to possess the fruits of their exercise and thereby *choose* the means of their disposal. The talented should only accrue unequal benefits from their talent if such inequality is to everyone's benefit. From a liberal-egalitarian perspective, and contrary to a libertarian one, the naturally disadvantaged have a legitimate moral claim on the resources of the advantaged, and the latter have a moral obligation to supply them.

What would a market-based libertarian education system look like. The libertarian ideal would be a largely privatized education market in which parents were free to deploy the resources they have a right to command in choosing an education for their children. Since the talented will have accrued greater resources than the untalented, they will have the most choice and be able to secure the best education for their children. And this is only fair; the talented parents would be reaping their just deserts. The untalented would not secure the best education for their children and this would also be fair and just. On the other side of the transfer, schools will enhance their market by making themselves attractive to the talented parents and denying access to the children of the untalented. Liberal-egalitarians might add at this point that the schools that fail in this mission inevitably become the 'sink schools' catering for the children of the untalented.

Libertarian justice in the distribution of educational goods looks paradoxically unjust from a liberal-egalitarian point of view. Hence the debate surrounding current market-orientated educational reforms in Britain. They do not constitute a fully privatized free market system but rather the introduction of quasi-market mechanisms into a system that remains substantially regulated by the state. I am thinking, of course, of such mechanisms as 'parental choice', the publication of test results in the form of school league tables, schools opting out of local government control into grant-maintained status, and the reintroduction of selection and setting in schools. Such mechanisms provide a basis for redistributing educational goods in favour of the children of those who are relatively well-endowed with resources of talent, property and wealth.

Some libertarian theorists are only too aware that social circumstances such as poverty and ethnicity prevent many children from realizing their natural talents and abilities in life. They may therefore support a minimum of state intervention to secure a measure of equality of opportunity without undermining the primary role of the family unit in deciding what education is best for its children. Beyond that, libertarians argue the state's responsibility for education should end. Equality of opportunity some libertarians would argue is quite consistent with a libertarian theory of distributive justice. Since education should be distributed in favour of the naturally talented, then the theory is undermined if children do not benefit from them purely because they are socially rather than naturally disadvantaged. And since it is difficult to sort out the socially from the naturally disadvantaged, an adequate minimum of education to safeguard equality of opportunity for all is necessary.

The British philosopher of education James Tooley (1995) is among those libertarians who argue, following West (1970), for a minimum adequate standard of education to safeguard equality of opportunity. He believes, however, that although a national inspectorate would need to monitor the extent to which schools provided such an education, it need not require a state-enforced curriculum. Schools operating and competing in a free market will tend, he argues, to arrive at an agreed core curriculum, specifying a minimum adequate education, for themselves.

Tooley (1995) claims that the idea of a guaranteed and adequate minimum level of social provision for all, including for education, was what Rawls was seeking in his formulation of his two principles of justice: an assurance that inequalities in the distribution of goods did not deprive but benefited the disadvantaged. He argues that Rawls' attempts to justify his principles as those which people in a pre-social state of ignorance about the positions they would occupy in society – 'the original position' – would rationally choose, fail. According to Tooley, Rawls not only fails to justify his principles as those which a rational person would choose from the 'original position', but he also fails to show how they might deliver an adequate minimum standard of provision at all. Hence, the disadvantaged might secure greater equality of educational opportunity from a market-based construction of an adequate minimum education than one constructed on the basis of Rawls' liberal-egalitarian principles of justice.

Tooley might well be right in a way, but his discussion of an adequate minimum education for all highlights for me what is truly at stake between a sophisticated and non-technocratic liberal-egalitarian conception of distributive justice in education, and the equality of opportunity ideology which underpins market-based educational reforms, and is frequently justified by a libertarian view of the rights of the individual. I would hypothesize that an adequate minimum education, specifying a safety net below which no pupil should fall in a market-based distribution of educational goods, whether it was planned by the state or constructed through the market, would look very different to the adequate minimum education planned from a Rawlsian and Stenhousian perspective. The latter as we have seen would give considerable priority to a general education which emphasized equality of access to cultural goods as a resource for reflecting upon the problems of living and the fundamental issues of human existence. It would cultivate individuality of response within a fraternal classroom culture that embodied equality of esteem and modelled society as the community of educated people. Such an education would be framed by aims and principles of procedure as frameworks for curriculum development in schools. It would have little use for planning by objectives. This is the conception of education which many school improvement researchers over the past twenty-five years have tried to give birth to through their collaborative work with teachers.

I would imagine that a market-based and equal opportunities orientated adequate minimum education would largely consist of a core curriculum of basic and social skills together with techno-scientific knowledge and skills that were deemed essential for wealth creation and productive enterprise. One would indeed have a minimum education based on outcome specifications. In this respect, it would match the model of schooling which informs school effectiveness research. However, a thorough-going market-based system would have little use for the findings of school effectiveness research. Brown, Duffield and Riddell (1995: 12–13) have already indicated this in their case studies of 'effiective' and 'ineffective' schools with differential socio-economic status intakes. They showed that the 'effective school' containing large numbers of low SES pupils still had difficulty marketing itself to middle-class parents, in spite of the fact that it shared similar characteristics to the 'effective' school that attracted middle-class parents. They also found that the 'ineffective' school with large numbers of high socio-economic status (SES) pupils had little incentive to improve because it continued to attract middle-class parents. In the parental choice market, 'outcomes' are important but not as indicators of technical efficiency. They are important as indicators of what Stenhouse (1967: 118) described as 'the accord between the culture of the school and the culture of . . . the pupils' "destination groups" '. Stenhouse admitted that he was claiming much greater weight for the influence of adult social groupings over the destinations of pupils than 'many educationalists would care to do' (p. 118). All this explains why school effectiveness researchers have had to admit that school effects compared with socio-economic background effects account for differences in achievement much less than they originally believed.

In the light of the above considerations, one can perhaps understand why Reynolds sees market-based reforms as the enemy, and wants those working in the school improvement paradigm to join forces with school effectiveness researchers to fight them. The problem with such collaboration is that although the two groups share some common commitment to a liberal-egalitarian concept of justice in education, they have very different visions of its educational implications. I do believe however that, at this present time, it is important to establish greater dialogue between educational researchers about the conceptions of the social ends of education, and of the means of realizing them, which are embedded in their research methodologies.

Postscript

On 19 March 1996, as I was completing this book, the *Guardian* newspaper carried a headline 'Blunket sanctions pupil opt-out'. Beneath it, John Carvel reported the reactions of David Blunkett, now Labour secretary of state for education but then shadow secretary, to the increasingly disturbing problem of growing numbers of alienated and disaffected pupils in secondary schools. It is a problem I predicted would be a direct consequence of the introduction of the National Curriculum.

> As someone who believes that human nature consists of dynamic qualities or powers which are quite resistant to social engineering, the consequences of the proposed national curriculum will be disastrous. By neglecting 'the inner being' the proposed curriculum will unwittingly alienate young people from their own natural powers, which will

nevertheless manifest themselves on a massive scale in ever new and sophisticated forms of human destructiveness.

(Elliott 1988a: 51)

Blunkett and the Labour Party were proposing, once the latter came to power, to get all pupils at post-14 to do more work experience outside schools and to encourage many to do vocational training for National Vocational Qualifications (NVQs) at local further education colleges. Blunkett argued, somewhat naively I feel, that a Labour government would ensure parity of esteem between academic and vocational courses in education 14–19. Blunkett wrote in an article for the newspaper:

It is time to recognise that young people who have become disaffected in their final years of compulsory education may get a better chance to make something of their lives if they are encouraged to take up vocational opportunities outside the traditional environment of the school.

Blunkett and the Labour Party have only partially grasped the problem of disaffected pupils. They have grasped the alienating effects of the academic curriculum on a significant proportion of young people, an effect which Stenhouse and many teachers in the old modern schools recognized thirty years ago. However, they have not fully grasped the nature of that alienation.

It is not simply that the academic subject-based curriculum provides them with little opportunity of success in the labour market, but that it does nothing to help them make sense of their lives in a way which motivates them to take responsibility for shaping the conditions of their existence. This is because it disconnects knowledge acquisition from their values (see Elliott 1991b), and prevents pupils from using the cultural capital of society to construct a meaningful vision of their future as individuals in society.

Overcoming a sense of alienation is not simply a matter of catapulting the disaffected into the labour market armed with a portfolio of NVQs. As I argued in Chapter 4, the labour market, operating to advance the economic ends of advanced societies, has the potential to create new dependencies, if individuals do not accept responsibility for shaping the economic conditions of their existence in a way which empowers them to fulfil more fundamental human needs. Alienated pupils in schools, as we have seen (Chapter 3), extend well beyond the sphere of the disruptive and non-attending. There are numerous high achievers leaving school and even university who are unhappy because their education has not given them much opportunity to explore where their values lie and what they want from life.

The construction of alternative 'vocational tracks' (narrowly defined) at post-14 is only part of the answer to the problems of dissaffection and alienation in schools. What is lacking in the Labour proposals, is any appreciation of the need to conceptualize a common general education, as opposed to a narrowly conceived vocational education, in a form which provides all pupils with equal access to what Stenhouse called the 'house of culture'. Such a conceptualization has been explored in this book. It emerged in Britain as a response to the proposal to raise the school leaving age to sixteen, in the face of increasing evidence that large numbers of pupils were dissaffected from the academic subject-based curriculum and leaving early to take unskilled jobs, while others stayed but under-performed. Innovative curriculum experiments, like the Humanites Project, demonstrated that a reconstructed general education could do much to minimize and reduce pupils' feelings of disaffection and alienation from their experience of schooling.

Of course, thirty years ago pupils had little difficulty in finding some form of paid employment. I am not arguing against the importance of schools giving more priority to the provision of vocational training. Under the Labour proposals, schools will coordinate the vocational provision pupils receive outside their boundaries. The problem with them is that they will have the effect of excluding many pupils from a general education after the age of fourteen. The proposals may serve the purpose of giving certain pupils greater equality of opportunity with respect to the labour market, but they are essentially unjust because they will have the effect of distributing the stock of cultural capital in society very unequally indeed. This perhaps explains why the proposals enjoyed the support of the last Conservative government. It is rather tragic that a political party which was founded on a committment to equality and social justice appears at a time of profound social change to be incapable of formulating an appropriate concept of education for the times.

7

Environment and School Initiatives (ENSI): An International Innovative Curriculum Experiment

In this chapter, I will attempt to show how the OECD (CERI) Environment and School Initiatives (ENSI) Project constitutes an invaluable resource for policy-makers concerned with the problem of how to construct a general education curriculum for basic schooling in our rapidly changing and increasingly complex modern societies. The design of the project was influenced by the work of Stenhouse some twenty years previously, and I shall indicate its similarities with the Humanities Project in the course of this chapter. As a contemporary example (the project is still operating after ten years) of a pedagogically driven process model of curriculum, ENSI represents the best living example of a planning option policy-makers tend to neglect (as I argued in Chapter 2 with respect to national curriculum policy-making in England and Wales and the work of Stenhouse).

The policy-making context

ENSI was launched in 1986 by the OECD Centre for Educational Research and Innovation (CERI) in response to a proposal submitted by the Austrian Government. The CERI governing board decided to include the project in the Innovation Exchange Programme for a two-year period, to be concluded by an international conference in Linz, Austria to discuss 'findings'. Participation by OECD member countries was voluntary. Interestingly, neither the USA nor Britain chose to be involved at this stage. The eleven participating countries were all part of Continental Western Europe. This may well reflect differences in the balance of preoccupations in member states, along the lines discussed in a previous chapter, when comparing Beck's theory of modernization with the view of Handy. In Continental Western Europe, governments were having to respond to the rise of powerful 'grass roots' social movements concerned about the risks techno-economic developments were posing to the quality of the environment. In the USA and Britain, 'grass roots' environmental pressure groups appeared to be less influential a decade ago in getting environmental risk issues to the top of the political agenda, which was dominated by a pre-occupation with the 'economy' and issues about the distribution of socially produced wealth (although largely excluding consideration of the means of production itself as a problem).

Hence, the launching of ENSI, it might be argued, constituted an indicator of a transition in some advanced countries towards a more reflexive form of modernization in which governments responded to the growth of oppositional social movements and their critiques of the environmental impact of the means of wealth production. This response not only constituted an acknowledge-ment that 'the development of environmental awareness' should be given priority as a curriculum aim, but also an acknowledgement of the principle of subsidiarity with respect to curriculum decision-making. The principle is well expressed in calling the project 'Environment and School Initiatives'. In the context of many countries' national curriculum policies, which prescribed from the centre both the knowledge content and the organizational frames in which it is to be transmitted, ENSI was a significant innovation, but inasmuch as it anticipated a new policy-making trend it was a trend-setter.

This perhaps explains why ENSI has continued to secure strong endorse-ment in the countries which made the heaviest investment in it from the beginning, and unlike many radical innovations has refused to quietly wither away and die. Following the Linz conference in 1988, the CERI board decided that ENSI had been so successful as an innovative experiment that its demon-strable potential should be further developed and its status upgraded to a major OECD programme. Thus ENSI 2 was launched with enhanced support within member countries and from the OECD (CERI) Secretariat. More coun-tries became actively involved, including the USA, the UK (Scotland, Northern Ireland), the Republic of Ireland and Australia. And greater stress was placed on understanding the policy context of ENSI as an innovation in certain self-selected countries. In March 1994, at the end-of-phase 2 conference in Bruns-wick, Germany, a strong case was made by country representatives for the continuation of ENSI as an international network. In early 1996 ENSI 3 was launched as a self-supporting international network under the general auspices of OECD (CERI), but funded by contributions from participating countries.

ENSI has become something of a curriculum lighthouse in the turbulent seas of social change which educational policy-makers are trying to navigate as they sail out of the twentieth and into the twenty-first century. Its guid-ing ideas have been extensively tested in schools, and the interaction between theory and practice richly documented in three OECD (CERI) publications entitled *Environment, Schools and Active Learning* (Laine and Posch 1991),

Evaluating Innovation in Environmental Education (Pettigrew and Somekh 1994) and *Environmental Learning for the 21st Century* (1995b). I will now examine these ideas and their impact on practice in ENSI schools with a view to clarifying their implications for curriculum development more generally in complex advanced societies.

The contribution of ENSI to rethinking the curriculum can be summarized as follows:

1 The process model of curriculum planning.
2 The pragmatic epistemology underpinning the curriculum.
3 The idea of learning as a dynamic process.
4 The local environment as a resource for, and the site of, action learning.
5 The role of schools as a community resource for the construction of local knowledge.
6 The idea of networks as learning systems which transcend the traditional boundaries between schools and society.
7 Curriculum decision-making as the design of innovative experiments at the school level.
8 Teacher-based action research as a basis for school initiatives and quality control procedures.

Each of these general ideas, which underpinned the design of ENSI and informed a great deal of practice in participating schools, are interlinked and together form a coherent and comprehensive 'curriculum theory'. In what follows, I will explore the relevance of these ideas to the changes occurring in modern societies and how they shaped the design of the project, and provide examples of how they informed curriculum and pedagogical development in participating schools. Towards the end of the chapter, I will explore the implications of this set of ideas for designing, in the context of a general education for basic schooling, a national curriculum framework which empowers teachers and schools to respond to the challenge of social change.

Social change, individualization and the process model of curriculum planning

Peter Posch (1991), a consultant to the Austrian authorities at the initial design stage of ENSI and one of its principal architects, has argued that environmental education both destabilizes some of the 'perennial tenets of schooling' and yet can provide some 'potential answers to some of the dilemmas they create' (see Posch 1993). He lists these tenets as follows:

◆ predominance of systematic knowledge;
◆ disciplinary specialization;
◆ transmission-mode of teaching;
◆ top-down communication.

The 'curriculum' is usually understood as a programme of study:

* aimed at the acquisition of predefined knowledge structures which are largely derived from the historic academic disciplines; and
* designed to support a transmission mode of teaching which reinforces 'the retention of the systematic character of knowledge and its reconstruction by the student'(Posch 1994), and involving a form of communication that establishes the teacher's control over the content and process of learning.

The first 'rational' step in planning a curriculum conceived in this way is to specify the intended learning outcomes or 'objectives' in terms of systematically organized knowledge. Any other approach to curriculum development is assumed to lack 'rationality'.

The advantage of such a curriculum model, as Posch (1993) has indicated, is that it enables schools to 'maintain a close relationship with the outcomes of academic knowledge production'. Such outcomes have traditionally constituted the educational 'gold standard' in western societies, and therein lies a significant problem. They may have been an appropriate source of educational standards in the relatively stable societies of the past, but how appropriate are they in the turbulent and complex modernizing societies of today? Do they not require a shift towards a more dynamic conception of the curriculum and educational standards. Posch (1994: 157) claims that 'The prevalent cultures of teaching and learning are still attuned to a relatively static society, in which the necessary knowledge, competences and values are predefined and stored in curricula tests and accredited text books'.

He argues that the future culture of teaching and learning will need to 'comprise contraries' to achieve a better balance between static and dynamic elements, which is necessary if schools are 'to find answers to the social changes presently occurring'. The strengths of pre-specified frameworks, which include giving educational processes a focus and sense of direction, will need to be retained, while constructing them in a form which supports and leaves space for dynamic elements within the pedagogy, and makes them less of a 'straight-jacket' for teachers.

It is clear from the evidence cited earlier that some OECD countries are attempting to construct curriculum frameworks at the policy level which create a better balance between 'structure' and 'openness', 'prescription' and 'discretion', 'static' and 'dynamic' qualities. Such frameworks are tending to acknowledge the significance of educational processes beyond that of their instrumental significance for the acquisition of pre-standardized bodies of static knowledge.

The significance of this shift towards a greater focus on process is that it opens up new possibilities for integrating systemic approaches to educational change at the policy level with a concern to support teachers and schools in meeting the challenges of social change. This approach can be contrasted with another attempt to reconcile systemic approaches to curriculum reform with school initiatives. The latter consists of designing a minimalist framework using the traditional 'objectives' model which leaves schools and teachers curricular time and space for their own initiatives. Such an approach is also evidenced in some OECD countries. For example, the Dearing Review of the National Curriculum in England and Wales has reduced the extent to which teaching and learning time in schools is pre-structured by national requirements, but the model of curriculum which underpins the framework specifying those requirements has not shifted; the framework has simply been 'pruned' or 'slimmed down'. What the shift to a greater emphasis on process rather than content and outcomes implies is the construction of a different kind of framework based on a different model of curriculum, a framework which both 'structures' teaching and learning and supports them as dynamic processes open to being shaped by teachers and students.

The design of ENSI's curriculum framework was influenced by Stenhouse's (1975) articulation of a 'process model' of curriculum design as an alternative to an 'objectives model' (see also Stenhouse 1970b, for a critique of the use of 'objectives'). The key features of the process model are:

1 A pre-specification of content, not in terms of the specific knowledge and skills to be learned, but in terms of the kinds of complex, value-laden, human and social situations which raise the central issues and problems pupils are likely to encounter during the course of their lives.
2 Statements about an educationally worthwhile way of handling this type of content specified in terms of 'pedagogical aims', which refer not to the knowledge outcomes of the learning process but to the intrinsic values which structure and give form to that process.
3 A specification of standards derived from the 'pedagogical aims' formulated as principles of procedure rather than content objectives.
4 Advice on how to identify and diagnose the concrete pedagogical problems and dilemmas teachers face in changing their practice to realize the values expressed in the aims and standards, and how to generate and test experimental teaching strategies, or 'action-hypotheses', for addressing such problems.

For Stenhouse, a framework developed on the basis of this model constitutes a specification for an innovative educational experiment to be carried out by 'teachers in the laboratory of the classroom'. It implies the idea of the teacher as a pedagogical researcher. Designing a process curriculum is, as I explained in Chapter 2, a matter of designing an innovative experiment in education – an action research project. This is why such a curriculum framework combines 'prescription' with 'openness'. What is prescribed is an experiment. It is also a systemic framework inasmuch as it displays the relationships between elements of education – curriculum, aims, process, methods, content, teacher development, evaluation and assessment – as a coherent whole. One might argue that a curriculum framework based on a process model is a necessary condition of any systemic approach to curriculum change which is seriously committed to the principle of subsidiarity and to helping teachers and schools meet the educational challenges social change is increasingly posing.

These challenges can all be linked to the paradoxes and dilemmas inherent in the individualization process (see Chapter 4) which characterizes advanced modern societies. Posch (1994) has summarized the major challenges as:

1 The negotiation of rules.
2 Social continuity.
3 Dynamic qualities.
4 Reflection and a critical approach to knowledge.

The first challenge stems from the liberation of people from traditional social ties mediated by systems of authority relations. Posch argues that social structures – the norms and conventions which regulate human conduct – can no longer be reproduced by deference to authorities because the latter have lost their power to legitimate obedience to such norms and conventions. What constitutes socially acceptable conduct is now a question to be answered on the basis of interpersonal negotiation rather than resort to social authority. Posch cites contemporary family relations as an example. What is allowable and not allowable is no longer decided on the basis of parental authority but a negotiated matter between parent and child. Conflicts arise between teachers and pupils when the latter encounter in schools a 'culture of predefined demands' which leave little space for negotiation. Schools in general, argues Posch, have not yet found ways of coping with a process of social change in which the 'negotiation of rules and norms is gaining importance'. This aspect of social change identified by Posch challenges schools to design a curriculum which, rather than representing a culture of predefined demands, is negotiable with pupils and supports, rather than constrains, creative and critical thinking.

The second challenge stems from the declining power of traditional forms of social authority to maintain continuity in social relationships. This consequence of the individualization process, Posch argues, is accompanied by a trend towards the instrumentalization of social relations in which people defect from stable ties for the sake of short-term gains, and lose capacities for mutual trust and the exercise of social responsibility. Can schools create situations, Posch asks, where the young can experience continuity in relationships by learning to collaborate with and value others in more than instrumental ways without feeling they are being socially coerced. The fundamental challenge for schools here is, I believe, to realize a learning process which respects and fosters the individuality of all pupils while at the same time fostering a sense of mutual respect and community. In the last chapter, I examined how Stenhouse conceptualized such a process and its links to Rawls' theory of justice.

The third challenge arises from the growing complexity of the economic and social conditions which impinge on people's lives and the inability of centralized decision-making agencies to control them. In this context, the 'centre' becomes more dependent on people at the 'grass roots' to exercise initiatives in controlling those conditions, and people begin to develop the motivation to seize control. Posch (1994: 156) argues that 'more and more individuals will have to be able to cope with unstructured situations, define problems, take positions and accept responsibility for them'. By way of examples, he cites on the one hand the limited power of governments to control the production and consumption of energy and their growing dependence on individuals within the population to exercise their own initiatives, and on the other the 'well educated skinhead' who rephrased the Cartesian proposition, 'I think, therefore I am' in terms of 'I throw stones, ergo sum'; perhaps expressing a growing desire on the part of the young 'to influence the conditions of life and to leave traces in their environment'. There is a need, argues Posch, for frameworks which enable the young to develop those dynamic personal qualities that are necessary if people are to take responsibility for shaping their environment in a constructive way. 'Can schools', he asks, 'provide opportunities to the young to experience that they can make a difference'.

The fourth challenge stems from an increasing consciousness on the part of citizens that they live in a risk society, where the consequences of techno-scientific developments are ambiguous. On the one hand, people become increasingly dependent for their well-being on applications of scientific knowledge in all areas of their lives, while on the other, they become increasingly aware of the risks to their well-being these applications produce. Scepticism and doubt about the uses of science grow with increasing dependence on scientific knowledge. According to Posch, this paradoxical situation may imply that definitions of what constitutes useful knowledge can no longer be left to 'authorities' and scientific experts, but become matters for negotiation involving 'more and more peripheral and smaller social units'. In this context, processes for establishing 'local truth' need to be established, Posch argues, with the result that communication between local agencies and units becomes increasingly important, since differences of perspective have to be handled as part of the process.

The implication of all this, for Posch, is that public confidence in scientific knowledge will depend not so much on the traditional rules and methods of data gathering and analysis scientists employ to verify its content, but on a social process which involves citizens in determining what constitutes socially worthwhile knowledge and enables them to exercise control over the scientific production of risks to their well-being. Can schools, asks Posch, provide opportunities for the young to develop both an appreciative and critical stance towards knowledge?

As I indicated earlier, Stenhouse believed that the provision of such opportunities was the function of the humanities curriculum and that such a curriculum should include the critical study of scientific knowledge, viewed not as objective truths but as dynamic ideas produced by historically and socially situated 'human minds' and encoded in texts. From this perspective, the study of science involves critically decoding scientific texts as part of our cultural heritage, or what Karl Popper (1972: 117–18) called 'World 3', in contrast to studying science as information about an objective world of material things, 'World 1'.

The ENSI project can be viewed as an invitation for schools and teachers to participate in an imaginative curriculum experiment designed to meet the educational challenges posed by the dimensions of social change identified by Posch.

The 'pedagogical aims' of ENSI were formulated as follows:

1 To help students develop an understanding of the complex relationship between human beings and their environment through interdisciplinary enquiry.
2 To foster a learning process which requires students to develop 'dynamic qualities' connected with exercising initiative and taking responsibility for the environment.

From these aims, four key principles of procedure or process standards were derived:

1 Teachers should help students experience the environment as a sphere of personal concern by involving them in the identification of problems and issues in their locality.
2 Students should examine these problems and issues as a subject for inter-disciplinary learning and research to develop usable local knowledge.
3 Students should be given opportunities to shape the environment as a sphere of socially important action, and therefore be involved in decision-making and the development of procedures for monitoring these decisions.
4 Students should accept the environment as a challenge for initiative, inde-pendence and responsible action.

In addition, this framework specified a second-order process principle which indicated the kind of support teachers and students needed to change the traditional culture of teaching and learning and thereby begin to realize the aims and standards specified:

5 Students and teachers should systematically reflect on their activities by involving themselves in action research.

In ENSI, action research had three major support functions:

♦ to help teachers cope with the complex problems they needed to face in bringing about significant pedagogical change;
♦ to provide a context for the systematic development of new competences;
♦ to establish a way in which teachers could exercise accountability by gen-erating accounts of their practice for professional and public discussion.

The above framework (see Posch 1993) implies a radical shift in the established culture of teaching and learning, although this may not be apparent at an initial glance. Within the context of ENSI activities, its potential to support such a cultural shift was frequently cited. Scotland's National Report claims that:

> The process of examining ENSI principles, transferring and applying these to individual school situations, planning and executing innovative projects with pupils and involving members of the community provided a challenging agenda.
>
> (McAndrew and Pascoe 1993: sec. 6.3)

When used as a guiding framework for action research – innovative experimentation in schools – it enabled teachers to question the assumptions and beliefs which underpinned their customary practice:

> the schools were asked to carry out a process of review. This reflective exercise resulted in teachers questioning current practice, both content and methodology. Presentation of the ENSI principles at school inservice meetings inevitably led to interesting and meaningful debate.
>
> (McAndrew and Pascoe 1993: sec. 6.3)

> If the ENSI project was something different, if one can say it was successful, it is not because it has introduced elements of environmental education into the curriculum of over 200 schools, but because it showed how it is possible to modify 'tacit knowledge' (Polanyi, 1966), the implicit images that teachers have of learning and knowledge.
>
> The ENSI teachers were not given curricular or materials, but a set of values, both environmental and educational, on which to build their own contributions to the project, some more general objectives and the concrete situations – the school initiatives regarding the community – within which they were to be carried out. ENSI created contexts which led teachers to reflect on their own practice and to modify it.
>
> (Meyer 1995: 33)

The statements of aims within the framework were particularly provocative because they appeared to embody a contradiction, which according to Posch was quite deliberate:

> The project links two educational aims which prima facie seem to contradict each other: the promotion of 'environmental awareness' and the promotion of 'dynamic qualities', such as initiative, independence and individual responsibility. The promotion of environmental awareness in schools is frequently associated with a conservationalist spirit and hostility towards economic technological development. On the other hand, the development of dynamic qualities is associated with a positive attitude towards economic and technological development and a disregard for

the environment. However, environmental awareness and dynamic qualities can also be regarded as interdependent. The environment offers on the one hand a unique context for the development of human creativity, initiative and organisational skills. On the other hand, the broad distribution of these skills in the population is considered an indispensable prerequisite of a sustainable society.

(Posch 1993: 448)

This account of the 'dual aims' of ENSI is grounded in the kind of analysis of social and economic change provided by Beck and Handy. The side-effects of technological development on the quality of the environment become as, if not more, significant factors in the growth of social complexity as their impact on people's economic well-being. This is why 'the development of environmental awareness' ought to become a high-priority educational aim. Moreover, since central governments are finding it increasingly difficult, in the face of this complexity, to engineer solutions to problems in society, they will need to devolve more responsibility to the citizenry at the local level. This has at least three educational implications.

First, what counts as educationally worthwhile knowledge will increasingly need to be locally defined in terms of its relevance to the particular situations people encounter in everyday life, and the problems and issues of practical living they raise. Secondly, what counts as an educationally worthwhile process of learning will increasingly need to take an interdisciplinary form, since understanding the complexity of a concrete human situation involves grasping relationships between the various factors operating in it; relationships which cannot be grasped in terms of any traditional category of knowledge production. Thirdly, since future citizens will be expected to accept responsibility for effecting their own 'solutions' to the problems and issues of everyday life, the educational process will need to provide all future citizens with opportunities to develop those dynamic qualities associated with a pro-active rather than a passive stance towards life's circumstances. Posch summarises the rationale for including 'the development of dynamic qualities' as a central aim of ENSI as follows:

social complexity and insecurity are increasing and the decision-making capacity of socio-economic systems is decreasing. These developments in society have implications which affect schools. Abilities that traditionally have been demanded of the elites in society are now increasingly demanded of every citizen: the readiness and ability to take responsibility in *shaping* public and private affairs.

(Posch 1993: 448)

The aims of ENSI, we must conclude, are not inconsistent with each other, if we view them in the context of social changes which require ordinary people to accept responsibility for shaping the conditions which govern their existence. In this context, 'the development of environmental awareness' is not a passive process of acquiring factual knowledge but an active one disciplined by an acceptance of responsibility for shaping the environment in which pupils live, move and have their being. Environmental awareness develops interactively with the student's attempts to shape the environmental conditions in which he or she lives. ENSI embodies a coherent pedagogical perspective which is underpinned by a dynamic theory of knowledge.

Knowledge, the curriculum and action research

ENSI's dynamic theory of knowledge, implicit in its use of Stenhouse's process model of curriculum design, has its origins in a cluster of ideas associated with the twentieth-century American pragmatists Pierce, James and Dewey. Dewey (1960), for example, argued that reflective thought constituted a search for a kind of understanding that enabled one to act wisely and intelligently in a changing world. He contrasted it with the idea of reflection entailed by the Grecian theory of knowledge, claiming that the ancient Greek philosophers glorified the invariant at the expense of change and in doing so left us with the idea that reflective thought is a matter of acquiring knowledge by copying the objects of the environment in terms of their fixed and universal features. In doing so, they disassociated theory from the immediacy of practical judgement and decision-making; an immediacy which stems from the need to respond to problems and issues as they arise in the practical experience of living.

The Greeks, according to Dewey, left European societies with a legacy that became enshrined in their tradition of education. It was a legacy that located knowledge as a reflection of reality and that defined reality as the realm of fixed, static and invariant things (i.e. Popper's 'World 1'). From the perspective of this static theory of knowledge, reflective thought is the passive process of producing faithful copies of things; what Rorty (1980), a contemporary American philosopher whose deconstruction of analytic philosophy was informed by pragmatism, called 'the mirroring of nature'. This legacy rendered the realm of change as the 'appearance' at the surface of things, and since practical activity falls within this realm, it cannot yield knowledge and understanding.

A pragmatic theory of knowledge views reflective thought not as the process of 'copying' or 'mirroring' the objects of experience in terms of their invariant essences, but as the process 'of taking account of the ways in which more effective and more profitable relations with these objects may be established in the future' (McDermott 1977).

The epistemological underpinnings of the ENSI framework are important to grasp because they enable us to understand that the project is not simply a challenge to traditional approaches to environmental education but to the whole European tradition of education which has permeated curriculum planning and policy-making in modern societies. Many recent attempts to reform the curriculum in basic education can leave the tradition basically intact and some of these prop it up and make it more 'change-proof'. This is because they do not constitute any kind of challenge to the Greek theory of knowledge which has underpinned the tradition for centuries.

Hence, when we look at some examples of teacher-led curriculum reform policies, we find an absence of any strategies to challenge and destabilize the traditional pedagogical culture of teachers, which defines knowledge in terms of inert bodies of universally true facts ('subjects'), and thinking as the passive contemplation of fixed and unchanging essences in the nature of things. In the absence of strategies which challenge this culture, teacher-led reforms may simply consist of changes in knowledge content and the forms in which it is organized in the curriculum. Aware of the motivational problems they experience with students, teachers may change the content in an attempt to make it more relevant to students' lives and organize that content in terms of 'cross-curricular' themes, topics and projects, thereby believing they are introducing an interdisciplinary dimension to the curriculum. They may even change their teaching methods and introduce team-teaching, group learning, peer tutoring and more 'discussion'. But none of these changes in themselves need be indicative of any significant shift in the pedagogical culture of teachers. Its basic structure of underlying assumptions may remain intact.

Some curriculum policies can be described as 'standards-driven reforms'. Standards are defined in terms of learning outcomes, conceived either as fixed and unchanging facts and concepts (knowledge), or as behavioural responses called 'competences' or 'skills'. The former tend to be labelled 'academic standards' and the latter 'vocational standards'. Standards-driven reform policies tend be linked to a strategy of accountability-driven reform. Standards provide a basis for monitoring learning outcomes, making comparisons, and holding teachers and schools to account. They are seen as an indispensable foundation for quality assurance.

Standards-driven reforms take the Greek theory of knowledge for granted. The familiar distinction between knowledge-based academic education and skills-based vocational education (it is now fashionable to talk about 'competences' in preference to 'skills') is underpinned by this theory, since an academic education is not assumed to be directly related to the practical requirements of the workplace, while a vocational education is seen to match those requirements. Knowledge and competence are assumed to be very different kinds of learning outcomes, occupying the separate spheres of 'theory' and 'practice' respectively. Within the European education tradition, knowledge carries higher social status than competence. Hence, its association with education for an elite class.

Policy-makers have argued that standards-driven reforms leave teachers free to determine appropriate teaching and learning methods. What they fail to recognize, at least publicly, is the fact that defining standards exclusively in terms of knowledge and behavioural outcomes rules out an alternative way of conceptualizing the relationship between the aims of the curriculum and the teaching–learning process.

They rule out the idea that education involves enabling students to actively shape their own learning rather than having it shaped for them. From this perspective, curriculum aims will refer to the personal qualities students need to develop through an 'active' relationship with the content, and the curriculum specification will include reference to the teaching–learning principles implied by such aims. Curriculum planning from this alternative point of view will be pedagogically driven and directed to effecting fundamental qualitative change in the way content is handled within the teaching–learning process. Those who embrace this perspective might question standards-driven attempts at curriculum reform in the following terms:

* How can a teacher develop a child's artistic potential if he or she determines in advance what the child must do to produce a work of art?
* How can a child develop his or her capacity to appreciate poetry if the teacher continually predetermines what counts as a 'correct' response?
* How can a child develop a capacity to analyse historical evidence if a teacher predetermines the conclusions the child should draw?

The issue at stake in all these questions is whether education is about developing capacities for exercising *judgement*. A standards-driven curriculum policy appears to be inconsistent with a curriculum policy that supports an education for judgement. The latter is a personal and individual act and usually associated with problems that have no clear-cut or standard solutions. The application of means–ends rules to produce such solutions is inappropriate because problems of this kind are not technical problems. Rather, they are objects of *deliberation*, and often involve aesthetic, moral or political considerations. An education for judgement implies a pedagogically driven curriculum policy.

Pedagogically driven curriculum policies have the potential to challenge and destabilize elements of the traditional pedagogical culture of teachers. They are not about reforming pupils' learning experiences but about fundamentally changing them in line with a pragmatist theory of knowledge. From the perspective of a pragmatist theory of knowledge, the relationship between theoretical knowledge and practical competence looks very different than it does from the perspective of the mainstream European tradition. From the latter perspective, the processes of acquiring theoretical knowledge and developing practical competence are quite separate, although the latter will involve applying knowledge previously acquired. A pragmatist theory of knowledge, however, implies that knowledge is actively determined in competent performances of a certain kind. Pragmatism holds that ideas are only valid, and therefore count as knowledge, if they can be used to conceptualize and demonstrate how a situation might be improved. Hence, in this context, practical competence consists in abilities to construct knowledge by using ideas to formulate and effect desirable changes in the situations of everyday life. It is the competence to actively shape the conditions of one's existence.

The pragmatist theory of knowledge does not deny other forms of practical competence, such as technical skills and the ability to reproduce customary practices. From this point of view, technical competence involves applying means–ends rules or techniques, derived from causal theories about the operation of factors in the physical world, to accomplish certain tangible and measurable effects in that world. However, technical competence should not be confused with competent performance in the context of complex social practices. For example, driving a car requires a great deal of technical skill but practical competence as a driver involves more than this. It involves the exercise of due care and attention to other road users with respect to the practical situations that can arise during the course of a journey. However, not all displays of practical, as opposed to technical, competence involve the ability to use ideas to effect change. Dewey (1960: 3–25) acknowledged the role of custom and tradition in structuring our everyday social practices. Competent performance is often a matter of doing things according to customary practice. However, argued Dewey, this is not always sufficient to accommodate the future because new conditions are introduced into the social context of our everyday practices which render some of them problematic and challenge us to reflectively reconstruct them. It is in these circumstances that practical competence consists of the ability to construct knowledge by using ideas and theories to effect worthwhile change.

From a pragmatist point of view, the distinction between academic knowledge and practical work/life-related competences, frequently drawn in terms of a contrast between 'academic' and 'vocational' education, is not a good way of conceptualizing different curriculum goals in a rapidly changing society. The pragmatist theory of knowledge opens the way to envisioning a basic general education for all pupils which, although not 'academic' in the traditional sense, enables all pupils to use ideas as resources for intelligently shaping their own futures in a society which is open to continuous change, and where custom and tradition no longer provide sufficient guidance for conduct in many areas of life. Such an education would focus on common areas of human experience and support the development of capacities for discernment, discrimination and judgement in these areas. Its realization would require many teachers to make significant departures from their traditional pedagogical practice, shaped as this is by the largely dated theory of knowledge embedded in the European education tradition.

Moreover, from a pragmatist perspective, vocational education is not an alternative 'track' to an academic education. It complements the kind of basic general education I have outlined. The latter establishes both a context and preparation for a more individually differentiated induction into specific vocational practices. I use the term 'vocational' in the broad sense as a form of work, for which one may or may not receive payment, but which evokes an enduring commitment and interest as a vehicle for developing one's talents.

A basic general education, underpinned by a pragmatist theory of knowledge, would provide a context which enables individuals to locate their commitment to a specific 'vocation' (broadly conceived) to areas of experience and human concern they share in common with others in society. It would provide a preparation for a vocational education since, in addition to the acquisition of the technical knowledge and skills necessary for work in their chosen field and learning to perform activities according to the customs and traditions operating in it, the 'trainees' will, in a rapidly changing society, need to develop capacities for innovative experimentation in the 'workplace' as a means of changing and developing their vocational practice as and when appropriate. There is currently a great deal of interest in developing 'reflective practitioners' through vocational education and training programmes in further and higher education. The task is not an easy one when the prevailing pedagogy in schools, and the curriculum structures which support it, provide little opportunity for pupils to develop their capacities for actively shaping their lives.

Examples of pedagogically focused curriculum policies are rare. In the context of the OECD study on 'Teachers and Curriculum Reform in Basic Schooling', Norway appears to be such an example, because it defines a national 'core curriculum' in terms of pedagogical values and principles that are underpinned by a pragmatist theory of knowledge. Within contemporary philosophical discourse, much of the epistemology that underpins the 'European tradition of education' has been discredited, and there is a renewal of interest in the ideas of Dewey and other pragmatists as a basis for reconstructing our understanding of the nature of knowledge and its relationship to everyday social practices (Dewey 1966). Although much of this discourse is either actively resisted or unacknowledged by educational policy-makers and reformers, it is not going on in a social vacuum. It is an expression of the transformation occurring in modern societies, in which science is losing its authority as a source of infallible and unchanging truth and as the model of rational thought. It is preparing the ground for a new understanding of science and rationality, which is less disconnected from the complexities of practical living and therefore more useful in helping the citizenry to shape the conditions of their existence (Elliott 1993). Such an understanding is anticipated in the design of the ENSI project.

ENSI's advocacy of action research as a learning process, for both students and teachers, is very consistent with the dynamic theory of knowledge developed by the American pragmatists. Although he did not use the phrase 'action research', Dewey (1960), as I indicated above, advocated the transfer of experimental methods from the field of the natural sciences to everyday experience. This involves people initiating courses of action as 'experiments in living', and then continually adjusting and modifying them in the light of data about their effects. Such a process can be described as action research, not simply because human 'action' is the object of research but because it is an integral part of a process in which people reflect about their conduct by experimenting with it.

The acquisition of knowledge has always been a central goal of learning in the European/Western tradition of education, and attempts to shift learning processes in a more pupil-centred direction are often perceived as threatening the importance of knowledge in education. The experience of the ENSI project in action, however, suggests that the outcome of teachers experimenting with their teaching in the light of the ENSI framework did not result in a devaluation of the importance of knowledge, but a reappraisal of some of the established rules and precepts governing the way students acquire it (Elliott 1995a, 1995b).

In Sweden (see Axelsson 1995), ENSI teachers were experimenting with strategies for overcoming a shared problem they had identified from interviewing students; namely, of 'low student motivation' in environmental education lessons. At first, they identified the problem as a technical one linked to methods rather than subject matter; the 'how' rather than the 'what' of learning. However, they discovered that their experiments with different learning methods – project and group learning, for example – didn't work. Then some of the teachers went to the ENSI conference in Perugia on 'handling complexity' in environmental education and began to think of their problem as a 'curriculum problem' rather than simply a problem of technique. Looking at evidence of their teaching, they found they organized the subject matter for the purpose of knowledge acquisition in a highly reductionist manner; atomizing it into discrete knowledge elements and thereby detaching it from the purposes and value judgements that shape human experience of the environment. The Swedish teachers began to redefine their subject matter as a complex sphere of personal influence in which knowledge is acquired through purposive human action, and they created spaces for students to construct knowledge by reflecting on aspects of the environment they judged to be significant for their lives. The redefinition of their subject matter led them to understand the development of environmental awareness as part of a broader learning process of action research. When knowledge acquisition is an aspect of learning how to change one's conduct towards the objects of experience, it becomes a dynamic rather than a passive process.

What the Swedish teachers learned through their own action research was that pedagogical problems cannot be resolved simply by surface changes to their 'methods'. Teachers can change their methods at one level without changing the rules and precepts which structure the way students learn, for the latter are embodied in conceptualizations of subject matter, in curricula. Inasmuch as curricula shape pedagogy, the claim that a centrally planned curriculum leaves teachers pedagogically free is to misconceive the relationship between curriculum and pedagogy by reducing questions about the latter to technical questions about methods of learning. Many persistent pedagogical problems that teachers encounter in contemporary schooling can only be resolved by changing their understanding of the subject matter they teach.

The ENSI project provided numerous examples of how changes in pedagogy, accomplished through teachers' action research (see Elliott 1995b), were accompanied by changes in their understanding of the subject matter (see Elliott 1995a). Through undertaking action research into the problems of realizing the aims and principles of ENSI, teachers became involved in a process of curriculum theorizing. In challenging the assumptions and precepts embodied in their conceptualization of the subject matter, the ENSI framework enabled teachers to reflectively critique them by comparing their pedagogical consequences with those entailed by an alternative understanding of that subject matter.

I now provide two further examples of how the ENSI framework challenged teachers to reconstruct their understandings of the subject matter.

An Austrian teacher of geography and economics, Karl Schweitzer, produced a case study of his attempt to initiate project work with students at a commercial high school in the Oberwart District (see Schweitzer 1991: 88–93). In doing so, he was concerned about the submissive attitudes of the students. Only rarely were they ready to exercise personal initiative, and according to Schweitzer this was linked 'to the fact that that rural families tend to be father-dominated', a situation reinforced by the traditional 'up-front' teaching they received at school.

The students started the project with a letter expressing concern about the 'reckless construction activities and unrestricted production' in their district. The letter was sent to politicians and large industrial corporations operating in the area. It succeeded in getting politicians and top managers to agree to be interviewed by the students, including the mayor of Vienna. The latter told the Oberwart students that criticism wasn't sufficient to get results, so they decided to develop the project by undertaking 'painstakingly detailed work' to produce a 'cadastral map' of the waste deposits in the district. The map had a significant impact in the district and is a good example of the way in which the use of subject-based ideas (in this case 'geography') empowered students to shape the conditions of their lives. The idea of 'cadastral mapping' was used to conceptualize a particular practical situation, to generate 'local knowledge' about the geographic distribution of waste deposits, to give students some practical purchase on a local situation that impacted on their lives.

The map was publicly commended as an 'important aspect of practical environmental work which can essentially contribute towards increasing the general environmental awareness' (Schweitzer 1991: 89). It received the 'Award for Environmental Technology' from the Ford Foundation and a major award from the First Austrian Savings Bank, among others. This recognition strengthened the students' resolve to press matters further with officials and authorities responsible for environmental matters, and to hold 'information evenings' for citizens in each local authority in the district. At these meetings, the students presented a multi-media show which demonstrated damage to the environment in the 'immediate neighbourhood' and discussed methods of waste avoidance and recycling. At this point in the project, students were using ideas, drawn from technology and a range of scientific subjects, which transcended the traditional subject matter of geography. By way of follow-up, they helped to set up 'eco-tips' for shopping, the household, and gardens and orchards.

In parallel with this collaboration between students and local citizens to change their personal conduct, the project influenced the actions of the authorities. Illegal dumps identified on the map were shut down and collection points for problematic waste set up. In addition, local authorities began to employ consultants to advise on questions of waste disposal.

As the project progressed over a three-year period, Schweitzer observed the dramatic impact it appeared to have on the motivation and attitudes of girl students. Whereas the motivation of the boys declined towards the end of the project, the reverse was the case with the girls, and Schweitzer decided to search for the reasons as part of his on-going action research into developing dynamic qualities through environmentally focused project work. He initially considered a number of possible explanations and then designed questionnaires to test their feasibility. The first one he entertained, that girls were more easily motivated by a male teacher than boys, proved inconclusive, but the second and third hypotheses were illuminated by the questionnaire data. The second was that girls have more out of school time than boys because the latter are more involved in clubs. The third was that project work encourages girls to break away from their traditional role in the home, to distinguish themselves beyond it, and to gain independence and autonomy. He found that boys had little spare time. Their club membership was three times higher than that of the girls, a fact explained by the male-orientated provision for spare time activities in rural areas. This reflected the different treatment girls experienced at home from their brothers. They expressed a great deal of frustration about restrictions on their freedom outside the home.

These results illuminated some of the things the teacher observed during the project. First, he observed in talking to parents that many accepted project work out of school time as acceptable for their daughters because it was teacher-supervised and therefore 'controllable' and 'serious'. It created legitimate space for girls to participate in activities outside the home, and was preferable to them sitting around 'in the cafe'. Secondly, the teacher observed an information evening, in which the girls responded aggressively to some parents' attempts to belittle their competence as knowledgeable persons on environmental matters. He concluded that the project provided a space in which the girls could confidently 'act out the generation conflict with their elders'. Thirdly, the teacher noted more generally that the public events in the project increased the self-confidence of the girls considerably. One group of girls in particular began to operate completely independently of the teacher. Schweitzer (1991: 93) noted:

> Dealing with public authorities and representatives of the media became a matter of course for them, as was impressively confirmed during a live broadcast from Radio Burgenland . . . when two pupils acted completely unselfconsciously and participated in the broadcast without any problem.

He concluded that the project served this emancipatory function for girls because 'the environment' is a highly topical field of public discourse, and the self-contradictory nature and variety of the questions (complexity) it raises made it easier for the girls to handle generational conflicts with their parents and elders, since the knowledge they acquired of the field placed them in a strong position.

Schweitzer's case study has enormous implications for the planning of a basic education curriculum for the twenty-first century, providing a practical illustration of the emergence of Beck's (1992) 'risk society' in a particular local context. It suggests that if policy-makers are serious about motivating students to develop those dynamic qualities which enable them to shape the conditions of their existence, then they should be giving the study of environmental issues which impinge on students' lives a central place in the curriculum. It also indicates how schools can influence the individualization process in advanced modern societies. It is perhaps not entirely fanciful to view the contrast, between the environmental project and 'sitting around in the cafe', in terms of dynamic versus passive ways of breaking away from traditional authority-based social ties to family and community; the latter preparing the way for the transformation of the young into units of conspicuous consumption and the former empowering them to accept responsibility for shaping and negotiating the conditions of their existence within their families and communities.

My second example of how ENSI helped teachers reconstruct their understanding of subject matter is taken from Scotland, where a strong tradition of environmental studies in the mainstream curriculum existed long before fifteen schools became involved in Phase 2 of ENSI in 1990. However, the opportunities ENSI gave for reflection, discussion and action research on current practice, in the light of its aims and principles, resulted in many teachers questioning whether the environmental studies tradition in Scotland constituted 'environmental education'.

Teachers in ENSI schools began to make a distinction between 'environmental education' and 'environmental studies' (see McAndrew and Pascoe 1993). The latter tradition emphasized cross-disciplinarity in which environmental themes were identified but their elements organized in the curriculum within the traditional subject categories. In this context, local studies using project and fieldwork methods tend to be structured by pre-specified and subject-specific knowledge and skill objectives. The construction of local knowledge is instrumental to the acquisition of subject knowledge. In 'environmental education', the reverse is the case. The acquisition of subject knowledge is instrumental to the construction of local knowledge because it is the latter which provides the basis for intelligent environmental action. McAndrew and Pascoe (1993) claim that the ENSI framework, in prompting an 'exploration of values and attitudes in pupils' and 'a consideration of the place of participatory action and involvement', enabled teachers to reconceptualize environmental education and its implications for curriculum planning. They argue that the principles of encouraging community-focused actions and constructing local knowledge provided 'the connective tissue which gave clear purpose and coherence to planning, implementing and evaluating actions'.

Work in Pumpherston Primary School, one of the fifteen schools in Scotland that participated in Phase 2 of ENSI, illustrates the changes in teachers' understanding and practice described by McAndrew and Pascoe. The school, situated in a village just outside a new town, produced a reflective case study of their work in the ENSI project, and a documentary account of their environmental project entitled *Caring for Our Environment* (Crandles and Kite 1995).

At first, teachers at Pumpherston felt that they had little to contribute to ENSI. However, in reviewing their environmental education policies in the light of the ENSI framework, they saw an opportunity for developing further the community-focused work they had initiated in two previous projects.

> On analysing the school's environmental education aims however, it became apparent that we were concerned not only to raise awareness for environmental issues but, that through meaningful activities, we could encourage the whole community to move with us in changing attitudes and values towards the environment . . . the review suggested opportunities for a wider focus involving the whole school and the community in a shared enterprise to improve the environment in which they lived.
>
> (SCCC 1993: 16)

A project was planned as a whole-school initiative and staff time allocated for this purpose. The initiative was called 'Take Pride in Pumpherston', and its principal aim was 'to give children a vision of the future that holds more than just the passive acceptance of what is there; that through empowerment they can influence the reality in which they live. They *can* make it better' (SCCC 1993: 117).

Each class participated in a survey of the village to identify areas for action. The pupils designed a questionnaire and interviewed local people as well as taking notes on their observations around the village. They then brainstormed the data for ideas: 'We could not do everything that people asked for. Some ideas were not possible, because they were too difficult. Other ideas cost too much money' (SCCC 1993: 7).

The children selected projects they could carry out for themselves under the following headings:

Brighten the school	*Brighten Pumpherston*	*Safety*
Window Boxes	Flower Beds	Road Survey
Flower Beds	Trees	Road Signs
Trees	Pond	
	Mural	

Each class took responsibility for one project. The total enterprise was coordinated by a 'quality circle', responsible for overall planning and consisting of six students elected by peers, one parent, one grandparent, one community education worker, one teacher and one non-teaching staff member. Then cooperation of the local press was elicited to publicize the projects – which received many offers of help as the 'message was spread' – and a parent group was established to assist with class visits and fieldwork, and not simply as childminders. Community involvement was further extended by the provision of ten weekly sessions about local environmental issues attended by ten to fifteen adults, and meetings and discussions arranged by the children with people from different sectors of the community.

The children identified what they needed to know in order to carry out their projects and called in experts to advise them (e.g. a wildlife photographer, an ornithologist, the Forestry Commission, a Countryside Ranger and an art specialist). In addition, a range of reference material was made available to help them carry out important background research for the projects, including researching local history as a basis for designing a wall mural in the village.

The Pumpherston case study describes the considerable change of role that the project required of teachers and emphasizes the importance of creating a climate of support within the school as a whole:

> ENSI Project involvement created a context for teacher development in a number of ways. It was vital to create a climate in the school which would support the teachers as they undertook projects that were innovative in different ways. They were being asked to deal with areas of content perhaps unfamiliar; employ fieldwork and a range of active learning situations with pupils; and consider the pedagogical challenges posed by giving the children so much ownership and decision-making power. ENSI actually involved considering a change of emphasis – from stressing the importance of content (traditional knowledge) to process (skills and attitudes) and new arrangements for how learning would take place. This required an implicit change in the role of the teacher – the teacher as a facilitator to give encouragement and social support – for the children needed to be secure and confident to feel free to question or to explore their ideas.
>
> (SCCC 1993: 24–5)

Teachers' responses to the Pumpherston project indicated not only that changes had occurred in their teaching methods, but more fundamentally, in their conceptions of the subject matter of environmental education and their role in mediating it to children. For example:

> The importance of the focus on the local environment. The lasting effect of the work on the children.

> I was made much more aware of the 'child educating the teacher'. I had to stand back. I have been able to use this approach several times now and in other areas of the curriculum.

> I had to depend on other people outside the school to support me a lot. I now realise how helpful and interested in our work they are.

> There's more to knowledge than just subjects.
>
> (SCCC 1993: 25–6)

These comments suggest that when the subject matter is viewed dynamically, as a complex sphere of personal influence rather than a static body of unchanging knowledge, the pedagogy will reflect a different relationship between the teacher and knowledge. Students will have more space to determine what counts as significant and useful knowledge and, in doing so, will need access to sources of ideas beyond their teachers, who cannot be realistically expected to know in advance everything that their students might usefully consider in deciding on a plan of action.

The teachers at Pumpherston developed an appreciation of the expertise located in the local community or nearby, and how they as teachers could facilitate their students' learning by helping them to gain access to these local experts. The ENSI project in Pumpherston Primary School was not just community-focused but community-resourced. It created a community-wide learning support network which perforated the boundary between school and community and constituted an educational partnership between them.

In many of the participating schools, ENSI was not part of whole-school curriculum planning. It operated either in a particular subject slot for some age groups or as an extracurricular activity or a mixture of the two. In these schools, the project was often dependent on enthusiastic volunteer teachers. The degree of institutionalization was low, since it did not disrupt existing patterns of curriculum organization, which were subject-based, or involve a 'critical mass' among the school staff (see Elliott 1991c: 19–36). This is not to say that ENSI was an insignificant innovation, but its significance was symbolic rather than instrumental to school change. Its value from a school management perspective tended to be measured in terms of 'good for community relations' rather than 'good for education'.

In Pumpherston, things were different. All the teachers were involved in curriculum planning, and all pupil groups participated. Although much of the work took place in 'environmental studies' time, 'the wider environmental education opportunities in the other curriculum areas were also developed' (SCCC 1993: 2–3). Since 'environmental studies' is an established organizational category in the Scottish curriculum, it was perhaps easier for Pumpherston to accommodate the interdisciplinary logic of ENSI than for schools in other countries.

The whole-school response to the ideas embodied in the ENSI framework at Pumpherston revealed the potential of this framework as a basis for restructuring schools as social organizations, and the significance of curriculum planning in the restructuring process. So often discussions about the need to restructure schools ignore the curriculum dimension. Yet radical restructuring involves profound changes in the pedagogical culture which underpins schools as organizational systems. This culture is embedded in the curriculum and there can be no fundamental change at the systems level without curriculum and pedagogical change, only change in the surface features such as 'school climate'. ENSI is a rare example of a *pedagogically driven restructuring of schooling*. The fact that this approach has, to date, not realized its full potential in this respect, is partly due to a widespread failure to recognize that the key to improving schools as systems lies in destabilizing the pedagogical culture they support, and that this cannot be accomplished without fundamentally changing the curriculum. I shall return to this issue later when I discuss school self-evaluation.

There is a sense in which the headteacher and staff of Pumpherston 'deschooled' their school in the curriculum planning process. The boundary between the school and the community became more porous in a number of senses. Firstly, the locality became as much a site/location for learning as the classroom. Secondly, a community-wide learning support network was constructed, which included parents, other community members and agencies, local experts, in addition to professional teachers. Thirdly, responsibility for coordinating and overseeing initiatives was given to a quality circle made up of children, school staff, parents and a community representative.

It might be argued that, through ENSI, Pumpherstone Primary School made significant advances towards bringing about its death as an organization called a school, and towards its rebirth as a radically new kind of organization; namely, as a learning system which operates through a social network. We could see Pumpherston and other ENSI schools, moving however falteringly in a similar direction, to be at the 'cutting edge' when it comes to designing learning systems for basic education in the twenty-first century. In this context, sites now known as schools may become centres for designing, developing, coordinating and evaluating community-wide learning support networks; places where members of the network meet, and where children gather for certain purposes but are not contained.

The idea of networking across established organizational boundaries – teachers with teachers, students with students, schools with their communities

– has always been central to ENSI's vision of educational change and flows from its analysis of social change (see Posch 1995a, 1995b). Posch (1995a: 47) has defined the essential feature of a 'dynamic network' as 'the autonomous and flexible establishment of relationships to assist responsible action in the face of complexity and uncertainty'. He goes onto argue that 'Dynamic networks contradict one of the traditional assumptions of schooling: the assumption of a separation of school and society. If dynamic networks develop it is difficult to say where the educational organisation ends and where society begins' (p. 48).

Such developments were well evidenced in a number of ENSI schools, in varying phases of advancement, and perhaps most notably at Pumpherstone. They cannot be dissociated from the epistemological assumptions which underpin the curriculum. The separation of school and society is an implication of a theory of knowledge which dissociates the processes of knowledge acquisition from the practical affairs of everyday life, and any attempt to overcome this separation can only succeed if educational practitioners come to adopt a more pragmatic theory of knowledge as a basis for pedagogical action.

The three examples I have used to illustrate the use of ENSI's curriculum theory in action – developments in Swedish, Austrian and Scottish schools – do not deny the need to maintain continuity in our education systems. While they demonstrate the power of professional and community-wide networks to support teachers' and students' learning respectively, they also demonstrate a distinctive role for schools as centres for curriculum planning, for facilitating worthwhile learning experiences on the part of students, for coordinating learning support networks, for generating locally useful knowledge, etc. What they imply is a restructuring of the roles and functions of schools in society rather than their elimination. But such restructuring implies more than reform in the sense of simply improving schools by making existing roles and functions more efficient and effective. It implies changing the structures of belief and value which underpin schools as organizational systems, and thereby generating new conceptions of their roles and functions. I will examine this issue in some detail in the final chapter.

I have tried to show that ENSI constitutes a pedagogically driven rather than a standards-driven, or even an exclusively teachers-driven, curriculum change process. This doesn't imply an absence of educational quality criteria, but rather an alternative account of them. The ENSI framework specifies quality criteria in terms of pedagogical aims and principles of procedure, rather than in terms of pre-standardized learning outcomes. Its use does not underplay the importance of assessing students' learning achievements. It simply does not provide a pre-standardized view of learning outcomes, because this is inconsistent with students determining these things for themselves as part of the learning process. The assessment of individual students' learning in this context may be a more complex matter of judgement rather than marking to a standard, but this should not diminish the importance of teachers gathering, assessing and reporting evidence about students' achievements. Pedagogically driven curriculum frameworks and policies focus attention on the conditions which enable worthwhile learning to occur, and are based on the view that the criteria for evaluating the quality of pedagogy can be specified without also having to specify learning outcomes. Evaluating pedagogy and assessing learning outcomes, as I argued earlier, are different processes.

Not unconnected with this point is the emphasis in ENSI on the production of local knowledge. If what students need to know is self-determined and relative to what they can use to shape the conditions of their lives, then pre-specified knowledge objectives are inappropriate. But this does not deny the significance of the academic disciplines as learning resources, or the importance of teachers as the mediators of the conditions of access to such resources. What changes are the rules and precepts governing the ways teachers give their students access to the contents of disciplines. When these contents are viewed as structures of ideas and methods of inquiry for students to use in thinking about solutions to the complex problems and issues that impact on their lives (see Stenhouse 1975: ch. 7), then the pedagogy will be quite different to one structured by prespecified content objectives.

In this context, worthwhile knowledge is not a static quality but a dynamic one constructed within the pedagogical process. However, the balance between static and dynamic elements, which Posch believes it is necessary for the culture of teaching and learning to maintain, is preserved. As bodies of information, the contents of the disciplines are static elements and only become dynamic as they are pedagogically transformed into 'useful' ideas for students to explore. Teachers need to understand the academic disciplines in both their static and dynamic aspects, as a store of static information and as dynamic structures of ideas for thinking about real-life problems and issues.

A process model of curriculum design does not neglect the significance of curriculum-as-content. What it does is specify the pedagogical principles for transforming static into dynamic content. The teaching of subject content in the light of such principles will require a closer cooperation between subject specialists than is possible within the established patterns of subject-based curriculum organization. The latter tend to support a transmission mode of teaching, which views the disciplines largely as stores of 'static knowledge'. Rather than destroying teachers' subject expertise, teaching arrangements which support interdisciplinary learning (e.g. team-teaching) can extend teachers' understanding of their subject as a store of useful ideas.

The use of the process model need not rule out the pre-specification of subject content. For example, Stenhouse's Humanities Project, rightly regarded as an exemplar of the process model, generated an organized selection of multi-media material reflecting content drawn from a variety of disciplines on the basis of its potential relevance to discussions of controversial issues in classrooms aimed at the development of 'understanding'. This content-specification differed from the traditional syllabus in a number of ways.

First, it was regarded as a specification of 'evidence' for a point of view, a value-position, a perspective on a human act or social situation and therefore as open to critical discussion. It was explicitly designed to foster a critical approach to 'knowledge'. In the traditional syllabus, the organization of content presumes its treatment as fixed and certain knowledge, and is therefore frequently explicitly structured by knowledge objectives. Stenhouse believed that specifications structured by 'objectives' were inconsistent with the idea of content as 'evidence' for critical discussion (see Stenhouse 1975: ch. 7). Secondly, the Humanities Project's content-specification did not imply any predetermined notions of progression or sequence in learning. The order and sequence in which items were introduced to students was for teachers and students to negotiate within the pedagogical process itself. Thirdly, the relevance of any element in the specification to the development of 'understanding' was treated as hypothetical and to be determined through the pedagogical process. Stenhouse's project centrally specified a 'foundation archive' of evidence to provide initial support for teachers embarking on a radical innovation, but viewed it as open to continuous reconstruction in the light of teachers' research into the usefulness of items as evidence for discussion. Teachers were free to eliminate and add items to the archive over time.

From the perspective of the process model, the 'curriculum-as-content' is a hypothetical and provisional specification in the process of being continuously tested and reconstructed by teachers and students at the local level. There is no reason why the construction and continuous reconstruction of such a specification should not be nationally coordinated, although it would be self-contradictory to argue that content should be nationally prescribed as mandatory. As a hypothetical and provisional content-specification, designed to support a particular form of teaching and learning, it presumes that teachers will be free to select some items of content rather than others, and to experiment with items that have not been included. The function of a centrally coordinated content-specification would be to support curriculum decision-making at the local and school level rather than pre-empt it, in which case procedures would need to be established for (a) constructing an initial specification of content in consultation and negotiation with teachers, and (b) eliciting and processing subsequent feedback from teachers about the relevance and value of particular items and which additional ones, in the light of their experience, should be included.

The Norwegian national curriculum appears to have many of the features one would associate with the process model. I have already indicated that a framework of pedagogical aims and principles lies at its 'core'. Following the construction of this framework, procedures were established for involving subject teachers in specifying curriculum content in a form that is consistent with and relevant to the 'core' aims and principles. In addition, the curriculum gives teachers a generous amount of space to determine content which may not command a national consensus, but can be justified in terms of its local relevance.

Designing the whole curriculum at the national level

What might a national framework for the whole curriculum look like, if it were based on the general ideas which underpin the ENSI project? What implications would it have for our understanding of the principle of subsidiarity in curriculum decision-making? How would it compare with other kinds of frameworks as a basis for enabling future citizens to take responsibility for shaping the conditions of their existence in increasingly complex and rapidly changing modern societies? Such a framework would consist of the following four components.

1 *A classification of the kinds of complex problems and issues which impact on people's lives*, including 'environment', 'cultural diversity', 'health', 'poverty and wealth', 'family life', 'sexuality', 'work and leisure', 'law and order', 'education', 'religious belief', 'the impact of science and technology', etc. There is no definitive set of categories for classifying the problems of living in advanced modern societies. Categorizations may differ somewhat from one country to another and over time in the same country, because they will reflect concerns that are relative to time and place. The important thing is that a set of curriculum categories is comprehensive in scope and that each category captures the complexity of the problems and issues it includes, sufficiently so to avoid too much overlap between categories and a fragmentation of focus.

It is important not to confuse these 'life-themes' with 'cross-curricular themes', because the same labels are often used to name them. The latter are classifications of subject-contents which pick out common dimensions across the subjects. As curriculum categories they are secondary to the subject-based categories, which constitute the primary organizing categories for the traditional curriculum. 'Life-themes' are categories for classifying the problems and issues which arise in everyday life, and constitute the primary organizing categories for an 'alternative curriculum'. It then becomes possible to classify subject-content in interdisciplinary forms; in terms of its usefulness and relevance to the problems and issues covered by each life-theme. However, such classifications of content, which as I have argued should always be treated as hypothetical and provisional, are secondary to, and dependent on, the classification of problems and issues of everyday life.

Although the ENSI framework can be understood to cover only one category, and not the whole of a life-themes curriculum, it is open to a more holistic view of 'the environment' as a curriculum category, covering problems and issues which emerge in human transactions with their social and cultural as well as their natural and physical environment. The project defined the category in this broader sense, although the projects which emerged in schools tended to define environmental issues largely in terms of people's transactions with their natural and physical environment. The broader sense of 'environment' makes it an inclusive curriculum category covering all of the more specific 'life-themes'. Viewed in these terms, the ENSI framework of pedagogical aims and procedural principles can be interpreted as a specification for a teaching and learning process which applies to the whole curriculum rather than part of it. Perhaps this would be quite appropriate as a form of curriculum organization in Beck's (1992) 'risk society'.

2 *A specification of the pedagogical aims and principles which ought to govern a learning process that focuses on the problems and issues of everyday living.* Such a specification can be formulated in very general terms, to indicate the broad aims and principles which should shape the teaching–learning process in general for the whole curriculum. But it should also spell out the implications of these aims and principles for the handling of particular life-themes. Different aspects may need to be emphasized for different themes.

A specification of a teaching–learning process in terms of the educational aims and principles it should realize is open to continuing clarification and elaboration, in the light of teachers' reflections about their practice. The function of such a specification is to support the reflective transformation of educational practice by teachers, and this is impaired if they come to regard it as the purveyor of fixed meanings.

Pedagogical aims and principles are *open conceptions* of an ideal teaching–learning process. They provide teachers with an orientation for their work rather than a fixed end-point, and they do not take the form of operational rules which prescribe concrete actions. The means of realizing the educational values such aims and principles express in practice, the pedagogical strategies, are appropriately a matter for situated judgement, and determined at the classroom level. Hence, the significance of action research within the process model of curriculum planning.

Long ago, Aristotle argued in his *Ethics*, that there is a sense in which the meanings of our value-concepts are necessarily vague, because they can only be operationally defined in the actions we take to realize them. If educational practice is intrinsically ethical in character, rather than simply being a technical means of producing outcomes which can be defined independently of such means, then reflection about pedagogical aims, and the principles they imply, cannot be separated from reflection about the means of achieving them. In the context of education viewed as an 'ethical practice', pedagogical strategies constitute acts of interpretation. In reflecting about their teaching–learning strategies, in the light of a set of aims and principles, teacher-researchers will ask whether such strategies constitute a valid interpretation of them.

The answer involves two dimensions of reflection: on the strategies in the light of the aims, and on the aims in the light of the strategies. Reflection on practice constitutes an interactive process of deliberating about both means and ends together. In undertaking action research, into the ways they operationally define a set of pedagogical aims and principles, teachers also develop their philosophical understanding of educational value-concepts. This kind of action research does not dissociate philosophical from empirical inquiry.

As I indicated earlier, many of the teachers involved in the ENSI project developed their understanding of the project's rather vague and ambiguous statements about the aims of environmental education by researching the strategies they adopted to realize them. Although ENSI teachers achieved greater clarity about the aims they were asked to realize through action research, and as a result greater commitment to them, Aristotle's point about the open nature of value-concepts remains a valid one. The fact that teachers developed their understanding of the aims of environmental education does not imply that they progressed towards some fixed end-point, some definable and measurable standard of perfect understanding. As with all value-concepts, developing one's understanding of educational concepts is a never-ending task, because they are always open to experience and reinterpretation according to the circumstances teachers face at a particular time and place. This is why the understandings the ENSI teachers developed of the aims of the project, tended to vary from one country to another, such variations reflecting differences in the social and cultural locations of the innovation.

3 *An interdisciplinary, hypothetical and provisional specification of 'core' subject content in relation to each life-theme for teachers (and students) to test experimentally in the teaching–learning process.* Such specifications will again be open to continuous revision in the light of teachers' action research. They may be accompanied by (a) the production of a centrally coordinated national archive of illustrative resources which can be accessed by teachers, perhaps via the internet, and be continuously developed in collaboration with them, or (b) suggestions for compiling an electronically accessed resource archive at the local level.

4 *A specification of guidelines for a process of action research by teachers to enable them to develop strategies for realizing the pedagogical aims and principles in practice, and to provide interested 'stake-holders' with evidence – about the pedagogical problems they addressed and the solutions they adopted – as a basis for informed discussion and debate.* Examples of such guidelines are the self-study manual produced by Stenhouse and his associates for teachers in the Humanities Project (see Stenhouse 1970a) and those produced to support teachers' action research in the ENSI project (see Elliott 1994).

Implicit in the kind of framework outlined above is a rather different interpretation of the principle of subsidiarity to those which underpin standards-led and teachers-led curriculum development. In the standards-led model, educational standards are set by central agencies in terms of fixed targets or objectives which refer to well-defined and measurable learning outcomes. The centre gives teachers and schools varying degrees of freedom to devise the means of achieving these standards and holds them accountable for the technical effectiveness and efficiency of the strategies they use on the basis of test results. Some central agencies may prescribe a particular way of organizing curriculum content in a programme of study aimed at achieving the desired outcome standards, leaving teachers free only to make decisions about teaching and learning methods, while others leave them free to devise both programmes of study and teaching–learning methods.

Whichever level of subsidiarity applies, in terms of the balance between centralized and local decision-making, standards-driven curriculum development can do little more than reform existing educational practice by making it more efficient and effective. More fundamental change would require a shift in the theory of knowledge which underpins established practice, and this would undermine the model of standards-led development for it is essentially a model of centralized social engineering. Such a shift would entail, as we have seen, a more dynamic learning process, which makes it increasingly difficult to pre-specify and standardize learning outcomes and the task of assessing them too complex for central agencies to handle.

I argued earlier that in advanced modern societies the established culture of teaching and learning has to change fundamentally, if the vast majority of our future citizens are to develop the dynamic qualities which will enable them to shape the conditions of their existence and thereby accept responsibility for their future. Equal educational opportunities for such development is essential to the development of advanced modern societies as participatory democracies. The alternative lies in the development of more sophisticated forms of totalitarian control over human behaviour than communism and fascism were capable of demonstrating.

Centralized social engineering in the form of standards-led curriculum development cannot deliver the fundamental changes in pedagogy that will need to occur if our future citizens are going to be anything more than passive consumers in a society controlled by market forces and governed by market values. Nor, as I also previously argued, will a policy of teacher-led curriculum development, in which government washes its hands of all responsibility for leadership in the curriculum field and simply 'decentralizes' this function, deliver fundamental pedagogical change on a sufficient scale. The teacher-led curriculum reforms in Britain during the 1960s and early 1970s amply demonstrated this. If we mount national curriculum policies on an interpretation of the subsidiarity principle that entails a crude form of decentralization, we shall not develop a curriculum that gets much purchase on fundamental pedagogical change.

A pedagogically driven national curriculum framework of the kind I outlined above, which is underpinned by the same general ideas as those which underpinned the design of both the Humanities Project and ENSI, implies a different interpretation of the principle of subsidiarity to both the standards-led and teacher-led approaches. In both these latter approaches, subsidiarity is not seen as a means by which the centre actively empowers teachers to take responsibility for fundamentally redefining and reshaping their pedagogy.

Within the pedagogically driven approach to curriculum development, subsidiarity implies that the central agencies adopt positive roles aimed at empowering teachers fundamentally to redefine and reshape the processes of teaching and learning. In this context, as I argued with respect to Stenhouse's conception of the humanities curriculum (see Chapter 2), a curriculum framework constitutes a specification for an innovative experiment to be carried out by teachers. As such, it is a framework which is open to being continuously developed – redefined and reshaped – by teachers, as they devise and test pedagogical strategies for realizing the aims and values which define the innovation. In this context the roles of central government agencies are those of:

1 Leadership in setting and communicating a vision of worthwhile pedagogical change to teachers, in a form which secures their commitment to the innovation as a worthwhile curriculum experiment. The curriculum framework structures the vision, but it is an open structure which enables teachers to contribute to the continuing reconstruction of the vision on the basis of their action research.
2 Support for teachers' action research into the problems of realizing the innovation's defining aims and principles in practice.
3 Coordinating the development of the curriculum framework, and the vision it 'captures', by processing feedback provided by teachers on the basis of their action research.

Rather than disempowering teachers as active agents of educational change, as both the standards-led and teacher-led approaches tend to, the roles of central agencies in pedagogically driven curriculum development, as they are depicted above, empower them fundamentally to change their practice. They are the roles performed by the central team of the Humanities Project and the national coordinators and pedagogical support persons in the ENSI project. The evidence contained in the national evaluation reports of both projects suggests that many participating teachers made significant progress in changing their practices in quite significant ways.

The kind of curriculum framework I have outlined implies *partnership, collaboration, cooperation* and *reciprocal accountability* between central agencies and teachers operating at the local level, in a context characterized by *mutual trust* and *free and open communication* (transparency of intentions). Teachers' accountability for their actions is not based on the presumption of the standards-driven approach: that they cannot be trusted to perform effectively if some form of external evaluation and surveillance by the central agencies is absent. It is based on the presumption that teachers are capable of consciously self-monitoring their practices through action research, and therefore of producing accounts of those practices for the purposes of public discussion and using it to elicit developmental feedback. The Humanities and ENSI projects both generated a comprehensive database about the practices of participating teachers in schools. In both, it largely consisted of case study data generated by the teachers themselves, and grounded in their action research. On the basis of the ENSI data, national coordinators, pedagogical support persons and OECD (CERI) consultants were able to identify and clarify both the problematics and potential of ENSI as an innovative experiment in schools. It enabled them to make comparisons across schools and across countries, and on this basis to develop better strategies for supporting and coordinating the work of teachers. ENSI amply demonstrated, as did the Humanities Project some twenty years earlier, how well-supported action research can establish the conditions of mutual trust which enable teachers to face, share, report and openly discuss negative aspects of their practice.

If governments seriously want to prepare their future citizens to take responsibility for shaping the conditions of their existence in society, then they will need to develop national curriculum policies which actively empower teachers to change fundamentally the prevailing pedagogical culture in their schools. The ENSI project constitutes a valuable resource in this respect because it indicates the lines along which such policies might be developed.

8

The Politics of Environmental Education: A Case Story

Introduction

In the previous chapter, I discussed the relevance of the OECD project on 'Environment and School Initiatives' (ENSI) for curriculum planning and policy-making in advanced modern societies characterized by continuous change, high complexity and the process of individualization. In this chapter, I tell a backroom story about the struggle to introduce ENSI into England and Wales at a time when policy-makers and officials were launching the National Curriculum, and viewing the project to be inconsistent with its premises and precepts.

At the heart of this case story is the conflict between the two different conceptions of curriculum change examined in this book: socially engineered standards-driven reform and pedagogically driven innovative experimentation. As I have tried to show, each constitutes a different response to social change and embodies a different vision of education. What is at issue in the conflict between these rival conceptions of curriculum change is the extent to which the mainstream European education tradition, which is both modified and maintained by standards-driven policies, constitutes an appropriate basis for responding to the changes taking place in the wider society.

Before focusing on what happened to ENSI in England and Wales during phase 2 of the project, I will set these events in the context of a broader story about the origins, design and initial phase of the project prior to the question of its introduction to schools in England and Wales. In doing so, I touch on some of the features of the project covered in the previous chapter.

Origins, birth and beginnings

The project was designed in a novel form for OECD (CERI Projects), which were typically designed as 'information exchanges'. As I explained in the previous chapter, the project constitutes an international curriculum development informed by a set of educational aims from which were derived a number of pedagogical principles specifying a desirable teaching–learning process. I have also described how the curriculum design fitted the 'process model' Stenhouse formulated for the Humanities Curriculum Project in Britain during the late 1960s, as did the design of Bruner's 'Man: A Course of Study' (MACOS) at the Educational Development Centre at Harvard (see Bruner 1970: ch. 2; Stenhouse 1975). What characterized the development of process models of curriculum design in Britain and the USA in the 1960s was their opposition to a rational model of curriculum planning which emphasized the detailed behavioural specification of learning outcomes: a model which carried the approval of government agencies in their attempts to render education more economically accountable at a time of scarce public resources.

Peter Posch (1988), at the University of Klagenfurt in Austria, the major influence over the design of ENSI, had from the early 1970s networked with curriculum theorists and developers in the English-speaking world. The Austrian Government was interested in an inter-governmental initiative in the field of environmental education and used Posch as a consultant in formulating a successful proposal to the OECD. Posch's achievement was to secure political legitimation for a 'process model'. It deserves the attention of curriculum historians because it constitutes either a landmark in the political history of curriculum planning, or an interesting deviation.

As we have seen, a 'process model' of curriculum design expresses a number of educational values which a so-called 'rational model' appears to neglect, such as relevance to the personal experience of students through a focus on the problems of everyday living, an active learning process through which students construct/reconstruct knowledge through their own research, and the need to transcend established subject boundaries in developing practically useful knowledge and understanding.

In introducing these values through the design of the ENSI project, Posch invited schools to initiate curricula which challenged the assumptions about learning, knowledge and curriculum organization which are built into the cenralized curriculum policies of many countries. The process model, as I have hopefully demonstrated (see Chapters 2 and 7), leaves greater scope for school- and teacher-based curriculum initiatives than one which, by emphasizing content objectives, dissociates knowledge from personal experience, reinforces passive learning and organizes knowledge in tightly bounded parcels.

The ENSI project cast the school in the role of generating concrete knowledge about the local environment for community use rather than of merely transmitting abstract knowledge in dissociation from its local applications and uses. In the previous chapter, I gave some examples of ENSI schools fulfilling such a role. Within ENSI schools, relevant curriculum content was determined by learning needs that emerged in the course of complex transactions with their local communities. In a context where schools aspire to break down the boundaries between themselves and their communities to generate local knowledge, learning outcomes cannot be predicted and pre-determined in advance. In securing political legitimation for ENSI from a number of member countries, the OECD has provided them with an opportunity to re-examine the appropriateness of their existing national curriculum policies for meeting the challenge of the environment.

I am unsure of the extent to which the representatives of the member states who participated in phase 1 of the project were fully aware of the implications of their enthusiasm for ENSI. But they were certainly aware of the symbolic significance of international curriculum development in the field of environmental education. National governments were being challenged by pressure groups to demonstrate a commitment to improving the environment. In the field of education, what could have symbolically expressed such a commitment better than a government's endorsement of a programme which encouraged schools to play an active role in shaping their local environment? It was the symbolic significance of ENSI, at a time when environmental issues were high on the political agenda, that secured its endorsement by a number of OECD member countries.

However, there was also another factor at work. The metaphor of the 'market' was beginning to drive economic policy-making, with its emphasis on enterprise and the need to 'emancipate' public services and citizens from the bureaucratic structures of the state. ENSI's emphasis on the development of 'dynamic' rather than 'passive' qualities echoed the enterprise values of emerging market societies. Its focus on school-initiated curriculum development in response to local concerns echoed an acknowledgement on the part of many governments of the need for public services to be less controlled by the state and more locally accountable to their clients.

From a political perspective, the rhetoric embedded in ENSI's design appeared to embrace the values of an enterprise culture in a market-orientated society. From an educational perspective, it appeared to embrace the progressive educational values of liberal humanism. It thus appealed to politicians and educationalists alike. Posch's skill in designing ENSI was that he made them appear to be congruent and thereby secured both political and educational legitimation for the project. In the UK, however, political legitimation was not secured with respect to the project in England and Wales.

In Chapter 2, I explained how a process model of curriculum design came to be associated in the UK with the emergence of the action research movement (see Stenhouse 1975; Elliott 1991a). How the aims and principles which specify a worthwhile teaching learning process are to be realized in practice is open for schools and teachers to determine in their particular circumstances. They call for intelligent professional judgements and decisions grounded in developing professional understandings of the problematic situations they encounter in bringing about educational change.

Posch built teacher-based action research into the design of ENSI. It was hoped that ENSI would generate a database on 'change issues', in the form of case studies constructed by teachers on the basis of their reflections about the problems and potential of developing environmental education curricula in the light of the project's aims and principles. I was asked to carry out a comparative analysis of the phase 1 case studies with a view to identifying generalizable 'findings' (see Elliott 1991a). These 'findings' were discussed at an end of phase conference in Linz, Austria, for all the participants in the project – students and teachers as well as academics and administrators.

The major findings discussed at Linz were summarized in a preparatory document (not publicly available) produced in the spring of 1989 for phase 2 of ENSI:

> The positive outcomes of innovative school initiatives were basically linked to teaching/learning factors, motivation of student interest and participation, heightened awareness of environmental problems, increased interest in science subjects with an understanding of relevance to daily life. The action research methods encouraged teachers to reflect on the quality and relevance of their approaches to teaching. It gave them a new and deeper insight into the performance of their students, stimulating formative evaluation methods rather than relying on traditional forms of assessment.

However, the case studies produced by teachers at phase 1 also provided evidence that:

> Environmental education seems to challenge both the educational systems and the community's tolerance for innovative practice. The measure of this challenge is an indication of both the relevance and the complexity of environment as a subject of study. Environmental education transcends the boundaries of traditional subject areas as it is not only a body of knowledge to be learned, but an active orientation to fundamental societal problems to be applied in the present and the future; prevention of environmental hazards depends on the conscious and unconscious choices of ordinary people.
>
> Environmental education in most member countries is still marginal to the mainstream curriculum.

The experience of phase 1 in the schools (see Laine and Posch 1991) was considered by the CERI governing board to be sufficiently positive to merit further development work in participating countries and an extension of access to countries not previously involved. For phase 2, it was decided to emphasize even more the significance of action research in helping schools and teachers to confront the problems of change, and to strengthen the national support for helping them to undertake such research. In phase 1, it was noted that the quality of the case studies, and the insights they reported, varied according to the quality and level of support teachers had received for reflecting systematically on the problems of pedagogical change. The design of phase 2 recommended the establishment of 'pedagogical support' personnel as distinct from those national coordinators who primarily had administrative and liaison responsibilities. The major function of such individuals was to assist schools and teachers to undertake action research which focused on certain key issues that had emerged from the phase 1 'findings'. These were as follows:

1 How are the complex relationships between human beings and their environment best represented and explored through the curriculum?
2 How are the value issues raised by human action on the environment best handled by teachers?
3 How can the study of local environmental problems be linked to global and generalizable issues?
4 How is knowledge generated by the environmental sciences best used to inform student research into local problems?
5 What are the organizational conditions for establishing interdisciplinary and project-based work, in a form which is part of the mainstream curriculum and accessible to all students?
6 How can the development of dynamic qualities be assessed and recorded?

Perhaps the most fundamental problem which emerged in phase 1 was that of realizing the aims and principles of ENSI within mainstream curriculum provision. The case study data portrayed a certain pathology of innovation. In some cases, ENSI was assimilated to the existing subject-based patterns of curriculum organization, where learning remained essentially a passive process of knowledge acquisition dissociated from an active and direct engagement in, and with, the local community. In other cases, ENSI's aims and principles were realized by small groups of teachers and students operating outside the framework of mainstream curriculum provision. These groups did much to bring rewards and recognition to their schools for enterprise and initiative in relation to local environmental issues. But they left the organization of mainstream curricula provision for environmental education untouched.

It was felt that action research by teachers would be insufficient as a basis for changing curriculum frameworks in schools shaped by external policies. What was also needed was an analysis of government environmental policies and the extent to which their educational and curriculum policies were matched to them. It was felt that the design of phase 2 of the project should incorporate a policy analysis perspective as a means of sensitizing governments to the practical issues of realizing those policies in the pedagogical practices of schools. The data gathered by teachers in the schools around the issues agenda cited above would provide a context for the policy analyses. This marks a new development in the OECD's conduct of policy analysis, since it is not normally grounded in the experience of those involved in grass roots development.

The fate of ENSI in Britain

Britain did not participate in phase 1 of ENSI, although a representative attended the initial negotiations, which involved the National Association for Environmental Education. I am not aware of the advice given by that association to government officials. The reasons for Britain's decision not to take part are unknown, but there are factors which might be significant to understanding that decision. In the mid-1980s, environmental issues were not high on the political agenda, compared with some other European countries. The activities of 'green' pressure groups tended to be viewed as part of a broad left-wing alliance whose influence the Conservative government was determined to minimize. Also, it is quite possible to speculate that ENSI was perceived as a potential political obstacle to the centralizing thrust of educational decision-making in Britain.

As phase 1 was in 'mid-flight' during the summer of 1987, the newly re-elected Conservative government announced its plan to make sweeping reforms of the educational system in England and Wales. The bedrock of the reforms was the introduction of a national curriculum into a country which 'had long been noted, by contrast with its European partners, for a decentral-ised curriculum with responsibility firmly in the hands of the professionals' (Pring 1989). In other words, at a time when the European countries participating in phase 1 of ENSI were beginning to entertain the idea of delegating curriculum initiatives from the centre to the periphery, the British Government was, some would say not untypically in the context of the European Community, going in the reverse direction. It is interesting that, politically, the idea of 'the market society' appeared to be legitimating these opposing trends. Other aspects of the British education reforms were clearly aimed at making schools less regulated by the bureaucratic controls imposed by local government and more responsive to the 'social market'; for example, through schools managing their own budgets, by giving parents greater choice of schools and greater powers over the ways they are run, and by allowing schools to opt out of local government control.

In November 1987, the Education Reform Bill for England and Wales (Scotland and Northern Ireland have devolved powers with respect to education) began its voyage through Parliament. The curriculum framework enshrined in it, with the exception of technology, looked very much like the traditional subject-based curriculum that had established itself in the old selective British grammar schools. It appeared to leave little room for curriculum reforms which many schools had initiated, in their attempt to make the curriculum more relevant to the needs of the majority of the nation's children during the period of reorganization into a comprehensive system from the 1960s onwards. For many, the National Curriculum appeared to be 'setting the clock back'.

By the time phase 1 was coming to an end in 1988, the schools in England and Wales were beginning to embark on the process of implementing a state-controlled curriculum shaped by a 'rational model' of planning. The national framework identified dimensions and themes like 'multicultural', 'health' and 'environmental' education across attainment targets in a variety of subjects. Although guidance was issued to schools on ways of introducing and handling cross-curricular themes within the National Curriculum, it fell under the heading of 'non-statutory' guidance.

As the Linz conference loomed and discussions began about a proposed phase 2 for ENSI, I wrote to the National Inspector (HMI) responsible for curriculum matters at the Department of Education and Science (DES), suggesting that the government should support the participation of British schools in phase 2. I had opposed the government's national curriculum proposals from the outset, in a speech to the North of England conference attended by the secretary of state for education (see Elliott 1988b). My interest in getting schools in England and Wales involved in phase 2 was to provide a context which enabled them creatively to offset some of the anticipated negative side-effects of the National Curriculum and assessment framework on the quality of teaching and learning in schools.

In the preceding years, school-based curriculum development, often as part of government-sponsored schemes like the Technical Vocational Educational Initiative (TVEI), or the reorganization of the public examination system at 16+, had yielded a considerable transformation in pedagogical practices. Teaching–learning processes had become more student-centred and focused on real problems in everyday life, and involved the development of dynamic rather than passive qualities in students. Schools had generated new ways of assessing students' personal development for diagnostic purposes.

From my point of view, the design of ENSI was consistent with the above changes in British schools, while many aspects of the new National Curriculum were not. ENSI would provide a context in which the creative achievements of our schools could be harnessed to the development of environmental education internationally. It would also provide a supportive context in which schools could continue to innovate, and maintain the direction of change they had been moving in prior to the National Curriculum. Through participation in the phase 2 programme of action research, teachers would be able to appraise realistically just how much of a straitjacket the National Curriculum imposed upon them, and make out a well-argued case to the secretary of state for amendments and changes to statutory orders. I felt that involvement in a government-sponsored project, within a politically high-profile area like environmental education, would provide the schools with some leverage over the process of implementing the National Curriculum. It appears that some people at the DES felt the same way.

In response to my request to HMI, the inspector with a national brief for environmental education was given permission to attend the Linz conference and asked to report back his impression of the project prior to any decision being taken about the participation of English and Welsh schools. He returned very impressed and enthusiastic about the outcomes of ENSI phase 1. However, he suggested that the DES might have strong reservations about supporting phase 2 of ENSI. The project did not align neatly with the development of the National Curriculum. Schools could be tempted to apply for exemption from certain statutory requirements. DES officials certainly appreciated the possible significance of the government's commitment to phase 2, although one could argue that they adopted an over-narrow interpretation of national curriculum requirements.

What began to emerge during 1988 were rather different interpretations of the practical implications of the National Curriculum. Some officials at the DES gave out the message that the national curriculum framework implied a subject-based pattern of curriculum organization in schools. The National Curriculum Council (NCC), on the other hand, a government body charged with the responsibility of helping schools to implement the curriculum, gave out the message that the organization of the curriculum, to deliver the content specified by the targets and attainment statements, was entirely up to them. The NCC was having to cope with the practical problem of curriculum overload in schools, and therefore pragmatically finding itself endorsing a degree of cross-curricular contact between subjects through topic-based and modularized courses.

Following the Linz conference, an OECD representative and I held a meeting with officials at the International Relations Division of the DES. A few days previously, prime minister Thatcher had made a significant speech on the environment, which suggested that the British Government would be placing it high in its policy priorities in the future. In the light of this, the officials told us that phase 2 of ENSI would have little problem in getting government support and that money could probably be secured for funding a pedagogical support unit. Later, the OECD representative met officials at Schools 3 Branch of the DES. I had originally planned to attend the meeting, but a person at Schools 3 informed the OECD that my presence was not necessary at this point in the negotiations. In contrast to the visit to the International Division, the OECD did not encounter a positive attitude to ENSI at Schools 3.

Shortly after these events, I attended a conference in Northern Ireland, where a leading expert on environmental education from England told the audience that the DES had, following the Thatcher speech, started to give environmental education a high priority. He told the following story. Immediately after the speech, the secretary of state for education asked his officials to retrieve from the files an HMI report on the place of environmental education in the

National Curriculum. He had previously decided that environmental education would be taught as a part of the geography curriculum. After the Thatcher speech, he crossed 'geography' out, and replaced it with the words 'No. I cross curriculum theme'.

The political climate appeared to offer a possibility of securing government support for ENSI. However, different messages were being signalled to different audiences. To the OECD headquarters in Paris, officials from the International Division were signalling a positive message of support. On the other hand, Schools Branch at the DES were signalling reservations about the project's compatibility with national curriculum requirements.

The outcome of these ambiguous messages was that some schools in England and Wales officially became participants in phase 2 of ENSI, but the project received no government support. There was no financial support to appoint a national coordinator. The HMI could not, by virtue of his role in the system, take on the coordinating role. He did, however, secure permission from the DES for a small involvement of schools on a voluntary basis. As civil servants, bound to carry out government policy, the officials at the DES felt they had no evidence that ENSI would enable schools to put the National Curriculum into practice. The HMI secured support for phase 2 of ENSI from three local education authorities (LEAs). In each LEA, clusters of phase 2 schools were to be coordinated by a local schools adviser, leaving the HMI inspector simply to serve as a link between the local coordinators and the OECD in Paris. He felt he could not play an active role in selecting the schools and coordinating phase 2 activities in them. This approach to establishing phase 2 in England resulted in some 'misunderstandings' of the inspector's role in Paris, where he was expected to be, and was effectively treated as, the national coordinator, quite contrary to all the firm messages given to the OECD.

However, although phase 2 of ENSI entered the English system through this approach, it left the problem of establishing a pedagogical support unit for the project at the national level. No offers of the necessary financial support came from Britain. The OECD programme officer expected me to head up the pedagogical support, given my experience of phase 1 of ENSI and my leading role in developing action research based approaches to curriculum development in the UK. I decided, in consultation with HMI, to seek funds for the pedagogical support unit from the private sector of industry and business.

The political context of the introduction of phase 2 of ENSI in England is well reflected in the HMI's account of an initial letter he had written to the chief education officers of prospective local authorities in June 1989. Hehad described the project, and the extent of international collaboration in phase 1, as he had experienced it at the Linz conference. The chief education officers were then informed of the OECD's desire to involve British schools, and of the inspector's offer to be an initial point of contact by making soundings with a small number of LEAs known for their experience and commitment in the field of environmental education.

The HMI inspector's letter informally took soundings from three LEAs about the possibility of them participating on the following basis:

1 Involving a small number of schools.
2 Nominating a member of the LEA advisory staff to serve as the local coordinator.
3 Accepting research support from a central unit.
4 Reminding them of the commitment to the National Curriculum.

The HMI inspector asked the chief education officers to indicate whether they would like their LEA to be involved. If so, the OECD would approach them formally.

In the summer of 1989, I submitted a proposal to the Laura Ashley Foundation (a charitable trust) for financial assistance, following an advertisement they had placed in the *Guardian* newspaper indicating that the trustees had 'a particular interest in schemes to increase awareness of the need to preserve the natural environment'. I also discussed the proposal with John Rae, the then director of the foundation, on the telephone. He felt it was the kind of proposal the trustees might be interested in and was willing to place it before them at their next meeting. John Rae had been headmaster at Westminster School, and was a liberal educationalist with a national reputation.

Prior to the trustees' decision, John Rae had left his position at Laura Ashley for another appointment. The decision was a negative one for me, but the national newspapers announced that the trust had awarded a substantial amount of money to the DES and World Wildlife Fund (WWF) on the basis of a joint proposal they had made to promote an 'Enterprise in the Environment' award scheme in schools. This scheme involved schools competing for awards on the basis of projects carried out by students into local environmental problems. The kind of project work specified by the scheme corresponded almost exactly to ENSI principles. I felt ENSI had been hijacked by the secretary of state. My analysis of the event went as follows:

◆ It confirmed a well-known suspicion that the British Government held towards the activities of international organizations like OECD, UNESCO and, of course, the EEC.
◆ The spectacle of a government agency obtaining substantial funding from a charitable organization to sponsor its schemes was dubious and an abuse of political power and privilege.
◆ It involved a political strategy of curriculum marginalization for the kind of environmental education that ENSI represented. Small groups of teachers and children could execute a project without it forming part of a school's mainstream curriculum provision, rather like they did in many phase 1 schools. The scheme was symbolically significant, enabling the government

politically to display a concern to promote environmental education in schools, while rendering it instrumentally or practically insignificant for the curriculum reforms it was actively promoting.

• It clarified government strategy with respect to environmental education. That policy was to appear to support environmental education while doing very little in practice. An integral part of this strategy was to encourage non-government organizations – charities and industry – to get involved with the provision of curriculum materials and even in-service training for teachers.

In October 1989, I shared elements of this analysis with the ENSI programme officer, by letter:

> I have had further discussions with the person who is managing things at the Laura Ashley Foundation until a new director is appointed. There is another meeting in the next few days, but she did not seem optimistic. She said it could take months to reach a decision. It is clear that the DES has leapfrogged the project by getting the Laura Ashley Foundation to fund their 'Enterprise in the Environment Award' scheme. Believe it or not the basic idea of the scheme is for children to investigate the environment in their local communities. How do you think this happened? When I suggested to the person at Laura Ashley that the OECD project had been leapfrogged, she did not dissent. I think the Director of educational programmes at CERI ought to know about all this because it is an indicator of the British government's attitude towards OECD initiatives (in my humble biased opinion).

Knowing that I have a tendency to use conspiracy theories to explain events, I was somewhat relieved shortly afterwards to find aspects of this particular conspiracy theory confirmed. A meeting was organized between officials at the DES, HMI and the local coordinators. In addition to English representation, inspectors from Wales, Northern Ireland and Scotland were invited. One of the Welsh representatives asked whether involvement in the ENSI project was compatible with the requirements of the National Curriculum. The DES official chairing the meeting explained reservations on this matter at the DES and pointed out that the 'Enterprise in the Environment' award scheme had been launched to marginalize the role of this kind of environmental education on the school curriculum, while at the same time to promote it at the periphery.

I managed to obtain a small amount of money from my own university to cover travelling expenses to schools and thereby offer them a minimum of pedagogical support. But I continued my efforts to find more substantial funding. In Scotland, matters were different. The Scottish Office, rather than the DES, is responsible for educational provision, and it had agreed to fund the employment of a full-time pedagogical support person. An HMI (Scotland) inspector took official responsibility as 'national' coordinator. In Northern

Ireland, the education office appointed one of its inspectors to coordinate phase 2 of ENSI. It linked in with schools participating in the Republic of Ireland, and it was agreed that pedagogical support for schools involved throughout Ireland would be provided by a unit at Trinity College, Dublin.

In Britain, we had a situation in which the government positively supported the participation of Scottish and Northern Irish schools in phase 2, but remained highly ambiguous with respect to the participation of English and Welsh schools. The national curriculum legislation only applied to England and Wales, although the Northern Ireland and Scottish Offices were busy developing a common curriculum along similar lines.

In the spring of 1990, I contacted the education office of WWF (UK), since they had expressed an interest in the OECD project. The head of that office had attended an initial meeting in Paris of member countries who might wish to participate in phase 2, and of course would have been involved in the DES/WWF bid to Laura Ashley. I met someone from WWF to discuss the possibility of securing funding for a pedagogical support unit, after which I submitted a written proposal. Following that submission, I telephoned the education officer and was told that funding was now unlikely, due to internal 'financial difficulties' that had suddenly become apparent.

In my search for funding, HMI knew of an interest in environmental education at a private 'middleman' agency which undertook educational projects for industry. This agency had been asked by two multinational companies to produce a comprehensive environmental education resource package for use in schools, and they had hired in a retired HMI inspector to assist. I met the director of the agency and explored the possibility of securing funding from the multinationals for the pedagogical support unit, in exchange for giving them an opportunity to have the potential of the package evaluated through action research in ENSI schools. The package's sponsors turned out to be more interested in the creation of a tangible product than in the pedagogical development of the teachers who had to handle it in classrooms. Its symbolic value as an artefact which could be placed in the hands of ministers of state to demonstrate the sponsor's concern for the environment appeared to override any concern for its practical value to teachers. Nevertheless, the agency asked me to act as their curriculum consultant for the production of the package. I agreed in the hope of building bridges for the future. I ended up introducing the package at the end of 1991 to a large audience of politicians, civil servants (from the DES and the Department of the Environment) and business executives in a conference hall near the Houses of Parliament in Westminster. I failed to obtain any funding from the multinationals for ENSI phase 2 in England as a result of my efforts.

At the Westminster event, I managed to snatch a moment with a minister for the environment, and suggested that his officials in attendance might like to have a word with the DES officials who were present about the level of priority the DES was giving to environmental education. He waved at the crowd in the room: 'Isn't this event evidence of our commitment?' He left me before I had a chance to reply.

I found myself in the middle of a complex situation. The British Government's lack of support had forced me, as a matter of deliberate policy, I was concluding, to seek funds for ENSI from the private sector. It eventually became clear to me (perhaps it should have done sooner) that the significance of private sector involvement in environmental education may not be dissimilar to that of the British Government. Both are primarily concerned with the construction of politically symbolic acts which publicly signify concern for the environment, rather than with the construction of effective and educationally worthwhile pedagogical practices for environmental education.

Let me backtrack on this story. In the autumn of 1990, following the opening of negotiations with the 'middleman' agency, it was suggested to me that another possible source of funding might be the Teachers' Branch of the DES and that I should submit a proposal to a certain official in Schools 3 Branch, who would then forward it across. I was told that I had to demonstrate the value of ENSI's pedagogical approach to helping teachers implement environmental education within the requirements of the National Curriculum. I was also advised to remove too much reference to the international dimension of pedagogical support; for example, helping teachers to share and compare their data with that gathered by teachers in other participating countries.

I constructed a fourth version of my proposal in the light of the NCC's newly published non-statutory guidelines for environmental education (Curriculum Guidance 7). I tried to demonstrate the compatibility of ENSI aims and principles with the aims of environmental education specified in the NCC's guidelines, and with the alternatives to subject-based curriculum organization outlined in that document. I argued that all the alternatives described were consistent with ENSI's interdisciplinary approach. Finally, I demonstrated the relevance of the issues agenda of phase 2 to the realization of the specific and general aims set out in the document for environmental education. The proposal was sent to the DES on 25 October 1990. The following features were highlighted in presenting the submission:

1 Its congruence with suggestions for handling environmental education in the context of the National Curriculum, as outlined in the NCC's Curriculum Guidance 7.
2 Its support for a learning process which emphasizes the importance of developing well-informed environmental concern, and capacities for decision-making and intelligent action with respect to the environment.
3 Its encouragement for the development of first-hand enquiry and personal/social skills.
4 Its support for reflective teaching and the sharing of experience and expertise between teachers in and across schools.

Evidently no money was forthcoming from Teachers' Branch, and the DES decided it would be more appropriate to send my proposal to the NCC for consideration. It was now public knowledge that tension over who controlled the implementation of the National Curriculum was growing fast between the DES and the NCC. An official told me that my proposal had been well received by one of the NCC committees. Eventually, I received a note from the assistant chief executive of the NCC informing me that I had submitted an unsolicited proposal in an incorrect format. Would I please send in the additional information required? No mention was made of the fact that the proposal had been submitted to the DES and not to the NCC, or of the fact that the latter had received it from the former. I was caught in what appeared to be a rising tide of conflict between the DES and the NCC. The fact that my proposal came to the NCC via the DES was not likely to advance my prospects as much as I might have hoped.

On 18 March 1991, I received a rejection letter from the assistant chief executive to my fifth version of the proposal:

> Dear John
> *Developing community focused environmental education through*
> *action research in schools: an international curriculum project*
> The proposal you submitted late last year under the above title has now been considered by the Curriculum Review Committee.
>
> In considering your proposal the Committee had to bear in mind Council's priorities in its forthcoming programme of work. These will concentrate on the core and other foundation subjects of the National Curriculum. I am sorry therefore that the Committee was unable to recommend support for this proposal.
>
> I wish you success in your search for funds.

Since the NCC is a government body, it was now (the spring of 1991) absolutely clear that the British Government was not giving any practical, as opposed to symbolic, priority to environmental education in English and Welsh schools, in spite of the Thatcher speech of the previous year and the impending 1992 environmental summit in Brazil.

In March 1991, the HMI inspector for environmental education brought together teachers, advisers and teacher-trainers in England, together with key figures internationally and non-government organization (NGO) representatives who supported environmental education in Britain. A national conference was held in Manchester. Besides discussing significant issues in establishing environmental education in the curriculum, and considering how complex and controversial issues could be handled, the possibility of creating a network to support and sustain the exchange of insights and experience was also raised. At this conference, I had a further discussion about the fate of my proposal with a DES official. He told me that there was a possibility of obtaining funds from the DES's research allocation. After the conference, he wrote to me requesting a revised submission:

> When we last met I promised I would explore further sources of financing for this project following your proposal being turned down by the National Curriculum Council.
>
> There is the possibility of money being made available from the Department's research budget, although this will as usual depend on decisions taken in the light of other bids and available resources.
>
> I think the best course would be for you to make a revised application to us including any updated information you have on e.g. costs and outcomes. Please let us know if there are no such changes and we will use the previous version.

The official went on to inform me that he was being moved on to another post, but assured me that he would make his successor aware of the proposal. My reply on 13 May included the following remarks:

> If you have any queries please do not hesitate to give me a ring but since this must be the sixth version of the proposal I am keeping my fingers crossed and hoping this is sufficient for your purposes. One additional piece of information which may be relevant is that so far such pedagogical support as we have been able to give to schools in this country has been funded by our School of Education's research committee. This was merely pump priming money to the tune of £1500. This simply covered my travel and subsistence costs to meetings in participatory LEAs. This money runs out at the end of July and it will be impossible for me to obtain any more. Effectively this means that in the absence of additional funding I shall have to withdraw giving any support to particular schools in this country. So I would certainly welcome a decision from the DES as soon as possible.
>
> I am very sorry to hear that you are leaving the job . . . No doubt our paths will meet again in the not too distant future. In the meantime many thanks for your assistance and help.

In July 1991, his successor wrote me a nice letter with more bad news:

> I put your submission dated 13 May to the Teacher's Supply and Training Branch, who hold a research budget, for consideration, as there is no research allocation for Environmental Education within this Branch.
>
> Unfortunately I now find myself in the unpleasant position of having to convey negative news. Although it was acknowledged that your proposal would result in the development of useful material about the application of action research in relation to environmental education, it was not rated as a particularly high priority in relation to other competing demands for very limited resources at the present time.

At this point, my money from the university for a minimum of support to phase 2 of ENSI in England ran out. I informed the OECD of the decision and rang the DES official. She suggested I might approach WWF, who evidently had not spent all the Laura Ashley money for the 'Enterprise in the Environment' scheme, which she informed me was to be terminated shortly. She also indicated that she would support my application to WWF. I no longer had any stomach for the battle and, with a bad taste in my mouth, decided to admit defeat.

By the autumn of 1991, the LEAs were in a state of disarray as their influence over schools became undermined by schools taking control of their own budgets. The local coordinators of ENSI phase 2 could no longer sustain their role. HMI were also being affected by a government proposal to cut their numbers drastically and remove them from their traditional school inspection role. Inspection services in schools were to become privatized. The HMI inspector for environmental education and I concluded that there was no alternative but to abandon phase 2 of ENSI in England, at least as far as providing any external support and liaison were concerned. The International Division at the DES became concerned about our conclusion to 'abandon ship' and called us to a meeting. Earlier the project officer at the OECD had contacted them and faxed the following message to my secretary:

> X [DES official] says there are funds available in his division and that John needs to call him about it.

At the meeting, it transpired that only about £2000 was available. This was clearly insufficient as a basis for support and I agreed that it should be distributed to the schools for help with costs incurred as a result of their participation. I certainly could do little with it as a basis for maintaining an adequate level of pedagogical support for action research. ENSI phase 2 marched on, but if it remained in England and Wales it did so invisibly. But this was not the end of the story. As ENSI enters phase 3 in its tenth year, the British government has finally decided to support the participation of schools in England and Wales.

9

What Have We Learned from Action Research in School-based Evaluation?

Introduction

This final chapter constitutes a personal reflection on what I think I have learned from my experience of participating both as a teacher and an academic facilitator in school-based action research over the past 30 years (see Elliott 1991a: chs 1, 2). In this book, I have tried to explain why the profound changes occurring in advanced societies challenge us to reconceptualize a general education which all pupils, regardless of their natural talents and abilities, can benefit equally from. I have argued that such an education will imply radical changes in the way curriculum content is selected and mediated to pupils, and that this implies a role for teachers as action researchers. Questions about curriculum and pedagogical strategies are central to questions about improving the quality of pupils' experience of schooling. They can only be answered through innovative curriculum experiments, carried out by teachers in 'classrooms', in collaboration with pupils and peers. As we have seen, this is a different view of school improvement to the one perpetuated by school effectiveness research. The latter tends to emphasize the significance of the school as a social system, rather than curriculum and pedagogy, as the major determinant of quality in schooling. Most of the things I have learned from working with teachers on school-based action research projects raise fundamental issues about the relationship between the classroom practices of teachers and the school as a social system.

I will now locate my own developing understanding of a perceived tension between top-down systems approaches and bottom-up classroom action research approaches to school and curriculum development, in a broader theory about the relationship between human actions and the systems in which they are located. In addressing them, I shall draw quite heavily on a single theoretical resource; namely, the 'theory of structuration' proposed by Giddens (1984). The reason I shall do so is that it helps me to clarify a number of beliefs and convictions which have emerged from my experience. Having clarified the task I have set myself, I hope that what I have to say will make a contribution to the school improvement debate.

Some understandings of the problems of educational change developed in the context of school-based action research:

*   Individual teachers cannot significantly improve their practices in isolation without opportunities for discussion with professional peers and others operating in a significant role relationship to them.
*   Attempts to change the pedagogical practices of teachers by changing schools and social systems through hierarchically initiated and controlled reforms tend to be resisted and are likely to fail.
*   Different approaches to school-based evaluation imply different views of the relationship between the pedagogical practices of individual teachers and schools as social organizations. Neither administratively led organizational reviews nor privatized self-reflection on the part of individuals are likely to make any significant impact on the quality of pedagogical practice in schools.
*   The institutionalization of an effective process of school-based evaluation can be facilitated or frustrated by school administrators and educational researchers, but it can only be realized through the free association of individuals networking across the system to collaboratively study their practices.

The central issue: What is the relation between structures and personal agency in shaping the pedagogical practices of teachers?

The educational action research movement has largely been concerned with improving the quality of teaching in schools by focusing on classroom transactions, situation and events. It has assumed that teachers operating in those physical spaces known as classrooms, with students socially organized into classes, have the power to effect significant changes in their practice.

Some educational researchers (e.g. on school effectiveness) and practitioners argue that such an assumption is unwarranted, since individual teachers' practices are shaped by the structural features of schools as social systems. These structures limit and constrain what it is possible for teachers to do in their classrooms. Changes in the classroom practices of individual teachers are therefore dependent on prior changes in the system as a whole and beyond the power of individual teachers to effect. The only people who have the power to reform social systems are those who have responsibilities for effective organizational functioning within them (e.g. administrators and managers).

The assumption that power to effect change lies in systems rather than the individuals who participate in them rests on the Parsonian view that organizational systems are constituted by a normative consensus about their aims and purposes. It is by virtue of this consensus of interest that systems have the power to shape the activities of their members. But systems constantly have to adapt to a changing environment and, according to normative functionalist theory, this is accomplished through a control centre which manages the social production of a consensus on aims and purposes – what are now fashionably called 'mission statements' – and adjusts the structures to accomplish them. From a normative functionalist perspective, 'management' is the agency that enables the system to be restructured. The power of the system over the activities of its members does not constitute oppression, since individuals allow the system to shape their activities because they share a vision of its functions.

This normative functionalist scenario posits hierarchically initiated organizational development as the key to improving classroom practice. School-based evaluation in this context is a very different enterprise to classroom action research, and in the British context is exemplified by the government-sponsored GRIDS project and its offspring, the Institutional Development Planning (IDP) movement. Such school-based enterprises tend to share the following characteristics:

- They are *hierarchically* initiated by school managers.
- The focus for evaluation is on system characteristics rather than the situated practice of individuals.
- The purpose of evaluation is *organizational reform*.
- The standards of evaluation are derived from statements about the *goals* and *purposes* of the school as a whole, which are produced by school managers through a process of negotiated consensus with teachers.
- Evaluation data take the form of quantitative measures of effective organizational functioning known as 'performance indicators'.
- The evaluation outcomes are *institutional development plans*.
- The process of evaluation tends to be couched in terms of cyclical and periodic reviews of organizational functioning.

The idea that educative power resides in schools as organizational systems rather than in the agency exercised by individual teachers in classrooms not only underpins a great deal of school-based evaluation, but also a great deal of what new passes for educational research. Couched in the terminology of 'school effectiveness research', it has spawned a whole new field of educational discourse and inquiry. Central to such research is the quest for generalizations about the relationship between the characteristics of schools as social organizations, often described in the discourse as 'school ethos variables', and the effective production of educational outcomes. Such generalizations provide school managers with the 'performance indicators' they can use to measure the effectiveness of their particular institution.

Let me now contrast this normative functionalist perspective with what might appear to be the naive perspective of classroom action research. From this perspective:

1 Evaluation is an aspect of teachers' attempts to innovate in their class-rooms in response to situations that render established practices problem-atic. It involves the self-reflexive monitoring of self-initiated change.
2 Evaluation focuses on pedagogically situated interactions between teachers and pupils and between the pupils themselves, and involves them in pro-cesses of data gathering and analysis.
3 Evaluation aims to transform pedagogical practices in schools.
4 Evaluation derives its standards for monitoring the innovation process from professed educational values embedded in the professional culture.
5 Evaluation gathers qualitative evidence to support teachers' judgements about the meaning and significance of their actions for the realization of professional values in particular situations. Which actions manifest these value qualities has to be determined *in situ* by formulating and testing action hypotheses in the light of evidence. In the context of action research, the gathering of evaluation data is not prestructured by indicators. Rather, it is an integral aspect of the teachers' quest through action research to discover which elements of practice are indicative of quality.
6 Evaluation results in specifications of quality indicators expressed as situ-ated action strategies for realizing professional values. Whereas function alist evaluations of systems imply a separation of research from evaluation (the former discovers measures of success, while the latter applies them), in action research they are one and the same process. This is because the discovery of quality indicators is an outcome rather than a precondition of evaluation construed as the self-reflexive monitoring of actions performed with transformative or innovatory intent.
7 Evaluation constitutes a continuous process of self-reflexive monitoring, which is a necessary condition of being able to sustain and realize the innovation in practice. Within the context of action research, evaluation is not cyclical and periodic as it is in the context of an organizational review: review–plan–implement–review. Action research as a process inte-grates planning, implementation and evaluation as aspects of a unified and non-sequential process of change. Implementation does not come after the planning. Rather, when the plan is finally 'on the table', it documents a successful implementation.

From a normative functionalist perspective, the classroom action research movement neglects the ways in which the system structures the activities of teachers in classrooms to limit and constrain their freedom to innovate. It is naive to assume that individual teachers can significantly transform their practices by reflecting on data they collect about their interactions with students in those physical spaces called classrooms. According to such critics, school-based action research projects fall within the misconceptions of a naive hermeneutics, which views action as originating in the intentional activities of free agents and grounded in their subjective interpretations of the situations and events they experience. The subjective interpretations of teachers are mere shadows, masking structural constraints on human action.

Inasmuch as classroom action research aims to transform the quality of teachers' practices by improving their interpretations of life in classrooms, it can indeed be represented as a hermeneutic process. But I am not so sure that it necessarily misrepresents the relationship between individual agents and their activities and practices. There are, as Giddens (1984) has pointed out, types of hermeneutic inquiry falling under the label of 'interpretative sociology' that give primacy in explaining human activities to the intentions and self-understandings of individual agents, and appear to neglect structural concepts. I would certainly argue that much of what passed for teacher self-evaluation in British schools during the 1970s and 1980s tended to assume that individual teachers were alone responsible for the quality of their practices and therefore had the power to change them if they wished without any reference to structural constraints.

The issue at stake here is whether you can have a type of hermeneutic inquiry which doesn't neglect structural concepts? Normative functionalist critics cannot ask this question without rendering their own assumptions entirely problematic. They must necessarily view classroom action research as a marginal enterprise in the quest to discover the key to educational change.

There is a 'critical paradigm' of educational action research which draws its inspiration from the idea of a critical social science developed by members of the Frankfurt School, particularly in the form articulated by Habermas. Such a paradigm is teacher-based and aims to improve their interpretations and practices in classrooms. It therefore incorporates a hermeneutic dimension, but at the same time, those who embrace it, such as Carr and Kemmis (1983), believe that pedagogy is shaped and constrained by external power structures. But the paradigm does not embrace the normative functionalist assumption that the power of schools as social systems to shape pedagogical practices depends on a consensus about their goals and purposes. Rather, it adopts the Marxist perspective that the power of social systems arises out of class-based conflicts of interest. As 'power containers' (Giddens 1984), systems 'resolve' such conflicts of interest through the operation of oppressive structures. Thus in capitalist societies, schools as systems are agents of oppression which foster the interests of some sectors of society to the exclusion of others. They reproduce unfair and unequal social conditions. Moreover, schools not only oppress certain categories of students by denying them access to the development of their capacities, but they also oppress teachers by preventing them from engaging in pedagogical acts that serve the interests of justice and equality.

Teachers can, however, according to 'critical educational theorists', emancipate their activities from the structures of domination that presently constitute schools as social systems. The initial step in this direction is for them to reflect about the ways in which their interpretations of classroom life are shaped by ideological structures which function to legitimate their activities and mask the structural properties they reproduce. This post-hermeneutic paradigm of action research involves teachers in the process of reflexively explicating the structural properties which shape their 'theories' and practices. Such enlightenment places them in a position to engage in strategic 'political' action aimed at dismantling the structures of domination and reconstructing the school as an organization in which the pedagogical acts of individual teachers are characterized by an absence of all constraints except the 'force of the better argument' (Habermas 1984).

In this ideal school, the pedagogical practices of teachers are not shaped by an organization defined in terms of power relationships, but one which maintains the conditions of free and open critical discourse. The outcome of such discourse, it is argued, is the production of a 'rational consensus' about pedagogical practices which are grounded in the democratic values of freedom, equality and justice. Inasmuch as conditions of free and open communication about practice are maintained within the school as an organization, individual teachers are empowered with capacities for rational action in classrooms. The ideal system is not antithetical to the idea of the teacher as a free agent in the classroom. To the extent that teachers' practices are free from power constraints, they are free to determine what constitutes good practice, but they cannot do this in isolation. It requires participation with other practitioners in a form of critical discourse that aims at the production of a rational consensus. Action to improve practice has to be enacted by teachers collectively on the basis of consensual understandings rather than individually. Only the enlightened collective has the power to resist the structures of domination. From this perspective also, the belief that individual teachers have the power to improve their classroom practices in isolation from each other is naive.

According to the exponents of this 'critical' paradigm, action research is a form of open collaborative discourse about the practice of schooling which empowers teachers collectively to improve their pedagogical practices. But one may ask how such a discourse is to be established if the system is not reorganized first. It is not sufficient to argue that the discourse emancipates teachers and empowers them to change the system, when the latter suppresses the possibility of such discourse in the first place. For some advocates of this paradigm the answer is supplied by the intervention of critical social scientists, who protect free and open discourse by generating critical theorems for teachers to reflect on the ways their understandings of practice become distorted by structures of domination.

We frequently talk about top-down versus bottom-up approaches to pedagogical change. If hierarchically managed organizational review constitutes a 'top-down' approach grounded in the presumption of a consensus about organizational goals, then 'critical action research' constitutes a 'bottom-up' approach grounded in the presumption of conflict between those who manage the system and those who operate within it and are oppressed by it. This implies that school-based action research is essentially an oppositional activity which generates conflict between administrators and teachers.

External researchers are cast in two quite different roles within the two approaches. In the context of hierarchically managed reform, they produce generalizations about effective organizational functioning which can be applied in management decisions and used to monitor their success. Such research will be underpinned by the presuppositions of a functionalist social science and employ quantitative measures which are assumed to secure freedom from value bias. In the context of emancipatory collective action by teachers, the researcher's role as a critical social scientist is far more interventionist and explicitly evaluative. Presuming a conflict of interest between managers and teachers, the critical social scientist takes sides and identifies with the teachers he or she defines as oppressed by the system. From this research perspective, the functionalist researcher also takes sides by identifying with those who maintain an oppressive system. There is no neutral standpoint for research: one either serves the interests of the oppressors or the oppressed.

Advocates of a critical educational science cast in the form of school-based action research and functionalists offer a similar critique of the hermeneutic paradigm I outlined earlier, and whose development I and colleagues in CARE at the University of East Anglia have become associated with; namely, that it is naive in neglecting the influence of external structural constraints on the autonomy of individual teachers. In spite of their differences, both functionalist and critical paradigms of school-based evaluation share two major assumptions, which leads them to confuse the kind of classroom action research I have been involved in with a form of teacher self-evaluation which is highly individualized and privatized: involving little sharing of data across classrooms and dialogue between teachers about the pedagogical problems and strategies evidenced in it.

The first major assumption is that structures exist externally to, and independently of, the situated activities of individual teachers in classrooms. They are posited as independent variables which shape and control those activities as a source of external influence. And this assumption rests on the further assumption that structures are properties of social systems. Since the school as an organizational system is perceived as an entity that exists externally to the situated activities that go on in the time slots and locations it allocates for them, it is assumed that constraints on such activities emanate from the system, and can only be identified by focusing attention on it.

The theory of structuration

Giddens has challenged both the above assumptions in developing his theory of structuration, a theory that resolves the dualism between 'structure' and 'agency'. According to Giddens (1984), systems are patterns of relationships across time and place. Thus in schools we find that teachers are allocated to groups of pupils in particular sites (classrooms) for 'periods'. The pupils will be grouped in certain ways (streamed across or within subjects, or mixed ability). They may have the same teacher for all subjects or different teachers according to subject. Teachers may be grouped together in subject departments or according to the age of the pupils they teach.

These administrative practices form only a subsystem within the total organization of roles and relationships in schools. Within classrooms, pedagogical practices display common patterns of interaction between teachers and pupils spread across time and place. They constitute the instructional system of the school. Then we have forms of social organization that are linked to curriculum and assessment practices.

Such 'systems' do not structure the activities of individuals because they do not exist outside them. They are simply the generalized patterns of conduct discerned in the activities of different individuals over time. It is the principles and properties inferred from such patterns that structure individuals' activities and explain the patterns themselves.

Giddens defines these structural properties as rules and resources. Rules are generalizable procedures applied in social practices. For example, in schools, there are general procedures for dealing with 'troublemakers', establishing discipline, grouping pupils according to ability, selecting, organizing and handling curriculum content, etc. Such procedures may be formulated and codified or simply remain implicit properties which regulate social organization. Resources, according to Giddens, are of two kinds: 'allocative' and 'authoritative'. The former refer to the capacities in a system to control material things, while the latter refer to its capacities for controlling people. In schools, capacities to acquire, produce and store curriculum materials in certain forms, like texts and computer software, enable teachers to organize their relations with pupils in certain ways rather than others. Texts enable pupils to process information independently of teachers and computer software enables pupils to play a more active and less passive role in the pedagogical relationship.

The principles and concepts that underpin the ways human beings are organized with respect to temporal-spatial regions, to their bodily positions and movements within these regions, and to tasks that provide opportunities for the development and expression of particular capabilities, all constitute manifestations of capacities to exercise particular forms of power over individuals. It is these ideas manifested in, but not reducible to, organizational patterns that constitute authoritative resources for structuring social practice. The implication of Giddens' theory of structuration for action research, as I have outlined it so far, is that 'systems' do not constrain what teachers do as such, because they are not the source of power over their activities. Rather, power originates in the principles which underpin 'systems'.

For example, in schools, pupils may spend most of their time in regions called classrooms under the supervision of a teacher, and within these regions they may be seated in positions facing the teacher rather than each other, and their movements away from these positions may be restricted. The tasks they are set under these conditions require the exercise and development of certain capacities rather than others, and may provide some pupils with better opportunities for self-development than others. Such patterns are underpinned by structural principles which generate within the school a particular form of disciplinary power associated with a need to transmit basic knowledge and skills of literacy and numeracy to large numbers of children.

As structural properties of social systems, rules and resources do not shape actions and interactions independently of the knowledge and consciousness of the individuals involved. For Giddens (1984), structures are 'both the medium and the outcome' of the practices they organize. They do not externally shape the actions of individuals because they do not exist 'outside' those actions. Rather, the structural properties of social systems are constituted and reconstituted in the actions of individual agents. Structure is 'internal' rather than 'external' to the consciousness of individual agents and is not to be equated with 'constraints'. Structures impose limits on what individuals can do, but at the same time enable them to do things. As properties of social systems, they do not generate power for the system to control individuals but rather generate power as a resource for individuals to bring about certain effects in their interactions with others. Teachers, for example, are empowered to do certain things in classrooms by drawing on rules and resources embedded in their professional culture.

Giddens' (1984) theory of structuration provides a basis for understanding a great many of the things we have learned about changing pedagogical practices through action research. We have learned from data gathered with teachers that their practices are highly routinized across time and place. The same individual tends to respond to similar situations which recur over time in the same way, and these patterns can be observed among teachers operating in different classrooms and schools. Moreover, when they become aware of what they are doing, many teachers find that it is not consistent with the ways they would prefer to describe their conduct, and they experience guilt. The assumption that underpins such guilt is that in reproducing certain patterns of conduct, they are as 'agents' intending to produce certain effects on pupils. For example, a teacher who discovers that he or she has a tendency to ask leading questions accepts that he or she is trying to get pupils to agree with a predetermined answer. The feeling of guilt tacitly acknowledges that he or she might have done otherwise to make his or her practice more consistent with the educational values he or she espouses.

Tacitly embodied in this example of teacher self-evaluation is a distinction between what Giddens calls 'practical' and 'discursive' consciousness. The 'notion of practical consciousness is fundamental to structuration theory' and it 'is that characteristic of the human agent or subject to which structuralism has been particularly blind'. In participating in the flow of routinized every-day activities, human beings are aware of what they are doing. They participate in the flow of action with intentionality (i.e. to bring about certain effects). Giddens calls this process the rationalization of human activities. Within the flow of actions, quite unself-consciously human beings know why they are doing them. By 'the rationalisation of action, I mean that actors also routinely and for the most part without fuss maintain a continuing "theoretical understanding" of the grounds of their activity' (Giddens 1984). In the context of the study of teaching, we talk about the importance of teachers understanding and critiquing the 'tacit theories' which underpin their practices.

Practical consciousness also implies that agents are involved in unself-consciously monitoring the flow of their activity and aspects of its physical and social context including the actions and reactions of others. The continuity of a practice over time depends on an agent's capacity to monitor what he or she is doing within the flow of the activity itself. Teachers who defensively claim that they naturally self-evaluate their practices when urged to do so by managers and administrators are correct. But this does not mean they self-evaluate in the way they are being urged to, namely by self-conscious monitoring. Practical consciousness should not be confused with what Giddens calls 'discursive consciousness', or the ability to describe what one is doing and why one is doing it to others. One must distinguish between self-monitoring and the reflexive self-monitoring of practice.

It is within the practical consciousness of agents that the structural properties of social systems are constituted as rules and resources to enable them to produce certain effects. Such rules and resources define their mutual knowledge or common practical culture.

Social systems do not exist independently of, and externally to, the situated activities of agents. They comprise, according to Giddens (1984), 'the situated activities of human agents, reproduced over space and time'. The reproduction of these patterns is accomplished by knowledgeable agents who know how to produce certain effects through their situated activities. Such knowledge is always mutual knowledge derived from a shared tradition or 'practical cultural'. The rules and resources of which such a cultural tradition consists are appropriated by individuals, not from an externally existing system, but from shared memory traces. It is the store of mutual knowledge, the practical culture, which structures activities into particular patterns or routines spread across space and time. This structuring of actions can only be accomplished through the processes of rationalization and self-evaluation carried out within the practical consciousness of individual agents. If individuals were not aware of what they were doing and why, social systems would not exist.

But all this does not imply that individuals are free to change their practices in isolation from other practitioners. Changes in the practices of individuals do indeed imply system change. But this is not a matter of changing an entity that exists independently of the agency of individuals. Rather, it involves the restructuring of their practical consciousness through the reconstruction of their store of mutual knowledge. And this is precisely the process involved in the development of discursive consciousness.

Discursive consciousness implies a capacity for discourse with others about one's practice and its effects. It is a capacity developed through the kind of classroom action research I have been involved with in schools. It has never assumed that reflexive self-evaluation is a process of isolated self-contemplation. Even when I have not worked with groups of teachers in schools, but with individuals drawn from different schools (as may be the case with teachers undertaking action research in the context of a part-time award-bearing university course), the process has normally involved them in trying to establish conditions in their schools for the discussion of classroom data with their peers and pupils. If this proves difficult to establish because the system of roles and relationships they are locked in manifests the kind of structural properties Simons (1985) refers to as 'hierarchy', 'territory' and 'privacy', then an outside academic facilitator may provide the discourse conditions under which discursive self-awareness can begin to develop. But this is always 'a halfway house' because, ultimately, the possibility of individual teachers changing their practice depends on their being able to legitimate such changes with their peers and the pupils they teach. This is why 'triangulation' methods – eliciting interpretative accounts of observational data from the points of view of the teacher, peers and pupils – have played such a central role in the action research projects I have been associated with.

The future of classroom action research as a change strategy

I have used Giddens' general theory of structuration to clarify and support the theory of pedagogical change that has underpinned the kinds of school-based action research projects I have been involved in. It is essentially the theory that pedagogical change fundamentally involves the collaborative reconstruction of the professional culture of teachers through the development of discursive consciousness. But the theory of structuration suggests that the participants in the discourse need to represent a wider range of roles and relationships than those of teachers, pupils and academic facilitators. The school as an organization embraces a complex system of roles and relationships, which includes a variety of subsystems. These subsystems may be so interlocking that it will be difficult to initiate change in one without corresponding changes in the others occurring. Discourse grounded in data about classroom practices needs to include school administrators, parents and employers, and teachers who have special responsibilities for curriculum planning and the assessment of pupils' progress. Moreover, the focus of school-based action research needs to be broadened to cover the range of practices represented in this wider group. Only in this way can the different cultures that shape practices within the different subsystems develop on a basis of mutual understanding. The kinds of discourse frameworks established for school-based action research in Israel by Keiny (1992) and her colleagues suggest that these broader collaborative research networks are beginning to emerge in schools. Even as far back as the early 1980s, some of the schools I worked with established contexts for administrators and parents to participate with teachers in discussions of classroom data.

As educational systems in many countries become more administratively decentralized, we shall witness a conflict between what Hargreaves (1991) has described as 'vision' and 'voice' change scenarios. The first is characterized by the power of the charismatic headteacher to secure the allegiance of individuals to his or her vision of the organization's goals as a basis for a hierarchical restructuring of the school. The second is characterized by a plurality of voices proclaiming their practical wisdom in a fragmented postmodern organizational culture. Hargreaves (1991) argues that:

> The challenge of restructuring in education and elsewhere is a challenge of abandoning bureaucratic controls, inflexible mandates, paternalistic forms of trust and quick system fixes in order to bring together the disparate voices of teachers and other educational partners.

References

Alexander, R., Rose, A. and Woodhead, C.A. (1992) *Curriculum Organisation and Classroom Practice in Primary Schools: A Discussion Paper*. London: Department for Education.

Axelsson, H. (1995) *Environment and School Initiatives*. Report No. 1, Department of Education and Educational Research, University of Göteborg.

Beck, U. (1992) *Risk Society: Towards a New Modernity*. London: Sage.

Brown, D. (1987) The attitudes of parents to education and the school attendance of their children. In K. Reid (ed.), *Combating School Absenteeism*. London: Hodder and Stoughton.

Brown, S. and McIntyre, D. (1993) *Making Sense of Teaching*. Buckingham: Open University Press.

Brown, S., Duffield, J. and Riddell, S. (1995) School effectiveness research: The policy makers' tool for school improvement. *European Educational Research Association Bulletin*, 1(1), 6–18.

Bruner, J. (1970) *Man: A Course of Study. Evaluation Strategies*. Washington, DC: Curriculum Development Associates.

Bruner, J. (1986) *Actual Minds, Possible Worlds*. Cambridge, MA: Harvard University Press.

Carlen, P., Gleeson, D. and Wardhaugh, J. (1992) *Truancy: The Politics of Compulsory Schooling*. Buckingham: Open University Press.

Carr, W. and Kemmis, S. (1983) *Becoming Critical: Knowing Through Action Research*. Victoria: Deakin University Press.

Colman, J.S. *et al.* (1966) *Equality of Educational Opportunity*. Washington, DC: US Government Printing Office.

Cooper, P. (1993) *Effective Schools for Disaffected Students: Integration and Segregation*. London: Routledge.

Corcoran, T. and Wilson, B. (1989) *Successful Secondary Schools*. Lewes: Falmer Press.

Coulby, D. and Booth, A. (eds) (1987) *Producing and Reducing Disaffection*. Buckingham: Open University Press.

Crandles, M. and Kite, A. (1995) *Caring for Our Environment*. Oxford: Oxford University Press.

Dearing, R. (1993) *The National Curriculum and Its Assessment: Final Report*. London: School Curriculum and Assessment Authority.

Department for Education (1992) *Choice and Diversity: A New Framework for Schools.* London: HMSO.

Department for Education (1993) *The Government's Response: Interim Report on the National Curriculum and Its Assessment.* London: DFE.

Department of Education and Science and the Welsh Office (1989) *National Curriculum: Task Group on Assessment and Testing. A Report.* London: HMSO.

Dewey, J. (1960) *The Quest for Certainty.* New York: Capricorn.

Dewey, J. (1966) *Democracy and Education: An Introduction to the Philosophy of Education.* New York: Macmillan.

Dorn, S. (1996) *Creating the Dropout: An Institutional and Social History of School Failure.* Westport, CT: Praeger.

Dreyfus, S.E. (1981) *Formal Models v Human Situational Understanding: Inherent Limitations in the Modelling of Business Expertise* (mimeo). Schloss Laxenburg, Austria: International Institute for Applied Systems.

Dyson, L. (1992) *Partnership: An Innovative Curriculum.* London: David Fulton.

Edmonds, R. (1979) Effective schools for the urban poor. *Educational Leadership,* 37(1), 15–24.

Elliott, J. (1988a) The state v education: The challenge for teachers. In H. Simons (ed.), *The National Curriculum.* London: British Educational Research Association.

Elliott, J. (1988b) Address to the North of England Conference (mimeo). Norwich: CARE, University of East Anglia.

Elliott, J. (1991a) *Action Research for Educational Change.* Buckingham: Open University Press.

Elliott, J. (1991b) Disconnecting knowledge and understanding from human values. *The Curriculum Journal,* 2(1), 19–31.

Elliott, J. (1991c) Environmental education in Europe: Innovation, marginalisation or assimilation? In K. Laine and P. Posch (eds), *Environment, Schools and Active Learning,* Part 1. Paris: OECD (CERI).

Elliott, J. (1993) Professional education and the idea of a practical educational science. In J. Elliott (ed.), *Reconstructing Teacher Education.* London: Falmer Press.

Elliott, J. (1994) Developing community-focused environmental education through action-research. In M. Pettigrew and B. Somekh (eds), *Evaluating Innovation in Environmental Education.* Paris: OECD.

Elliott, J. (1995a) Reconstructing the environmental education curriculum: Teachers' perspectives. In OECD (ed.), *Environmental Learning for the 21st Century.* Paris: OECD (CERI).

Elliott, J. (1995b) Environmental education, action-research and the role of the school. In OECD (ed.), *Environmental Learning for the 21st Century.* Paris: OECD (CERI).

Fitz-Gibbon, C., Tymms, P.B. and Hazelwood, R.D. (1989) Performance indicators and information systems. In D. Reynolds, B.P.M. Creemers and T. Peters (eds), *School Effectiveness and Improvement.* Groningen: RION.

Giddens, A. (1984) *The Constitution of Society.* Cambridge: Polity Press.

Goodson, I. (1994) *Studying Curriculum.* Buckingham: Open University Press.

Gray, J. and Wilcox, B. (1994) 'The challenge of turning round ineffective schools'. Paper presented to the ESRC Seminar on School Effectiveness and School Improvement, University of Newcastle, October.

Habermas, J. (1984) *The Theory of Communicative Action.* London: Heinemann.

Hamilton, D. (1994) Clockwork universes and oranges. Paper presented to the *British Educational Research Association Conference*, Oxford, September.

Handy, C. (1995a) *The Empty Raincoat*. London: Random House.

Handy, C. (1995b) *Beyond Certainty*. London: Random House.

Hanley, J.P., Whitla, D.K., Moo, E.W. and Walter, A.S. (1970) *Curiosity, Competence, Community; Man: A Course of Study, An Evaluation*. (2 vol. set.) Cambridge, MA: Educational Development Center Inc.

Hargreaves, A. (1991) Restructuring restructuring: Postmodernity and the prospects for educational change. Paper presented at the *Annual Conference of the American Educational Research Association*, Chicago, IL, April.

Hargreaves, D.H., Hestor, S.K. and Mellor, F.J. (1975) *Deviance in Classrooms*. London: Routledge and Kegan Paul.

Hopkins, D. (1994) School improvement in an era of change. In P. Ribbins and E. Burridge (eds), *Improving Education: Promoting Quality in Schools*. London: Cassell.

Howe, K.R. (1995) Democracy, justice and action research: Some theoretical developments. *Educational Action Research Journal*, 3(3), 347–9.

Irving, B.A. and Parker-Jenkins, M. (1995) Tackling truancy: An examination of persistent non-attendance amongst disaffected school pupils and positive support strategies. *Cambridge Journal of Education*, 25(2), 225–35.

Jenks, C., Smith, M., Acland, H., Bane, M.J., Cohen, D., Gintis, H., Heyns, B. and Michelson, S. (1972) *Inequality: A Reassessment of the Effect of Family and Schooling in America*. New York: Basic Books.

Keiny, S. (1992) *School-based Curriculum Development: A Process of Teachers Professional Development* (mimeo). Ben Gurion University of the Negev, Israel.

Kinder, K., Harland, J. and Wakefield, A. (1995) *Three to Remember: Strategies for Disaffected Pupils*. Slough: National Foundation for Educational Research.

Kymlicka, W. (1990) *Contemporary Political Philosophy: An Introduction*. Oxford: Clarendon Press.

Laine, K. and Posch, P. (eds) (1991) *Environment, Schools and Active Learning*. Paris: OECD (CERI).

Lash, S. and Wynne, B. (1992) Introduction. In U. Beck, *Risk Society: Towards a New Modernity*. London: Sage.

Lyotard, J.-F. (1979) *The Postmodern Condition: A Report on Knowledge*. Manchester: Manchester University Press.

MacDonald, B. (1974) Evaluation and the control of education. In D. Tawney (ed.), *Curriculum Evaluation Today: Trends and Implications*. London: Macmillan.

MacDonald, B. and Walker, R. (1976) *Changing the Curriculum*. London: Open Books.

MacLure, S. (1993) Patten: Poor marks for listening to teachers. *Times Educational Supplement*, 22 February.

Marquand, D. (1988) *The Unprincipled Society: New Demands and Old Politics*. London: Jonathan Cape.

McAndrew, C. and Pascoe, I. (1993) *Environment and School Initiatives (ENSI) Project in Scotland: A National Report and Case Studies in Environmental Education*. Dundee: Scottish Consultative Council on the Curriculum.

McDermott, J. (1977) *The Writings of William James*. Chicago, IL: University of Chicago Press.

Meyer, M. (1995) Quality indicators and innovation in environmental education. In OECD (ed.), *Environmental Learning for the 21st Century*. Paris: OECD (CERI).

National Curriculum Council (1993) *The National Curriculum at Key Stages 1 and 2: Advice to the Secretary of State for Education*. London: NCC.

Nozick, R. (1974) *Anarchy, State and Utopia*. New York: Basic Books.

Nuttall, D., Goldstein, H., Prosser, R. and Rasbash, J. (1989) Differential school effectiveness. *International Journal of Educational Research*, 13(7), 769–76.

OECD (1995a) *Teachers and Curriculum Reform in Basic Schooling*. Draft Report, June. Paris: OECD (CERI).

OECD (ed.) (1995b) *Environmental Learning for the 21st Century*. Paris: OECD (CERI).

O'Keefe, D. (1994) *Truancy in English Secondary Schools*. London: HMSO.

O'Keefe, D. and Stoll, P. (1995) Understanding the problem: Truancy and curriculum. In D. O'Keefe and P. Stoll (eds), *Issues in School Attendance and Truancy*. London: Pitman.

Perrone, V. (1989) *Effective Schools and Learning: Reflections on Teachers, Schools, and Communities*. New York: Teachers College Press.

Peters, R.S. (1966) *Ethics and Education*. London: George Allen and Unwin.

Pettigrew, M. and Somekh, B. (eds) (1994) *Evaluating Innovation in Environmental Education*. Paris: OECD.

Popper, K. (1972) *Objective Knowledge: An Evolutionary Approach*. Oxford: Oxford University Press.

Posch, P. (1988) The project 'Environment and School Initiatives' (mimeo). Klagenfurt, Austria: University of Klagenfurt.

Posch, P. (1991) Environment and school initiatives: Background and basic premises of the project. In K. Laine and P. Posch (eds), *Environment, Schools and Active Learning*, Part 1. Paris: OECD (CERI).

Posch, P. (1993) Action research in environmental education. *Educational Action Research: An International Journal*, 1(3), 447–55.

Posch, P. (1994) Changes in the culture of teaching and learning and implications for action research. *Educational Action Research: An International Journal*, 2(2), 153–61.

Posch, P. (1995a) Professional development in environmental education: Networking and infrastructures. In OECD (ed.), *Environmental Learning for the 21st Century*, Paris: OECD (CERI).

Posch, P. (1995b) Networking in environmental education. In M. Pettigrew and B. Somekh (eds), *Evaluating Innovation in Environmental Education*. Paris: OECD.

Pring, R. (1989) *The New Curriculum*. London: Cassell.

Pring, R. (1995) The community of educated people: The Lawrence Stenhouse Memorial Lecture. *British Journal of Educational Studies*, 43(2), 121–45.

Rawls, J. (1971) *A Theory of Justice*. Oxford: Oxford University Press.

Reid, K. (1987) Attitudes: Parents, pupils and teachers – the implications for professionals and practitioners. In K. Reid (ed.), *Combating School Absenteeism*. London: Hodder and Stoughton.

Reynolds, D. (1994) School effectiveness and quality in education. In P. Ribbins and E. Burridge (eds), *Improving Education: Promoting Quality in Schools*. London: Cassell.

Reynolds, D. and Sullivan, M. (1979) Bringing schools back in. In L. Barton and R. Meighan (eds), *Schools, Pupils and Disaffection*. Driffield: Nafferton.

Rogers, B. (1990) *You Know the Fair Rule: Strategies for making the hard job of discipline in school easier*. London: Longman.

Rorty, R. (1980) *Philosophy and the Mirror of Nature*. Oxford: Blackwell.

Rudduck, J., Chaplain, R. and Wallace, G. (1996) *School Improvement: What Can Pupils Tell Us?* London: David Fulton.

Rutter, M., Maughan, B., Mortimore, P. and Ouston, J. (1979) *Fifteen Thousand Hours: Secondary Schools and Their Effects on Children*. London: Open Books.

Sammons, P., Hillman, J. and Mortimore, P. (1995) *Key Characteristics of Effective Schools: A Review of School Effectiveness Research*. A Report for the Office of Standards in Education. London: Institute of Education.

Sayer, J. (1987) Why have you come to school today? A pathology of presence. In K. Reid (ed.), *Combating School Absenteeism*. London: Hodder and Stoughton.

Schon, D.A. (1971) *Beyond the Stable State: Public and Private Learning in a Changing Society*. Harmondsworth: Penguin.

Schools Council (1972) *With Objectives in Mind: Guide to Science 5–13*. London: MacDonald.

Schostak, J. (ed.) (1991) *Youth in Trouble: Educational Responses*. London: Kogan Page.

Schweitzer, K. (1991) 'Waste project – Oberwart Disctrict': Emancipation through environmental projects. In K. Laine and P. Posch (eds), *Environment, Schools and Active Learning*, Part 2. Paris: OECD (CERI).

Scottish Council on the Curriculum (1993) Take pride in Pumpherstone. Annex to *Environment and School Initiatives (ENSI) Project in Scotland: A National Report and Case Studies in Environmental Education* (C. McAndrew and I. Pascoe, eds). Dundee: Scottish Consultative Council on the Curriculum.

Silver, H. (1994) *Good Schools, Effective Schools: Judgements and Their Histories*. London: Cassell.

Simons, H. (1985) Against the rules: Procedural problems in school self-evaluation. *Curriculum Perspectives*, 5(2), 1–6.

Stenhouse, L. (1967) *Culture and Education*. London: Nelson Books.

Stenhouse, L. (1970a) *The Humanities Project: An Introduction*. London: Heinemann Educational.

Stenhouse, L. (1970b) Some limitations of the use of objectives in curriculum research and planning. *Paedagogica Europaea*, 6, 73–8.

Stenhouse, L. (1975) *An Introduction to Curriculum Research and Development*. London: Heinemann.

Stenhouse, L. (1983) Research as a Basis for Teaching in *Authority, Education and Emancipation*. London: Heinemann.

Taba, H. (1962) *Curriculum Organisation and Classroom Practice in Primary Schools: A Discussion Paper*. London: Department for Education.

Tattum, D. (ed.) (1986) *Management of Disruptive Pupil Behaviour in Schools*. Chichester: John Wiley & Sons.

Tooley, J. (1995) *Disestablishing the School*. Aldershot: Avebury.

West, E.G. (1970) *Education and the State*. London: Institute for Economic Affairs.

Index

CURRICULUM INNOVATION
A CELEBRATION OF CLASSROOM PRACTICE

Roger Crombie White

Curriculum Innovation is a celebration of teachers' achievements and creativity at the secondary level of schooling. It examines the historical and political contexts of curriculum development and control in the United Kingdom, and analyses the values and beliefs that have shaped the reforms in schools and colleges over the last two decades. It considers the extent to which these changes have acted to challenge the professional autonomy and status of teachers and lecturers, and reflects the views of those affected.

It provides an account of the current curriculum provision for the 14–19 age group – a contemporary 'map of the territory' – and highlights the ASDAN Award Scheme, one successful example of teacher-led innovation. As the pendulum begins to swing back from the centrally controlled and narrowly prescribed programmes of study and attainment targets of the National Curriculum, it is important to draw attention to such areas of good practice and identify the policy implications of these grass roots initiatives.

This book highlights not only the 'professional imagination' but also what it can achieve. It makes for inspirational reading and will be of great interest to students, teachers and lecturers, and anyone involved with curriculum development for the 14–19 age group.

Contents
Introduction – History of curriculum control – Professional autonomy – Curriculum ideologies and underpinning values – International comparisons – The curriculum map – Teachers as curriculum innovators – The profession's perspectives – The ASDAN award scheme: a case study of teacher-led curriculum development – Conclusion – Appendix: respondents to questionnaire survey – Bibliography – Index.

176pp   0 335 19756 6 (Paperback)   0 335 19767 4 (Hardback)

EDUCATION AND THE STRUGGLE FOR DEMOCRACY
THE POLITICS OF EDUCATIONAL IDEAS

Wilfred Carr and Anthony Hartnett

During the past decade there has been a series of radical changes to the educational system of England and Wales. This book argues that any serious study of these changes has to engage with complex questions about the role of education in a modern liberal democracy. Were these educational changes informed by the needs and aspirations of a democratic society? To what extent will they promote democratic values and ideals? These questions can only be adequately addressed by making explicit the political ideas and the underlying philosophical principles that have together shaped the English educational system. To this end, the book provides a selective history of English education which exposes the connections between decisive periods of educational change and the intellectual and political climate in which it occurred. It also connects the educational policies of the 1980s and 1990s to the political ideas of the New Right in order to show how they are part of a broader political strategy aimed at reversing the democratic advances achieved through the intellectual and political struggles of the nineteenth and twentieth centuries. The book proposes that a democratic educational vision can only effectively be advanced by renewing the 'struggle for democracy' – the historical struggle to create forms of education which will empower all citizens to participate in an open, pluralistic and democratic society.

Contents
Introduction: the politics of educational ideas – Education, politics and society – Democratic theory and democratic education – 'Gentling the masses': the nineteenth-century origins of the English educational tradition – 'Secondary education for all': the struggle for democractic education in twentieth-century England – The battle of ideas and the rise of the New Right coalition in England – The New Right offensive and the demise of democratic education in England – Conclusion: democratic education in the twenty-first century – Notes – References and bibliography – Index.

256pp   0 335 19520 2 (Paperback)   0 335 19521 0 (Hardback)

STUDYING CURRICULUM
CASES AND METHODS

Ivor F. Goodson

Studying Curriculum offers a fruitful and practical approach for analysing the inescapable political realities of the contemporary curriculum. It reminds us that what is socially constructed can also be deconstructed and reconstructed, and that notions of social equity and justice can be reconstituted within school curricula. As Andy Hargreaves notes in his critical introduction to this volume: 'such a combination of conceptual and political radicalism, and empirical and historical realism not only defines Goodson's scholarship but also demystifies the curriculum it addresses'.

Ivor Goodson explores how and by whom the curriculum is controlled. He examines how social background and origin, historical and political context, and school curriculum are interrelated. He takes a social constructionist approach, and plants this firmly in the 'middle ground' of subjects – their traditions, departments and politics. This enables both a rendering of the experience of those working within these traditions; and a reaching outwards to the structures and assumptions underlying those subject traditions.

Contents
Critical introduction – Curriculum reform and curriculum theory: a case of historical amnesia – On understanding curriculum: the alienation of curriculum theory – Curriculum history, professionalization and the social organization of knowledge – Behind the schoolhouse door: the historical study of the curriculum – Vocational education and school reform: the case of the London (Canada) technical school, 1990–1930 – Subject status and curriculum change: local commercial education, 1920–1940 – 'Nations at risk' and 'national curriculum': ideology and identity – Studying curriculum: social constructionist perspectives – Notes and references – Index.

160pp   0 335 19050 2 (Paperback)   0 335 19051 0 (Hardback)